AGEING AND GLOBALISATION

Martin Hyde and Paul Higgs

D1612589

P

First published in Great Britain in 2017 by

Policy Press
University of Bristol
1-9 Old Park Hill
Bristol
BS2 8BB
UK
+44 (0)117 954 5940
pp-info@bristol.ac.uk
www.policypress.co.uk

North America office:
Policy Press
c/o The University of Chicago Press
1427 East 60th Street
Chicago, IL 60637, USA
t: +1 773 702 7700
f: +1 773 702 9756
sales@press.uchicago.edu
www.press.uchicago.edu

British Library Cataloguing in Publication Data
A catalogue record for this book is available from the British Library

Library of Congress Cataloging-in-Publication Data
A catalog record for this book has been requested

ISBN 978-1-4473-2230-6 paperback
ISBN 978-1-4473-2231-3 ePub
ISBN 978-1-4473-2232-0 Mobi

Cover design by Policy Press
Front cover image: Istock
Printed and bound in Great Britain by CMP, Poole
Policy Press uses environmentally responsible print partners

Contents

List of tables and figures

Tables

Figures

List of acroynms

A4M	American Academy of Anti-Aging Medicine
ASAPS	American Society for Aesthetic Plastic Surgery
ASEAN	Association of Southeast Asian Nations
BAPRAS	British Association of Plastic, Reconstructive and Aesthetic Surgeons
CHIC	Cosmetics Harmonization and International Cooperation
CPI	consumer price index
DB	defined benefit (pension scheme)
DC	defined contribution (pension scheme)
EBRD	European Bank for Reconstruction and Development
ECSC	European Coal and Steel Community
ELSA	English Longitudinal Study of Ageing
ESAAM	European Society of Anti-Aging Medicine
EU	European Union
FDA	Food and Drug Administration
FDI	foreign direct investment
HLE	healthy life expectancy
IEG	Independent Evaluation Group (World Bank)
ILO	International Labour Organization
IMF	International Monetary Fund
INGO	international non-governmental organisations IPS International Passenger Survey
ISSA	International Social Security Association
ISSP	International Social Survey Programme
JAAM	Japanese Association of Anti-Ageing Medicine
JCI	Joint Commission International
LME	labour market exit
LMP	labour market participation
MNC	multinational corporation
NAFTA	North American Free Trade Agreement
NHIS	National Health Interview Survey
NIH	National Institute for Health
NMP	New Mobilities Paradigm
NMT	new medical technologies
OECD	Organisation for Economic Co-operation and Development
OPEC	Organization of the Oil Exporting Countries
PAYG	pay-as-you-go

PROST   Pension Reforms Option Simulation Toolkit
REACH   Registration, Evaluation, Authorisation and
            Restriction of Chemical substances
RIS   regional implementation strategies
SAGE   Study on Global Ageing and Adult Health
SERPS   State Earnings Related Pension Scheme
SHARE   Survey of Health, Aging and Retirement in Europe
SSA   Social Security Administration
UKAF   United Kingdom Accreditation Forum
UN   United Nations
UNECE   United Nations Economic Commission for Europe
WAAAM   World Anti-Aging Academy of Medicine
WHO   World Health Organization
WOSIAM   World Society Interdisciplinary of Anti-Aging
            Medicine
WTO   World Trade Organization
WVS   World Values Survey

About the authors

Martin Hyde is a lecturer in sociology at the University of Manchester. He has a degree in sociology and politics from the University of Bristol and a PhD in the sociology of ageing from University College London. He has a long-standing interest in cross-national comparative research on ageing. He has published numerous journal articles and book chapters on a wide range of issues from consumption to heath inequalities in later life. He has been involved in a number of large-scale studies including the English Longitudinal Study of Ageing (ELSA), the Survey for Health, Retirement and Ageing in Europe (SHARE) and the Swedish Longitudinal Occupational Study of Health (SLOSH). He also co-ordinates the Integrated Datasets in Europe for Ageing Research (IDEAR) network. He is an associate editor for *Ageing & Society* and *BMC Geriatrics and Gerontology.*

Paul Higgs is professor of the sociology of ageing at University College London. He has a degree in sociology from the Polytechnic of North London and a PhD in social policy from the University of Kent. He has co-authored with Chris Gilleard a number of books: *Cultures of Ageing: Self, Citizen and the Body* (2000); *Contexts of Ageing: Class, Cohort and Community* (2005); *Ageing, Corporeality and Embodiment* (2013); *Rethinking Old Age: Theorising the Fourth Age* (2015) *and Personhood and Care in Advanced Old Age* (2016). He is the co-author of *Medical Sociology and Old Age: Towards a Sociology of Health in Later Life* (2008) with Ian Jones and co-edited *Social Class in Later Life* (2013) with Marvin Formosa. Professor Higgs edits the journal *Social Theory and Health* and has published widely in social gerontology and medical sociology. He holds fellowships from the Academy of Social Sciences and the Gerontological Society of America.

Acknowledgements

As anyone who has ever written a book knows it is never just the product of the authors. Through its many stages and iterations, it benefits from the input of others, continually refining it and reshaping it. It is important to acknowledge their role in this process. The current book began life as a PhD thesis. Throughout this stage we benefitted from the wisdom, criticism and support of many people through conference presentations to coffee shop conversations. However, there are a few key people who require a special mention for their intellectual and material support. We would like to thank Chris Gilleard, Ian Rees Jones, Dick Wiggins, James Thompson and Graham Scambler for their input, arguments and encouragement throughout this period.

Turning a PhD into a book is a challenging task. However, we were assisted by an amazing publishing team at Policy Press who supported and encouraged us at every stage of the process. In particular, we would like to thank Isobel Bainton and Rebecca Tomlinson for all their hard work, guidance and support on this book. Without them this would have been a much harder and much less enjoyable experience. We would also like to thank the anonymous reviewers whose comments, on the proposal and the draft, were insightful and constructive. We are also extremely grateful to Chris Phillipson, the series editor, who worked with us to help us realise our vision for the book and ensure that it was accessible to a wide audience.

Finally, above all others we could not have done this without the support of our families and friends. Writing can often seem like a very solitary affair. Yet it would be impossible without the encouragement from those around you. We are both incredibly fortunate to have such understanding and supportive personal networks. In particular Martin would like to thank Lizzie Evans and Paul would like to thank Liz Higgs and Xavier Finnian Desmond Higgs. This book is dedicated to you all. Without your help and inspiration we would not have been able to finish it.

Preface from the series editors

Chris Phillipson (University of Manchester, UK),
Toni Calasanti (Virginia, Tech, USA) and
Thomas Scharf (University of Newcastle, UK)

As the global older population continues to expand, new issues and concerns arise for consideration by academics, policy makers and health and social care professionals worldwide. *Ageing in a Global Context* is a series of books, published by Policy Press in association with the British Society of Gerontology, which aims to influence and transform debates in what has become a fast-moving field in research and policy. The series seeks to achieve this in three main ways: first, through publishing books which re-think key questions shaping debates in the study of ageing. This has become especially important given the re-structuring of welfare states, alongside the complex nature of population change, both of these elements opening up the need to explore themes which go beyond traditional perspectives in social gerontology. Second, the series represents a response to the impact of globalisation and related processes, these contributing to the erosion of the national boundaries which originally framed the study of ageing. From this has come the emergence of issues explored in various contributions to the series, for example: the impact of transnational migration, cultural diversity, new types of inequality, and contrasting themes relating to ageing in rural and urban areas. Third, a key concern of the series is to explore inter-disciplinary connections in gerontology. Contributions will provide a critical assessment of the disciplinary boundaries and territories influencing the study of ageing, creating in the process new perspectives and approaches relevant to the 21st century.

Given the above aims, we are delighted that one of the first books in the series has, as its central concern, the exploration of the impact of global interconnectedness on the lives of older people. The authors of the book – Martin Hyde and Paul Higgs – have played a leading role in applying sociological perspectives to the study of ageing, most notably in furthering our understanding of the transformative role of globalisation. This book represents a major assessment of the links between later life and global change, drawing together a wealth of theoretical and empirical material. It will certainly be essential reading for those working in the field of ageing but should also have much wider impact on the social and health sciences more generally.

xi

ONE

Introduction

Today, for the first time in history, most people throughout the world can expect to live into their 60s and beyond. However, not only are people living longer but the world in which they are doing so has undergone a number of radical changes. Urbanisation has transformed the ways in which people live and today the majority of the world's population lives in cities. Not only has the way we live changed but so too has the way we work. Large parts of the developing world have become heavily industrialised drawing people away from agricultural labour into the factories. At the same time across the middle and higher income countries the loss of these industrial jobs and the rapid rise of the service sector has created new jobs and new, often precarious, ways of working. In both cases workers across the world are increasingly believed to be caught up in the global economic flows of trade and investment that encircle the world and bind countries together as part of a global market. Advances in transportation and communications have also appeared to shrink the world around us. Email and video calls make it possible to instantly speak to people thousands of miles away. Satellite television and internet streaming make it possible to watch foreign TV, news or sporting events from your home or even on the move. This movement of images and things is mirrored by the movement of people. Cheap flights have made it possible for many in the high income countries to explore the world, while millions of people are forced to migrate to escape war and poverty throughout other parts of the world. Alongside these changes there have been a number of global socioeconomic developments. On the one hand the world is now a wealthier place than it was in the past. On the other hand, it is also a more economically unequal place than at any time in recent history. It has been estimated that as few as 62 super rich individuals now hold as much wealth as the world's poorest 50% (Oxfam International 2015). All of these trends point to the importance of the changing nature of space to understand the world in which we are ageing.

It has become increasingly common to note that we 'age in place' and that place has an important impact on our experiences of later life. However, the places in which we age are undergoing a series of changes. We have moved away from a world in which nations were seen as the dominant spatial form to a world characterised by a series of overlapping spaces. These new spaces include global spaces, such as the global financial markets, regional spaces, like the European Union, and local spaces, such as industrial or technology districts like Silicon Valley. This series of transformations poses challenges for gerontology as well as for older people themselves. If we assume that notions of time and space are intimately interconnected then the changing nature of space raises many questions about how we see time, and ultimately, how we think about ageing. This raises a number of questions: what does it mean to age in the locations configured by the intersections between global, regional and national spaces? What does international mobility mean for theories of the life course? How is structured dependency theory affected if the nation state loses its central role in the construction of pension and retirement policies? What is the impact on the political economy of ageing approach if multinational corporations (MNCs) appear to have freed financial capital from the constraints put on them by the nation state and are now able to operate across a global economic landscape? What does it mean for cultural gerontology if people age in multicultural communities, or that the largest proportions of the world's older population will soon be found in the lower income countries of the developing world? How do we as researchers rise to these challenges, and how do we explore what these new ways of living occurring in these spaces mean for the experience and understanding of later life?

These questions and their answers are manifold because the issue of globalisation operates at many different levels. In addition, an important difficulty that we face is that many gerontological theories emerged alongside, or in response to, national policies and took the nation state as the taken-for-granted focus for their inquiries. Hence such theories are often ill-equipped to deal with the new spaces and the actors that now operate within them. Even when conducting cross-national comparisons, gerontologists have generally relied on the nation state as the most meaningful unit for comparison and assumed that the experience of ageing for different populations was determined by national characteristics or policies. This reality has changed and there are now new policy actors that operate at the regional level, such as the EU, and global actors, such as the World Bank, that operate above both nations and regions. Conversely there is also a growth of more localised devolved sub-national political units that are beginning to take control over policy making and which impact on the lives of many older people in areas such as healthcare spending, transport and so on. This complexity presents us with a mosaic of different types of actors operating across a variety of different spaces challenging the conventional focus on the nation state that has been emblematic of much of gerontological writing. However, in responding to these challenges, there is an equally real danger that gerontologists will un-reflexively adopt some of the more generalised theories around globalisation and end up replacing one overarching spatial framework, that of the nation state, with another, that of the global system. To a great degree this book is an argument cautioning against this tendency as the global represents only one of the varied landscapes of ageing in the current period. In our view gerontology often appears to be trapped within one or other of these spatial contexts and only addresses questions that seem specific to whatever level seems dominant, whether this is in terms of national policies, international trends or local initiatives.

An equally important point is that discussions of globalisation and ageing should not only be seen as intellectual one-way traffic. Globalisation theorists have generally overlooked age and ageing or have treated these subjects as relatively unimportant or unproblematic issues. Yet, given that ageing is a universal human phenomenon and because it impacts on every aspect of life, from health and finances to leisure and housing, population ageing affords us a unique opportunity to critically explore many of the claims that are made about globalisation. Consequently, in this overview of globalisation and ageing, we need to also ask what can the patterns and profiles of the ageing population tell us about the nature of globalisation, regionalisation, and the importance of local forms of living. Gerontology should not be limited to simply echoing the debates about the changing nature of space and globalisation but should also be using its knowledge about the nature of ageing and later life as a prism through which to actively inform them.

Undertaking this task is important, not simply because a more integrated approach to globalisation is increasingly necessary, but also because the continuing effects of the global economic crisis of 2008 have destabilised many of the assumptions and policies formulated in the 20th century for old age. The present global population has, on average, the longest life expectancy and the greatest proportion of older people in history. At the same time these changes have been accompanied by a greater global interconnectedness between nations, regions and even cities and towns. This is continually organising and reorganising the spatial and temporal foundations through which old age has been positioned and understood since the Second World War. Yet it is widely acknowledged that there is still relatively little research on the interconnections between globalisation and ageing. The research that does exist, it can be argued, often suffers from simplistic accounts of later life, globalisation or both. This book seeks to redress this gap in our knowledge and, by bringing these two issues together, develops a more detailed understanding of both arenas and the ways in which they interact that can be useful to students of globalisation as well as those concerned with ageing and later life.

Structure of the book

The book is organised into three parts. Part 1 addresses the main theoretical debates within both gerontology and globalisation theory while Part 2 draws on a range of empirical data to examine the different dimensions of ageing and later life. Finally, Part 3 concludes by assessing the potential impact of these chapters on our understanding of these new spaces, later life and the connections between them.

Chapter Two covers the ways in which the main social gerontological theories have dealt with the issues of space. Rather than repeat the conventional narrative about the historical development of these theories, they are divided into groups which correspond to two broad historical periods; the modern and the late modern. The main argument here is that the gerontological theories that took modernist spaces, such as the nation state, as their reference for understanding ageing are being fundamentally challenged by the emergence of these new spaces and the relations between them. What these spaces look like and how they interconnect are explored in Chapter Three. Here the arguments and evidence for the existence of alternative, global, regional and local, types of spaces are addressed. The chapter argues that we need to be aware that the evidence supports the contention that all of these spaces now co-exist alongside that of the nation state, and that it is important to develop theoretical models that allow us to examine the interrelations between the different spatial levels.

Part 2 contains four chapters. Chapter Four deals with the health and health care of older people around the world. Chapter Five explores the issues of employment, financial wellbeing and pensions. Chapter Six looks at the cultural engagement of older people around the world. Finally, Chapter Seven examines the political images and discourses, of ageing and later life.

All these chapters follow a broadly similar structure. As Martin, Metzger and Pierre (2006: 503) argue, the sociology of globalisation has two subject types:

> [Firstly to] try to identify, then explain, social processes common to (almost) all countries of the world (or more

accurately, common to all relevant entities) and which are 'going in the same direction', i.e. that convey a common evolution, leading to the thought that things are evolving towards standardization... Second, we refer to the social phenomena that immediately present themselves as global (that touch – almost – all relevant entities of the world) and, surely, themselves result from prior globalisation processes.

Following this approach, each chapter starts by examining the spatial patterning of the relevant dimensions of ageing and later life, whether for example that is health or income, through the analysis of data from a range of surveys in order to assess whether local, national, regional or global patterns are evident. These analyses provide an important basis from which to explore what appears to be the most appropriate spatiality for a given topic. However, given that such data do not permit a direct examination of the impact of actors operating in terms of different spatial logics, each chapter also assesses the impact of relevant global, regional and national actors on later life in the context of the topic under scrutiny. Finally, we conclude by drawing these various strands together. In each arena there is clear evidence that the conventional ways of thinking about ageing and later life have weakened. New temporalities around health and retirement as well as ageing itself have opened up. These in turn call for, and create, new types of spaces. However, it is equally important to note that we are far from witnessing the emergence of a global space of ageing and later life. Instead global, regional and national patterns are still clearly identifiable. This supports the central argument of this book that no single spatial logic can be said to be dominant but that different spaces overlap and confront each other across a range of dimensions. This conclusion is even more apparent when examining the key actors who seek to shape these new temporalities. A number of what have been termed 'epistemic communities' have emerged, around anti-ageing medicine, the new pension orthodoxy and active ageing, and are discussed in the penultimate chapter. Müller (2003) has defined epistemic communities as networks of knowledge-based experts, potentially drawn from a variety of fields, who share a common belief in 'specific truths, a set of normative and causal beliefs, patterns of reasoning, and discursive practices'. In each case the networks that we have identified comprise actors operating along different spatial logics which are united by common discourse and practice. In fact, in order to be successful these epistemic communities must align as many actors across as many spatial logics as possible. Those that fail to do so stand little chance of achieving their goals. Therefore, to properly understand the nature of ageing and later life today, and the ways in which key actors seek to direct these developments, social gerontology needs to move beyond simple theoretical models that privilege single spatialities and look instead at the complex 'heterarchical' interactions that exist across time and space.

The conclusion of this book can be clearly stated. It is that the processes that constitute globalisation are not capable of being understood in terms of a simple reductionism of one overriding logic that leads to 'the race to the bottom' as some writers have posited. Neither is it the case that 'globalisation' can be added unproblematically to existing gerontological theories in a 'do you want a side order of globalisation to go with your order' approach. We hope to show in this book that it is the case that global processes are having an effect on the experiences of ageing and old age, but so too are many other things, many of which are reconstituting the spaces of ageing in the contemporary world. Of significant note is that it is often older people themselves who, through their own social and cultural engagements, are responsible for reconfiguring the field of ageing and it this continuing engagement that ensures that the relationship between later life and the development of these new spatialities will be one of transformation rather than overwhelming determinism.

Part 1
Theories of ageing and globalisation

TWO

Theorising time and space in social gerontology

The themes of time and space occupy a central place within social gerontology (Baars 2015), however, these are generally implicit and often poorly theorised by researchers and writers in the field. Yet the ways in which we understand time, space and the interconnections between them impact on the ways we frame ageing and later life. As conceptions of time and space change so too do our theories of ageing. As a result, it is important to critically assess the *time-spaces* employed in social gerontology if we are to understand the potential impact of globalisation on contemporary ageing. In this book we use the term *time-space* to refer to how spatial and temporal regimes are interconnected and constitute one another at both the material and symbolic level. These time-spaces produce and are reproduced by a set of dominant ideas, practices and discourses. The transition from one time-space to another is reflected in a change in the relationship between these two constituent parts and leads to changes in the social, cultural, political and economic practices that were underpinned by the previous system. Therefore, those gerontological theories that were developed around earlier time-spaces focused on the nation state are being challenged by the emergence of new forms of space, from the local to the global. To explore what this means for our understanding of later life and for older people themselves we need to move away from the conventional narrative about the development of social gerontological theories and re-examine them in terms of the temporal and spatial frames which they deploy.

Social gerontology represents a broad church (Moody 2000, Victor et al 2007, Phillipson 2013a). It spans a range of disciplines from the biomedical through to the arts. Indeed, having been criticised for most of its history for being data rich but theory poor (Bengtson et al 1997, Harper 2000, Alley et al 2010), social gerontology is now faced with a seeming embarrassment of theoretical riches. However, the connection to empirical studies has not always as strong as it might have been (Hendricks et al 2010). Moreover, the changing terminology and often fuzzy theoretical boundaries have made it difficult to present a comprehensive and unambiguous picture of the state of theory within the subject. Nonetheless, it is possible to discern a conventional narrative of the theoretical developments within social gerontology. Phillipson and Baars (2007) have presented what could be described as a fairly orthodox version in which they identify three key phases in this development. The early phase, from the late 1940s to the 1960s in which ageing is seen as an individual and social problem, is characterised by activity theory and disengagement theory. In the middle phase, from the 1970s to the 1980s, ageing is seen as socially and economically constructed. This is a more diverse moment and includes modernisation and ageing theory, life course and age stratification perspectives before moving onto to structured dependency and political economy of ageing approaches. The present phase, from the 1990s onwards, is dominated by cultural and critical gerontological perspectives. They argue that these phases and the shifts between them reflect the different ways in which the relationships between older people and social institutions has evolved.

Time-spaces of ageing and later life

This conventional narrative provides a useful framework for exploring the historical development of social gerontological theories as well as setting the parameters of the debate about the meaning of later life. However, the framework leaves issues of time and space implied or neglected. Yet time and space form the twin axes along which ageing and later life are constructed and understood in all societies.

From a relatively conventional, but not uncontested, sociological approach to history it is possible to identify two relatively recent periods in history (Giddens 1991a, Francis 1992, Smart 1992). These are classified here as first modernity and second modernity (Beck and Lau 2005). Although this periodisation is generally formulated within a European context one can also see evidence of this shift in non-Western societies such as China, Japan and those of the Middle East (Elliott et al 2014). However, while debates about the presence and persistence of non-Western forms of modernity are important (Eisenstadt 1999, 2000, 2002), it is clear that many of the features of first modernity coalesced most clearly in Europe and America. In addition these nations were also critical in the export of modernist ideas and practices especially as a result of their colonial and imperial activities (Appadurai 1996, Wagner 2015).

It is important to note that each of these historical periods is embedded in its own temporal and spatial regime which produces and reproduces theories of ageing. Consequently, instead of viewing the development of social gerontology as an unfolding linear narrative, it is possible to identify two broad families of theories. Theories in each family share a similar set of temporal and spatial assumptions while differing from those in the other group. In the first group are the modernist views of ageing. This category contains disengagement theory, modernisation and ageing theory, age stratification and life course approaches, structured dependency theory and the political economy approach. The second group can be seen as representing the late modern take on ageing and includes both cultural and critical gerontological perspectives.

Modernist approaches to ageing and old age

Social gerontological theories of the mid to late 20th century reflected the temporal and spatial logics of first modernity. Giddens (1991a) identifies three key, interconnected, elements of modernity that set it apart from 'traditional' societies. These are the separation of time and space, the disembedding of social institutions and institutional reflexivity. He argues that, although all societies develop schema for understanding and organising time and space, in pre-modern societies 'time and space were connected *through* the situatedness of place' (1991: 16a). Modernity breaks this connection by emptying out time and disconnecting space from place. Another key factor in this separation was the disembedding of social institutions which Giddens (1991a: 18) defines as the 'lifting out of social relations from local contexts and their re-articulation across infinite tracts of time-space'. The principal institution that emerges from this process is the nation state that has sovereignty and ultimate authority over a given geographical area. Modernity also ushered in a new conceptualisation of time as abstract, linear, future oriented and measurable. Hence the rail networks that developed throughout the 19th century did more than simply connect space; they also coordinated time. Until then, village clocks, where they existed, were set and regulated locally, usually in relation to the sun, creating a great number of different local times within a given country. The coming of the train, and improvements in mechanical motions, meant that all clocks were steadily synchronised to 'railway time' (Giddens 1991b). Alongside this was the shift from the farm to the factory that not only created a new class of workers, it also replaced older temporal frames, of what Hareven (1994) calls 'family time', with a new, harsher, abstract 'industrial time'. These changes to the way in time and space were conceived had a radical impact on the organisation and conceptualisation of the life course. The modern life course emerged around the partition of life into three mutually exclusive, sequential stages of education, work and leisure (Elder 1975, Mayer and Schoepflin 1989, Hareven 1994, Settersten and Mayer 1997). Following these arguments, it is possible to group together a number of gerontological theories that use these referents, of the nation state and the standardised life course, to frame ageing and later life (see Table 2.1). The relative salience of time or space varies according to the primary focus of the different theories. Life course theories have clearly privileged the temporal dimension while structured dependency theory is arguably more focused on the spatial. However, all were based upon the notion of a standardised, fixed, linear life course and took the nation state as the key spatial reference.

Table 2.1. The spatial and temporal regimes of modern and late modern societies

Period	Time	Space	Time:Space	Life-course	Gerontological theories
First Moder-nity	Clock Industrial Standardised	National	Time=Space	Stand-ardised	Disengagement theory Modernisation and ageing theory Age stratification and lifecourse approach Structured depend-ency of old age Political economy of ageing
Late Moder-nity	Digital Multiple Accelerated Plastic	Post-national Global Glocal	Time>Space	Frag-mented Fluid	Critical gerontology Cultural gerontology

Disengagement theory

Disengagement theory probably best illustrates the taken-for-granted nature of assumptions about time and space employed by these early modernist theories (Facchini and Rampazi 2009). In Cumming and Henry's (1961) *Growing Old: The Process of Disengagement*, retirement, as a process and a status, is seen as a functional response for both the individual and society to older age. Retirement was believed to function for the individual, much like the 'sick role' did for medicine (see Parsons 1955, Williams 2005), by offering a socially sanctioned non-economically productive role. It was argued that this allowed older (male) workers to withdraw from employment without feelings of shame or inadequacy. This same process provided a social function by freeing up labour market positions for younger workers with new skills and ideas. Bromley (1981: 134–5) gives an account of this approach:

> One of the more obvious features of maturity and old age is social disengagement – a systematic reduction in certain kinds of social interaction ... It is normal in late maturity and encouraged by common social practices such as superannuation, limited terms of office, age limits and many social norms and expectations affecting behaviour ... The process looks like a sensible attempt on the part of the older person to distribute his [sic] reduced energies and resources over fewer but more personally relevant activities, to conserve effort and to escape from demands which he cannot or does not wish to meet.

Here we can see a considerable degree of similarity between functionalist ideas of the division of labour in society, with each person fulfilling their specific role, and the idea of the division of time within the life course, each period having its specific requirements. Early life is a period of socialisation. This is followed by mid-life, in which each citizen fulfils their (re)productive duties. Finally, the end of life is when individuals should withdraw from these activities. In this model retirement is not only a matter of individual biographical timing, it is part of a wider structure of social timing. Withdrawal from work and other activities is underpinned not just by social policies, around retirement for example, but by normative expectations of disengagement. It is the assumption that there is an affinity between individual and social calendars that leads to the conclusion that retirement represents both an individual and a social good.

Similarly, disengagement theory collapses the spatial distinction between the individual and society. Looking back on this theory from our historical location it is possible to identify a tension between the individual and social processes at work. However, in line with functionalist sociology the authors saw no such tension. For them what was good for the individual was good for society and *vice versa*. Thus, as Phillipson and Baars (2007) note, from this perspective retirement ceases to be (solely) an individual decision but it becomes a social problem. For functionalists in particular, but also for sociologists in general at this time, this meant it became a problem for the nation state. Thus retirement was seen as crucial for the health and productivity of the nation because it opened up employment opportunities for cohorts of young workers.

Life course and age stratification approaches to ageing

Of the all the theories identified within this modernist group, it is the life course theories as well as the age stratification approach which appear, *prima face*, to be most explicitly concerned with the temporal frames through which ageing and later life have been constructed. Advocates of the age stratification approach have argued that age classifications are not static, rather societies are composed of a number of age strata, made up of children, teenagers, middle-aged adults, and so on, which were dynamically interconnected (Riley 1971, 1973, 1974, Foner 1984). These strata were not fixed but were composed of different cohorts. Thus differences between age strata could be due as much to the different historical experiences of each cohort as any age related factors. For Ryder (1985) these birth cohorts, and their succession, were the 'demographic metabolism of society'. Each member of a birth cohort, which Ryder defined as 'those persons born in the same time interval and aging together' (1985: 12), occupies a 'unique location in the stream of history'. As each cohort enters these age strata they confront pre-existing age related norms and sanctions. These are the relics of past cohorts and bear the imprint of their historical experience. Thus each new cohort, forged during a different time, will seek to challenge these boundaries and assert their identity as an age group.

Writers from a life course perspective developed similar arguments although their focus was on the individual rather than on the cohort. They argued that in order to understand the situation of older people it was necessary to look at the entirety of their lives, along multiple dimensions such as work, family and housing, and the advantages and disadvantages that they had encountered (Elder 1994, Berney and Blane 1997, Blane et al 1999, Holland et al 2000, Dannefer 2003, Blane et al 2004, Ferraro and Shippee 2009). Of equal importance, and what distinguishes this approach from Eriksonian life stage theory, was the insistence on locating the timing and trajectories of the life course for different cohorts within their, different, historical contexts (Elder 1975, 1994, 1998, Gilleard and Higgs 2015).

Although the reliance on the notion of a standardised life course is obviously more explicit among these life course theories, it occupies an equally important place in the ideas of the age stratification approach as well. The life course approaches that are used in gerontology, as well as elsewhere (see Ben-Shlomo and Kuh 2002, Kuh et al 2003 for epidemiological uses), assume that individuals pass through a series of successive stages leading to later life. The number of stages in this sequence varies somewhat but generally corresponds to the familiar pattern of the 'three box model' of early life, education, employment and finally retirement (Dannefer and Settersten 2010). The recognition that there are differences between people as they age, accumulating advantages or disadvantages, contrasts with the use of fixed ages at which to explore these differences. The awareness of variable life trajectories is predicated upon an established, standardised life course. To employ a sporting metaphor, we may all run the race better or worse but we do so along the same course.

This holds true for age stratification theory too. While the primary temporal unit in this theory is the cohort a similar dynamic is evident; in this case it is successive cohorts who encounter and pass through these life stages rather than individuals or social classes. Thus the 'churning' that Ryder (1985) refers to is the result of the tension between demographic change and a pre-existing, established life course. Consequently, these theories rely on the standardised life course and (re)produce an image of old age as clearly defined and different from other age groups.

Both approaches also operate with a similar, although less explicit, spatial frame. These trajectories and transitions take place within the nation state. While the basic tripartite model of the life courses is generally seen as a common feature of Western societies at least, there is also an acknowledgement that the exact spacing of these temporal units differs between nations. Each country will have slightly different 'status passage' points because of variations in both social policies and cultural norms. For example in Europe there are differences in the ages at which individuals enter and leave formal education (Eurydice 2011). Similarly, the age at which people can retire from the workforce varies considerably between countries (OECD 2013). Given the importance of retirement in demarcating the beginning of later life for each of these theories, these national variations in social policy imply a state centric approach.

Similarly, from an age stratification perspective, differences in the culture and history of each country signify that the experience of each cohort is not only time specific, but is also space specific. It is often the unique nature of the national experience that defines one cohort from the next. For example, the fall of the Berlin Wall or the Vietnam War might act as a defining moment separating one cohort from the next within a specific country.

Modernisation and ageing theory

Modernisation and ageing theory also has the nation state as its primary spatial frame. Despite their focus on the 'global' trend towards the, apparently inevitable, modernisation of societies, Cowgill (1974) and Cowgill and Holmes (1972) rely on the nation state as the unit of comparison against which 'progress' towards this end can be measured. A central argument is that the societies of the 'developing' world will gradually come to resemble those of the 'developed' world. As a consequence, the status of older people becomes diminished. As noted earlier a key feature of modern society is the emergence of the nation state and as such societies can be compared with one another on the basis of their level of modernisation. This means, in part, that comparison can be made depending on the degree to which they are governed by a rational, bureaucratic, nation state rather than relying on traditional, local, tribal or kinship structures (Lerner 1964). The connection between theory and spatialisation is paramount.

Modernisation and ageing theory also rests on a 'dual' temporality. The first temporality is the overarching modernisation process. This reflects the broader modernist, scientific, Enlightenment notions of progress. As Massey (2008) has argued such approaches, by seeking to locate nations along a continuum of traditional to modern, represent time *as* space. From the perspective of modernisation and ageing theory, countries in the developing world appear as manifestations of developed nations at earlier stages in their history. The second temporality refers to the concomitant reorganisation of time within the nation state. One of the central characteristics of modernisation, according to its advocates (Lerner 1964, Inkeles 1969, 1998), is the emergence of policies governing the management of the life course. This is particularly evident in the development of, and participation in, formal education. A key indicator for this has been the employment of those of 'working age' in the formal (non-agricultural) sector. Cowgill and Holmes (1972) saw modernisation as a shift from the natural rhythms of 'family' time, in which older people were venerated, to the artificial, impersonal, dictates of 'industrial' time, which privileges the young. The spread of new technologies was also believed to disadvantage older people by devaluing their skills and experiences, which had developed during different times and the creation of new jobs for which they were ill-equipped. Similarly older people were also seen to be excluded from the spread of education as this became connected with childhood (Palmore 1971, Cohen 1994). In this view the emergence of retirement constituting the end of working life was seen as disastrous for older people, robbing them of both status and power. The progress of nations along the path of modernisation seems to inversely parallel the individual's forlorn journey to the industrial scrap heap of 'old age'. Both pathways reflect and reinforce the dominant temporal trope of modernity. Time is organised, standardised, linear and irreversible.

The structured dependency of old age: the institutionalisation of time and space

In a similar manner to modernisation and ageing theory, Townsend's structured dependency theory focused on the marginalisation of older people. However, it was also an analysis of the increased institutionalisation of the time and space of old age. He points to three key policy areas that have been responsible for this: retirement, pensions and residential care (Townsend 1981). Hence his work can be read as a description of the consequences of the struggle between competing spatial and temporal regimes for older people. In his seminal work *The Family Life of Older People* (1963), Townsend presents a picture of later life in the East End of London in the 1950s that was still largely localised but rapidly undergoing change. Central to this study were the negative consequences of the dissolution of kin-based community networks for older people. He explicitly situated the 'problem' of old age in a wider, political, debate about the shift away from the provision of care for older people by the family to care by the state. This transformation can be seen as a reflection of the shift from the spatial and temporal regimes of pre-industrial society to those of an industrial, modern, society (Townsend 1963). Although the majority of the older respondents in Townsend's study did not live with their adult children they lived in close proximity to them. They reported being in frequent contact, usually in person and often several times a day. Townsend argues that these dense kinship networks, especially in the form of regular contact between mothers and daughters, were crucial for maintaining the independence of older people. These kinship networks were overlaid with community and class relations. Although logically separable, in the East End of London during this period these two were practically the same. In fact, Townsend chose the location precisely because it was a long established working class community with a strong identity based around male employment in the dockyards.

However, Townsend was describing a world on the brink of change (Gilleard and Higgs 2005). Local forms of social life were giving way to the national. Kinship and community structures were being dis/

replaced by those of the nation state. Townsend describes the rise in both geographic and social mobility among the younger generations as tearing working class families apart. Sons no longer followed their fathers into the factories and shipyards of the East End but commuted to new office jobs in the City. He particularly lamented the weakening of the mother–daughter relation, the axis around which family support in later life was maintained, as daughters moved away with their husbands to start their new families away from Bethnal Green. He argues that these changes were in part a product of the post war housing policy as well as being the product of social change. Consequently, while he welcomed the clearance policy, which demolished the old Victorian slums and war damaged buildings, he bitterly opposed the new high-rise flats that replaced them. He argued that the shift from horizontal to vertical living made it much harder to maintain these traditional family structures. This in turn made older people much more reliant on the state. In the absence of family support older people who were perceived as no longer able to care for themselves were moved into either psychiatric institutions or old people's homes. He saw these as the direct descendants of the Poor Law institutions which had previously loomed in the public imagination. Following Goffman he viewed these homes as 'total institutions', referring to the residents as 'inmates' and the 'incarcerated'.

In *The Family Life* Townsend saw this as a personal tragedy for older people. However, by the time he published his 1981 paper on the *Structured Dependency of Older People* he saw this as part of a much more insidious spread of state control over older people. In this later work he argued that 'society creates the framework of institutions and rules within which the general problems of the elderly emerge and, indeed, are manufactured' (Townsend 1981: 8).

This is echoed by Hazan (1994: 14) who describes the deterioration of the status of older people through successive changes in their socio-spatial location:

> The allocation of space to the elderly at once indicates their place in the community and instructs it as to the overall structure of society and the nature of social relationships prevailing in it ... In biblical times, the 'elders', sages, wise men and leaders, as guardians of the community were allocated social and physical space at the gate of the town [the most prestigious position]. Today their situation is just the opposite. From the almshouse and the workhouse through community-sponsored 'old age homes' to the large

denominational charities, institutional care for the aged implies marginality and isolation from the mainstream of society.

From this perspective the spatial institutionalisation of older people was accompanied by, or even predicated upon, an equally insidious institutionalisation of time with the imposition of the state mandated retirement age. Here it is possible to read Townsend's work as a study of the, uneven, development of the standardised life course. In *The Family Life* he reports that there is still a good deal of variability in the ages at which men retire. This variability contrasts with what he saw as the uniformly negative experience of retirement. In this he was building on early post war concerns about universal state pensions and retirement. Contemporary commentators argued that the 'current proposals and plans to encourage or force people to retire from their jobs in the post war period are a threat to their best interests [because] idleness may result in serious personality disintegration' (Wermel and Gelbaum 1945). These concerns were echoed by Townsend (1963: 153) who reiterated the 'chief theme ... that retirement is a tragic event for many men'. As with the spatial relations of older people he is describing a changing temporality. Variable retirement ages were being replaced by a standardised, state imposed, retirement age. For Townsend this temporal institution was a cruel parody of the earlier spatial institutionalisation of older people in the Poor House. He argues that pensions (in the UK) were deliberately set at or below subsistence level to discourage indolence in later life and encourage saving throughout working life. However, this legacy, coupled with the forced expulsion of older workers from the labour market via retirement, has led to the institutionalisation of impoverishment in later life. This has doubly disadvantaged the working class (especially men) for whom the loss of employment meant not only the loss of income but also of social life. Hakim (1994: 66) writes

> Retirement from work might be conceived as such a rite of passage inasmuch as it may involve the ceremonial and often humiliating separation from a previous identity, but it confers no alternative identity, no social future.

Thus, from the structured dependency approach, retirement is not the start of a new time of life but represents the end of time. It is the fossilisation of time, the absence of a future.

The political economy of ageing and the contested temporalities of capitalism.

In advancing what he terms a political economy of ageing approach, Chris Phillipson (1982) presents a much more complex and contested set of temporalities around the construction of old age. He starts by demonstrating how the age and timing of retirement have fluctuated with the needs of capital. Alongside this he describes the emergence and institutionalisation of retirement. Thus his *Capitalism and the Construction of Old Age* can be (re)read as an exploration, in part, of this tension and of its resolution.

Phillipson's main argument in the book is that the labour market participation rate of older workers has been dependent on the demands of capital and is therefore variable. He states that:

> ... historically aging and retirement are closely intertwined. The number of elderly people influencing both the development of pension systems and formal retirement ages. However the relationship between demographic change and those related to work employment are more subtle than this statement would suggest. Alterations in the supply and demand for labour exert an independent force on retirement patterns. (Phillipson 1982: 6)

During periods of lower labour market supply, such as during wars, older workers will be retained or re-hired to fill gaps in the workforce. During times of economic constraint, such as a recession, companies will seek to lay older workers off to maintain their rate of profit. Other writers from the political economy approach have also pointed to the link between early retirement policies, such as the Job Release Scheme introduced in the UK in 1977, and mass unemployment (Dex and Phillipson 1986, Maule 1995, Desmond 2000, Taylor 2002, 2003).

Against this variability Phillipson notes the emergence of another, more standardised, temporality. He draws on the historian E. P. Thompson's (1967) *Time, Work Discipline and Industrial Capitalism* as a framework for interpreting the competing temporalities of work and leisure around retirement. Thompson describes the increased standardisation and rationalisation of working life under industrial capitalism as opposed to pre-industrial working life. This drive to standardisation reached its zenith with the emergence of the huge industrial complexes of the early to mid-20th century (Baran and Sweezy 1966, Lenin 1975 [1916]). Indeed Braverman (1976) has argued that monopoly capitalism is not just based upon the standardisation of the productive process but seeks to control the entire labour process through the discipline of the production line and Taylorist work planning.

For Phillipson this division between work and life has become the 'hallmark of industrial and monopoly capitalism' (1982: 57). The division of the day into a time for labour and a time of leisure became a metaphor for the lifecycle itself. The end of the working day was seen to correspond with the end of working life. He argues that '[o] ld age together with retirement has become a major stage in the lifecycle with older people being recognised as a distinct social and economic category' (1982: 38). As with Townsend he identifies the imposition of state retirement age as the principal manner in which this has been achieved. He describes the welfare state as 'the use of state power to modify the reproduction of labour power and to maintain the non-working population in capitalist societies' (1982: 77). From this perspective Phillipson argues that the state played an increasing role in the construction and maintenance of old age. However, the relationship between the nation state and capital remained uneasy. Unlike Townsend, Phillipson does not see the marginalisation of older people as a problem wholly created by the state. He describes it as a process produced by capitalist social practices and other organisations, such as Friendly Societies, to which the state had to respond. In the UK it did so with the 1946 National Insurance Act. This made the receipt of a state pension dependent on the condition of the cessation of paid employment. This heralded the dominance of a state mandated retirement age, as part of a standardised life course, over the more variable needs of capital.

Notions of spatiality are not as explicit as those of time in Phillipson's work. However, it is possible to trace the underlying spatial frame he employs by examining the principal Marxist theory on which it relies. As noted above Phillipson draws heavily on the concept of monopoly capitalism. In its Leninist (1975 [1916]) formulation this concept was used to examine and critique the imperialist expansion of the main capitalist powers. He argued that the sheer size of the 'combinations', in Germany and the USA in particular, have fused capitalism with the state leading to a period of imperialist competition between states to secure benefits for *their* capitalists. Thus, despite, or because of, greater international competition, a synergy emerged between the needs of capital and those of the nation state. This concept was developed more thoroughly by Baran and Sweezy (1966) in their classic work *Monopoly Capitalism*. Although they do not employ Lenin's terminology, state monopoly capitalism, they still see the relationship between the state and capital as integral and mutually reinforcing. They argue that

> ... we have not chosen to follow this precedent [of using Lenin's phrase] but rather to use the term monopoly capital or monopoly capitalism without qualification for two reasons. In the first place the state has always played a crucial role in the development of capitalism ... Under the circumstances to lay special emphasis on the role of the state in the state of monopoly capitalism may lead people to believe that is was of negligible importance in the earlier history of capitalism. Even more important is that terms like state capitalism or state monopoly capitalism almost inevitably carry the connotation that the state is somehow an independent *social* force co-ordinate with private business and that the functioning of the system is determined not only by the co-operation of these two forces but also by their antagonisms and conflicts. This seems to us a seriously misleading view. (Baran and Sweezy 1966: 75)

In both formulations, and therefore by extension in the political economy of ageing approach, the nation state as a combined economic and political unit emerges as the principal actor and focus of analyses. This conclusion is supported by Walker's (2005: 815) observation that the 'political economy of ageing is rooted in the relationships between social structure, individual socioeconomic status, gender, ethnicity, the life course and the state. Not surprisingly, therefore, its primary attention has been towards the nation state (especially the role of the state in social policies affecting older people)'.

However, as we argue, the utility of these standardised, modernist, spatial and temporal referents for understanding later life have been seriously called into question following the empirical and theoretical developments of the past few decades (Phillipson 1998, 2013a).

Ageing and later life in late modernity

As shown in Table 2.1 both cultural and critical gerontologists are situated, and situate themselves, within the spatial and temporal regimes of second modernity. This term and its collection of synonyms such as late modernity, reflexive modernity and liquid modernity all aim to provide a theoretical terminology for changes in the nature of modern societies where both a greater reflexivity and individualisation are seen to occur (see Giddens 1991a, 1994, Bauman 2000). Others have seen this transformation in terms of a move to post-modernity where the collapse of meaning has rendered Enlightenment values of truth and progress both problematic and lost in an endless process of self-referentiality (Baudrillard 1989, Harvey 1989). Not only are the knowledge claims of modernity challenged but also many of its institutions which are now seen as much more contingent than they have in the past. This development has had profound consequences for the understanding of old age and the structuring of the life course. As Gilleard and Higgs (2005: 1) reflect:

> The flux in the social organization of the 'post-modern' life course has rendered later life an increasingly contested field ... the cultural developments of the late twentieth century have generated a new set of terms by which the life course can be understood ... this 'cultural revolution' has destabilized many of the institutional structures underpinning the 'modern life cycle', at the same time 'disembedding' individuals from refuge in the 'community'.

In a similar fashion, although from a different perspective, Phillipson (1998: 29) states that:

> Critical gerontology, in fact, is built upon a number of assumptions about the nature of social change, in particular that which concerns the shift from a modern to a 'late' or 'postmodern' age... and the subsequent impact on the social position and identity of older people.

As a consequence of this shift to 'advanced' modernity, he argues that we have entered a 'period of crisis in respect of the identity of older people'.

Both positions identify the collapse of the standardised, modernist, life course as a central issue in the construction and circumstances of later life. For critical gerontologists this represents both a risk and an opportunity. In line with the earlier political economy of ageing approach the de-institutionalisation of retirement is seen as a response to the needs of a globalised, increasingly crisis ridden, form of capitalism (Laczko and Phillipson 1991, Biggs 2004, Biggs et al 2006, Westerhof and Tulle 2007, Asquith 2009). This shift in temporality away from an organised, socialised, life course to a more individualised life project has been accompanied by a shift in the burden of responsibility for wellbeing in later life from the state to the individual.

> Policies were therefore moving from traditional concerns with discrete problems in the fields of work, healthcare and housing to more integrated policies on ageing that touch on the lifestyles of older people more generally ... In doing so, the basic discourse of disengagement and decline which was related to state support was increasingly supplemented by a discourse of autonomy and participation, related to the value of individual responsibility. (Westerhof and Tulle 2007: 239)

Many have also argued that the move from chronologically based definitions of older age to the seemingly more positive representations of ageing have not only served to mask inequalities in later life but have (re)produced new discourses and practices of exclusion. Bowling (2005, 2006) has criticised the concepts of 'healthy ageing' and 'successful ageing' for re-medicalising later life and argued that these concepts represent a 'new ageism' in which the fear of ageing has been replaced by the fear of ageing with a disability. However, it has now become the individual's responsibility to ensure that they remain disability free. Thus, rather than ensuring healthiness in later life, this discourse ignores socioeconomic factors and ends up blaming the victim (Minkler and Fadem 2002, Angus and Reeve 2006, Katz and Calasanti 2015).

> Despite the fact that the discourse of positive ageing sounds positive, it is not. It is not positive because if you are incapable of meeting the benchmarks of a positive ageing experience, then you have negatively (or unhealthily, unsuccessfully, or unproductively) aged, and with it, you must bear the weight of failure as it is represented in the terms opposed to healthy, successful and productive. Positive ageing is also not positive because it is consistent with a deficit model of ageing – that is, old people cause us troubles. (Asquith 2009: 267)

The adoption of this discourse by policy makers, at the national and international level, is seen to fit with a broader, neo-liberal, assault on welfare (Asquith 2009, Phillipson 2013a, Rubinstein and de Medeiros 2015). In the UK Biggs (2001) has argued that the third age emphasis on choice, autonomy, activity and productivity accords with the Third

Way ideology. Thus despite appearing to be progressive, government policy is aimed at reducing future welfare expenditure, rather than promoting positive ageing (Polivka 2001). Biggs (2004: 47) concludes that in the present period of late modernity older people are caught between the twin perils of 'fixity and flux'. The former represents 'fixed social–cultural stereotyping that may deny or restrict possibilities for personal growth and meaningful social inclusion' while the latter is an expression of the post-modernisation of identity. However, both of these are seen as threats for older people. He notes that 'flux includes a second assault on identity. This arises from the fragmentation of standpoints from which to resist dominant constructions, increasing uncertainty and making personal coherence difficult to maintain'.

However some critical gerontologists also celebrate the emancipatory potential of the collapse of these restrictive age categorisations (Grenier 2012, Phillipson 2015). Drawing on the more humanistic tradition within critical gerontology there are those who see the demise of these overly determining age structures as an opportunity to reclaim older peoples' subjective accounts of their own ageing. This has led to an increased interest in biographical perspectives which aim to uncover the more fluid, reflexive, discursive practices through which older people construct their ageing identities (Wilson 1997, Phillipson 1998, Powell and Longino 2002, Twigg 2007, Gilleard and Higgs 2013). This biographical perspective reflects the multiple temporalities of ageing in second modernity. Central to this is the rejection of the master status of chronological age, with its associated narrative of biological and cognitive decline. Instead older people 'hold different age identities in different domains of functioning, such as physical, social and psychological functioning' (Westerhof and Tulle 2007: 248). Subjective age emerges as a more meaningful, individualised calendar against which people interpret their lives. This perspective is also seen to challenge the 'masculinist' focus of traditional gerontology and draws attention to the alternative identities and temporalities of marginalised groups such as women and ethnic minorities (Russell 2007, Hurd Clarke and Bennett 2015).

The plasticity of ageing, as opposed to the rigidity of chronological age, is a key feature of the cultural gerontology position. Crucially they argue that the institutional arrangements that underpinned the construction of ageing and older age in the post war period have been or are being substantially altered (Gilleard and Higgs 2005, 2013, Twigg and Martin 2015). Present cohorts of those entering later life are healthier, wealthier and more active than their predecessors. Consequently, traditional images of old age as a period of decline and dependency are steadily being replaced by more positive images of 'active', 'successful' or 'productive' ageing (Uhlenberg 1992, Pampel and Hardy 1994, Gilleard and Higgs 2000, 2005, Bass and Caro 2001, Weiss and Bass 2002, Katz and Marshall 2003, Metz and Underwood 2005). Marketers and the media are also re-packaging images of later life in line with the more active lifestyles of the population (Peterson 1992, Gunter 1998, Long 1998, Ekerdt and Clark 2001, Robinson and Umphery 2006, Simcock and Sudbury 2006, Moschis 2009). Alongside these improvements in wellbeing, the fragmentation of the temporal and spatial structuring of later life has driven and been driven by the increased agency of older people.

In place of the uniform passage into old age there is now a more fluid and open set of transitions into the third age. Peter Laslett (1987, 1996, 1997), who is credited with popularising the concept of the third age in the English speaking world, argues that the rapid increases in life expectancy have had a radical impact on people's perception of ageing and time. There is now the 'necessity of all persons having to *live in the presence of their future selves*' (Laslett, 1997: 1805, emphasis added). In Laslett's vision this necessity required people to take action to remain healthy to ensure an active third age for as long as possible. From this perspective entry into and exit from this period of life varied hugely and was not determined by chronological age.

Gilleard and Higgs (2000, 2002, 2005, 2013) have developed Laslett's concept of the third age. However rather than see it as a matter of personal planning and moral worth they argue that it is best understood as a 'cultural field' which has opened up the potential for the creation of alternative identities in later life. They argue that the rapid growth in the number and proportion of older people within society has, paradoxically, fractured the very idea of 'old age'. Instead 'we are beginning to see a variety of 'cultures of ageing' emerge, seeking to establish 'meaning' in ageing' (Gilleard and Higgs 2000: 22). The key driver of these 'cultures of ageing' has been the expansion of post war consumer capitalism. Their principal argument is that those cohorts who grew up in a period of mass consumption have a radically different approach to ageing and time than their predecessors. Significantly, although they argue that 'the baby boom generation broke the mould of the modern life course' (Gilleard and Higgs, 2002: 376), this is due principally to their generational experience rather than their demographic weight. This experience, which was marked by the decline of traditional industries, increased political freedoms, rising material wellbeing and the growth of consumerism, radically transformed intergenerational relations and the life course.

> If the interwar years had been a time when class based revolutions seemed imminent, the 1960s were a time when generational revolution appeared to be in the offing. (Gilleard and Higgs 2007: 16)

Drawing on Mannheim's (1952) seminal work on generations, Gilleard and Higgs (2005) argue that this experience created a 'generational habitus' based around consumerist lifestyles and the rejection of 'old age'. This focus on generations is crucial as it illustrates the multiple and overlapping notions of time. Here generation, as a cultural space, should not be confused with cohort, as a demographic unit. While cohort is uniform and measurable, generation is fuzzy and elusive. For Mannheim, generation could not be reduced to a single temporal frame but was instead marked by overlapping temporalities. He criticised positivistic accounts of generations (and social stability) for their mechanistic view of time where one generation simply succeeds another. In contrast he saw the 'time interval that separates generations [as] subjectively experienceable time' (Mannheim cited in Pilcher 1994: 486). Kettler and Loader (2004: 161) have argued that Mannheim's concept of time 'is 'hierarchical' rather than simply chronological, in that relations between past and present are mediated by structures of meaning that cluster and accumulate events and that differ in rates of change'.

A second important dimension which is also related to the spread of consumerism is the notion of the reversibility of time (Coupland 2009). Both cultural and critical gerontologists have drawn attention to the massive growth in markets for 'anti-ageing' products and practices. Gilleard and Higgs (2007) argue that the new consumer based lifestyles of the 1950s and 1960s eroded class distinctions among an emergent 'Youth'. As such 'Youth' looked to exclude the 'Other' of the older generation. As history's first teenagers entered later life they were reluctant to abandon these ideas.

> Old age – the attributed community of "the old" – forms a key boundary marking the limits of third age culture. The third age is defined both by the continuities of choice and the discontinuity of old age. Within the field is a conscious absence of an individualised old age. Old age is rejected as a collective choice because it seems to represent a return to the past. Communal representations of old age threaten to dissolve the life-styles of autonomous individuals, turning them into an amorphous collective mass grave, the burial

ground of individuality and choice. Old age is culturally
marginalised because those who were old and out of date
were the other that helped a generation define itself. As
the signifier of material and symbolic bankruptcy, old age
is simply not a choice. (Gilleard and Higgs 2007: 26)

Instead older people can now be seen to be actively engaged in the
continuous, indeterminate processes of what is referred to as 'identity
work' (Riach and Loretto 2009) or 'beauty work' (Clarke and Griffin
2008, Clarke et al 2009, Hurd Clarke and Bennett 2015) to create
socially and individually meaningful identities which are not based
on chronological (old) age but rather seek to undermine, conceal or
reject them. This has led to the growth of cosmetic surgery and of anti-
ageing products such as nutraceuticals, cosmeceuticals, health foods,
super-foods and lifestyle guides (Higgs 1995, Gilleard and Higgs 2005,
Vincent 2006, 2007, 2008, Vincent et al 2008). There now exists a
huge industry that promises its consumers that they can 'turn back the
ageing process' and 'look ten years younger' (Coupland 2009).

In contrast to the common temporal frame employed by these two
perspectives there are some slight differences in the spatial frames they
use. Although both clearly argue that the nation state has more or less
given way to global pressures they disagree on the relevance of local,
community based sources of identity for older people. While cultural
gerontology is clearly global in outlook, critical gerontology often
encompasses a number of views from the international to the glocal.

In spite of their (empirical) focus on Western Europe and North
America, Gilleard and Higgs (2005: 4) argued that the 'third age can be
treated as a 'global' construct, capable of being extended to all corners
of the world'. From this perspective third age cultures spread out from
their heartlands of the USA and the UK, where consumer markets
were most developed, to other countries as they are engulfed by the
wave of global consumer capitalism (Gilleard and Higgs 2015). As
such this will weaken and replace previous forms of social attachment.
They argue that with the spread of new lifestyles, travel and tourism as
well as internet technology have sealed the fate of local, place-based,
communities as a central source of identity in later life.

Late modernity has seen a blossoming of alternatives to
the community of place. These alternative communities
privilege sources of identity other than those given by ties
of work and family. In a post-work world, such alternative

communities provide options for new identities and a new sense of belonging. (Gilleard and Higgs 2005: 18)

Phillipson and Baars (2007) also identify globalisation as a defining feature of critical gerontology. They argue that 'globalization has produced a distinctive phase in the history of ageing, with tensions between nation state-based policies concerning demographic change and those formulated by global actors and institutions' (2007: 81). This is echoed by Walker's (2005) call that 'the political economy of ageing must adopt an international form if it is to interpret fully the changing relationship between old age and the state' (2005: 816). In *Old Age* John Vincent (2003) identified three ways in which this will affect older people. Firstly, widening of inequalities and increasing poverty will affect older people more severely given their pre-existing high rates of poverty. Secondly, hostile international capital markets will put pressure on social security spending. Lastly older people are less able to escape the effects of environmental degradation. Phillipson (2002) has further argued that there has been a fundamental rupture in the relationship between nationality and citizenship which, through social policies such as pensions, has underpinned modernist notions of 'old age' for many decades.

> Growing old has, itself, become relocated within a trans-national context, with international organisations (such as the World Bank and International Monetary Fund) and cross-border migrations, creating new conditions and environments for older people ... Globalisation, it is argued, has produced a distinctive stage in the social history of ageing, with a growing tension between nation state-based solutions (and anxieties) about growing old and those formulated by global actors and institutions. Ageing can no longer be viewed as a 'national' problem or issue but one that affects trans-national agencies and communities. Local or national interpretations of ageing had some meaning in a world where states were in control of their own destiny. (Phillipson, 2003)

Hence both nationality and citizenship are seen as being reconfigured within diverse global networks as the nation state seems to steadily lose its economic and political power. For many this represents a threat to the provision of welfare for the older population in the West as it seemingly undermines the basis of national citizenship without providing an adequate, supranational, alternative (Wilson 2002, Neilson 2003, Phillipson 2003). At the same time, in the developing world Polivka (2001) and Polivka and Borrayo (2002) identify globalisation as the main threat to the ageing populations as result of the imposition of austerity programmes and cuts in social spending.

However, although these writers see globalisation as a threat to other spatialities, namely the nation state, a number of critical gerontologists do not hold that these other institutions have been completely eclipsed. In particular, locally based organisations or structures are seen as relatively resistant to, or even reinvigorated by, global processes. Phillipson (2007: 321) argues that although globalisation might impact negatively on older people who have lived in the same area for a long time, it 'also gives rise to new types of movement in old age, and is constructing an expanding mix of spaces, communities and lifestyle settings'. This is supported by a host of studies on the experiences of older migrants among retirement migrants in Arizona's Sun Belt (McHugh 2000a, 2003, McHugh and Larson-Keagy 2005) or British and Swedish retirees in Southern Europe (Warnes et al 1999, King et al 2000, Gustafson 2001, 2002, 2008). Conversely Lewis (2009) has looked at the experience of older Cambodian migrants in the USA. Among this group she notes that a central feature in normal (and normative) discourses on ageing is the centrality of place. Phillipson and Scharf (2005: 72) also argue that contrary to the end of space argument in globalisation theory 'research on older people suggests that, globalising processes notwithstanding, the relationship between people and place is even more important at the beginning of the 21st century than it was a century or more ago'. This position is closer to Robertson's (1995) view of a 'glocal', rather than a completely 'globalised', world in which the global and the local are mutually constitutive. We shall return to this argument and its limitations in the next chapter.

Conclusions

The preceding discussion demonstrates a number of key points. Firstly, that time and space are intimately connected as explanatory concepts even though the ideas themselves might seem to be increasingly disconnected. Secondly, that our theories of ageing and later life rest upon and, in turn, reinforce particular time-spaces. Consequently, changes in the spatial and temporal architecture of any society or historical period will impact on the expectations and experiences of older people in other societies or time periods. This in turn demands that that we reassess the ways in which we understand contemporary ageing and later life. This can be seen in the way in which the temporal and spatial conditions of older ways of ageing were radically changed by the emergence of modernist social forms, such as the nation state and medical science. However, it has also been argued that the spatial and temporal assumptions on which these 'modernist' social theories rest may no longer pertain. Rather the shift to second modernity has been accompanied by a radical reorganisation of time and space which has also transformed old age. By extension we need to critically assess the utility of those older, modernist, gerontological theories that framed their understanding of ageing and later life within the confines of the nation state and the standardised life course. If these spatial and temporal references have become less stable, then the theories that were built on them must also have become less stable.

Changes in the temporal coordinates of ageing and later life are well documented in the de-institutionalisation of the life course and the emergence of a set of competing, non-chronologically age based set of identities for later life. Moreover, just as the nature of ageing and later life has become more fragmentary, so too has the space in which people age. The nation state is seen to have diminished as the principal space in and through which old age is constructed. Both cultural and critical gerontologists have seen globalisation as the key challenge to ageing and later life as well as to theories of them. Paradoxically, while there has been a collapse of the modernist time-spaces through which ageing has been constructed, principally the nation state, the use of globalisation within gerontological literature is increasingly problematic in understanding these changes. A key issue, although not one unique to gerontology, has been the absence of an agreed upon definition of what constitutes globalisation. Even when definitions are given they often fail to capture what is qualitatively different about globalisation and therefore appear to substitute one totalising set of spatialities, the global, for another, the system of nation states. This approach is too simplistic and fails to give due recognition to the multiplicity of spatial logics that now operate in today's world. This deficit has been partly recognised in the use by some authors of terms such as glocalisation alongside the realisation that other (local) spatial logics may also be important (Phillipson and Scharf, 2007). However, this approach is also still somewhat limited, as will be shown in the following chapter. Instead we argue that we need to look at the ways in which different spaces, from the global to the regional and the local, interact and to examine the ways that these interactions impact on different aspects of ageing. In order to do this, we need to critically assess what these different spaces are and how, if at all, they relate to one another.

THREE

Competing spatialities of ageing and later life

As the previous chapter has shown, gerontological theories are deeply embedded in the temporal and spatial regimes in which they operate and consequently they reflect the dominant time-spaces of their own historical locations. However, as key writers such as Giddens, Appadurai and Beck note, we are in the midst of a relatively long process of the re-spatialisation of the social, political, cultural and economic spheres. An important dimension of this has been a shift away from the national time-space operating as the dominant spatial logic (Giddens 1991b, Smart 1992, Appadurai 1996, Beck 1999). This has also brought about a reorganisation of the temporal and spatial coordinates of later life. Consequently, gerontological theories that explain ageing and later life in relation to national frameworks need to be reassessed. This is particularly important given that gerontology has yet to address the nature and form of this new world order. Chris Phillipson notes:

> Globalisation undoubtedly adds a further dimension to the nature of such risks and the different way in which they are expressed throughout the life course. Exploring the lives of older people as active participants in this new global environment will be a major challenge for critical gerontology in the twenty-first century. (Phillipson 2003)

Our aim in this chapter is to address this challenge and to contribute to the growing academic interest in the spatial relations of ageing and later life. Interest in environmental or geographical gerontology has grown apace over the past two decades. This has produced a range of work from retirement migration (Warnes et al 1999, King et al 2000, Warnes 2006), residential arrangements (McHugh 2000a, McHugh and Larson-Keagy 2005, Peace et al 2007) and the use of domestic space (Percival 2002). Up until the mid-1990s, however, the focus was very empirical. While this was important for exposing inequalities between older people in different places, the relative dearth of theoretical engagement was additionally problematic. From the mid-1990s onwards there were calls for more engagement with the cultural turn and for more critical analyses of the impact of geographical perspectives on our theories of ageing. In their review of the field Harper and Laws (1995: 200) identified two key areas that required investigation:

'… the age variable itself, its social and spatial construction … and, secondly, the geographical implication of the ageing of all societies'.

However, we are concerned with a much broader conceptualisation of space which encompasses not only the geographical but also the political, economic and social spaces in which ageing and later life take place. Our argument throughout the book is that, although we are witnessing the decline of the nation state as the dominant spatial unit through which to understand these political, economic and social processes, the system of nation states has yet to be fully replaced by a new spatial order. Instead what we see are the emergence of a number of different types of spaces ranging from the global, the regional to the local. The challenge of these new spatial logics for gerontology is not simply an empirical one. It also challenges the epistemological and ontological assumptions that underpin the 'methodological nationalism' (Wimmer and Glick Schiller 2002) of many modernist accounts of ageing and later life.

Moreover, if we are to understand what the emergence of these new spaces means for older people as well as the ways we think about later life, it is important that we are clear about what has replaced the former structures of old age. To this end it is necessary to have a clear definition of what is meant by globalisation and to be able to contextualise the broader debates around globalisation in the social sciences. It is equally important to explore the limits of globalisation as an empirical phenomenon. A key objective in this chapter will be to explore the extent to which other spatial logics, such as 'regionalism' or 'localism', can provide alternative frameworks for understanding ageing and later life. The salience of these other spatial dimensions is reflected in the apparent divergence within the gerontological literature between the increased use of globalisation as a theoretical frame and the growth of empirical studies that continue to point to regional, national and local differences in the organisation of later life. Consequently, it is important to assess the evidence that these different spatialities exist and what constitutes them before we can begin to examine whether they have an impact on ageing and later life. Yet, it also has to be acknowledged that while this attention to non-global spatialities is important, such approaches are also often limited to only one spatial frame. Thus the central argument of this chapter is that theories that rest on the dominance of one spatiality to the exclusion of others can only offer a partial framework for analysis. Our overall position is that contemporary society is made up of a mosaic of different spatial orders which are not necessarily reducible to one another. Social gerontology, indeed sociology in general, needs to move away from binary oppositions which posit one spatiality against others, and towards an acceptance of a more nuanced 'heterarchical' model which allows for the complex interplay of different spatial logics.

Globalisation

Globalisation, it is generally acknowledged, has become a buzzword, ubiquitously used but poorly defined. As yet there is no consensus about how to define it, when it began, what caused it and what its effects have been or will be (Bauman 1998, Scholte 1998, 2005, Goldblatt et al 1999, Held and McGrew 2003, 2007, Wolf 2004, Van Der Bly 2005, Cohen and Kennedy 2007). These are more than semantic issues. Despite the growing awareness of the importance of globalisation within social gerontology, definitions of what is meant by globalisation in the gerontological literature can often be ambiguous or even absent. The lack of a common vocabulary means that it is difficult to assess claims made about the impact, or otherwise, of globalisation on the lives of older people.

In line with Scholte (2005) we define globalisation as a 'reordering of social geography' rather than just seeing it as a simple expression of economics, politics or culture. Globalisation is the reconfiguration of space (and time) such that the global becomes the normative horizon for both structure and action (Thrift 1999, Therborn 2000, Held and McGrew 2003). Put more simply this means that people start to think and act in global rather than national terms. For example, businesses will look for opportunities from around the world rather than just within their national markets. Similarly, people might be as likely to look for jobs abroad as they would in their own country. At a very basic level the growth of cheap air flights and advances in information and communication technologies have created many opportunities for certain groups of people to be more globally mobile, thereby seeming to make the world a smaller place. This process of shrinking the distances between places has been given a number of different labels and definitions. Harvey (2006) refers to it as 'time-space compression' while Giddens (2002) calls it 'time-space distanciation'. Both terms aim to capture the idea that globalisation has made space much more permeable and pliable. Reflecting these ideas Held and McGrew (2007) refer to globalisation as a '*stretching* of social, political and economic activities across political frontiers'. While focusing on the novelty of globalisation itself as an explanatory category, Albrow (1996: 120) has argued that 'the shift from the transnational to the global in international affairs is one of the characteristic sequences in which globality crystallizes as a new level of explanation'. For him this is not the same as the simple increase in bilateral or multilateral agreements between states, rather globality implies a qualitative shift rather than a simple quantitative expansion of international activity. Castells (2000) has described the emergence of a global 'network society' which is marked by a 'timeless time' and a 'space of flows'. Thus, despite using somewhat different terms, central to each theorisation is the notion that the radical reduction in the time that it takes to traverse the globe either in real terms, such as long haul flights, or in virtual terms, such as email, has radically altered our perception of place and space.

Globalisation in this sense implies that social action takes place on a global level as opposed to that of other spatialities, such as the national level. Hence the persistence or disappearance of the nation state has become the key axis around which the globalisation debate has turned (Goldblatt et al 1999, Riain 2000). Beck (1999) observes that globalisation has problematised the modernist notion that social action takes place 'in the self-enclosed spaces of nation states'. Appadurai (1996: 19) goes further, arguing that

> ... the nation-state, as a complex modern political form, is on its last legs ... Nation-states, for all their important differences ... only make sense as a system. This system (even when seen as a system of differences) appears poorly equipped to deal with the interlinked diasporas of people and images that mark the here and now.

As the dominant spatial (and temporal) unit of modernity the fate of the system as a whole appears inseparable from that of the nation state. Bauman (2007: 2) argues that with the coming of liquid modernity 'the power to act effectively that was previously available to the modern nation state is now moving away to the politically uncontrolled global (and in many ways extraterritorial) space'. A common explanation for this assumed demise is the inability of the nation state to manage global problems which, by their very nature, transcend national boundaries. Hence there is an institutional mismatch between the configuration and capabilities of the nation state, which developed in response to the priorities of a particular historical age, and the demands of the global system. Put more prosaically, the modern state is 'too big for the small problems in the world and too small for the big problems' (Appadurai 1996).

For Giddens (2002) late or reflexive modernity is a cause and consequence of the increased globalisation of social action. For him globalisation is not simply a shift in the geopolitical locus of power but represents a radical reordering of the spatial and social modes of living. There has also been a shift in the time-space relationship. Under modernity the two coincided, in the form of the nation state (time=space) however, with the advent of late modernity and the increased globalisation of social action time has come to dominate space (time>space).

> Tradition is about the organization of time and therefore also space: so too is globalization, save that one runs counter to the other. Whereas tradition controls space through its control of time, with globalization it is the other way round. Globalization is essentially 'action at distance'; absence predominates over presence, not in the sedimentation of time, but because of the restructuring of space. (Giddens 1994: 96)

Following these arguments, a number of writers have criticised the state centric focus that is emblematic of modernist social sciences as being inadequate for understanding the present global condition (Scholte 1998, Urry 2002, Sheller and Urry 2006).

> globalization calls into question *a basic premise of the first modernity ... methodological nationalism ...* the globalization debate in the social sciences may be understood and developed as a fruitful dispute about which basic assumptions and images of society, which *units of analysis*, can *replace* the axiomatics of the national state (Beck 1999: 21, emphasis in original)

However, despite the claim that globalisation is now the normative frame of reference, it is important to remember that it is a multidimensional phenomenon. In contrast to writers who seek to identify a single underlying motor or explanation for globalisation we see it as a complex set of processes. At the most basic level a number of writers have argued that globalisation should be disaggregated into three separate (but related) dimensions: economic, political and social globalisation (Keohane and Nye 2000, Dreher 2006, Raab et al 2008). While

Beck (1999) has identified five different dimensions: informational, ecological, economic, cultural and the globalisation of labour and production, we have chosen to employ Arjun Appadurai's (1996: 32) conceptual model of globalisation 'as a complex, overlapping, disjunctive order' as a better way of understanding the phenomenon. He proposes 'that an elementary framework for exploring such disjunctures is to look at the relationship among five dimensions of global cultural flows that can be termed (a) *ethnoscapes*, (b) *mediascapes*, (c) *technoscapes*, (d) *financescapes* and (e) *ideoscapes*'. Hence rather than globalisation being reducible to a single factor, these 'scapes' make up the multiple and uneven '*imagined worlds*' of globalisation. He defines these as:

- *Ethnoscape* as 'the landscape of persons who constitute the shifting world in which we live: tourists, immigrants, refugees, exiles, guest workers and other moving groups'.
- *Technoscape* as 'the global configuration, also ever fluid, of technology and the fact that technology, both high and low, both mechanical and informational, now moves at high speeds across various kinds of previously impervious boundaries'.
- *Financescapes* as 'the disposition of global capital [that] is now a more mysterious, rapid and difficult landscape to follow than ever before'.
- *Mediascapes* as 'the distribution of the electronic capabilities to produce and disseminate information ... and the images of the world created by these media'.
- *Ideoscapes* as 'the concatenations of images, but also are often directly political and frequently have to so with the ideologies of states and the counter-ideologies of movements explicitly oriented to capturing state power or a piece of it'.

In Appadurai's theory each of these 'scapes' is constructed by social actors as imagined worlds similar to Benedict Anderson's (2004) idea of the nation as an 'imagined community'. However, he believes that we now live in globally imagined worlds rather than locally or nationally imagined communities. It is the relationships between these 'scapes' that create the contemporary cultural field. An important distinction that separates Appadurai's model from reductionist descriptions of globalisation is that these dimensions are not reducible to one underlying dominant factor. He goes further to argue that, because each of these scapes has developed its own set of internal constraints and goals, relationships between them are 'deeply disjunctive and profoundly unpredictable' (Appadurai 1996). Each follows different trajectories which are 'non-isomorphic' and as a result, they can confront and destabilise one another. Appadurai's key insight in developing this model was that globalisation was not just the expansion of global capitalism, nor was it simply leading to an inevitably homogenised global culture. Rather, he sought to demonstrate how modernity circulates through geographic, diasporic, imaginary and local spaces to produce irregularities of globalisation. Hence he uses the term 'scapes' to denote the uneven landscapes global modernisation (Martínez 2012).

While Appadurai has provided a template for investigation, and has identified the shift away from the national time-space as the dominant spatial logic, we would also argue that we have yet to enter a truly global time-space. This is not to deny that globalisation is a real phenomenon. But rather to argue that it is not the dominant spatial logic. Neither is it inevitable nor indeed is it irreversible. A closer examination of economic, cultural and political life reveals a far more complex pattern that cannot be simply understood through the binary distinction of the 'national' versus the 'global'. While we draw on Appadurai's conceptual model of the disjunctive nature of globalisation, we argue that it is necessary to extend this to include other spatial logics and look at how different actors attempt to organise these scapes across different spatialities. Appadurai sees these scapes as operating globally and accepts that there might be contradictions and disjunctures between them at the global level. However, we would contend that there are also spatial contradictions across the same scape. Thus actors might wish to promote or capture a certain set of ideas, an ideoscape, about ageing within a certain geographical space that might contradict or establish boundaries against encroachment from an alternative politics of later life that are also trying to achieve spatial dominance. For instance, one could identify a European ideoscape around ageing that the EU or other European actors wish to promote and maintain within their spatial and regional limits. In turn they might see this as a way of holding off a global ideoscape of ageing promoted by other actors such as the World Bank or IMF. The same could also be true of financescapes, such that certain countries might want to have control over their pension arrangements but regional or global actors seek to promote their particular financescape across those national boundaries.

These ideas form one of the cornerstones for our understanding of spatial processes. Just as Appadurai's scapes operate unevenly and disjunctively we also see spatial logics as multiple, heterogeneous and potentially contradictory. Correspondingly we need to consider not only the contradictions between scapes, for example how the financescape might be disjunctive with the ideoscape or the ethnoscapes of ageing, but also consider the spatial limits within those individual scapes such that there might be regional ideoscapes that may or may not be in conflict with each other but that create boundaries at certain regional spatial limits. Thus, although seeing globalisation as a process of re-spatialisation might better reflect the complexity of the underlying transformations these arguments are not without criticism. Many writers point to the persistence, emergence or resurgence of alternative, competing, spatial logics operating in the world today. As such an exclusive focus on the global is possibly too simplistic to contain the multiplicity of spaces in the contemporary world order. In place of a global era we are faced with a number of competing and coordinated spatial logics of which the global is only one and not always even the most important.

Regionalisation

In the preceding section we outlined the literature which identifies globalisation as the key spatial logic with which to understand social change. However, there those who argue that we are living in a more regionalised, rather than a more globalised, world (Hettne 2001, 2005, Beeson 2005, Dicken 2007). These writers contend that political, economic and sociocultural activities are increasing organised within supranational regional levels such as the EU, ASEAN and NAFTA (Hirst and Thompson 2000, Tshuma 2000). As Grimes (2012) has noted these regional projects have gained increased support as people and politicians search for alternatives to the US-led global financial system following the Global Financial Crisis of 2008. Crucially these arguments suggest that there are serious empirical and theoretical limits to globalisation. They also challenge the argument that globalisation has become the most appropriate spatial logic through which to understand ageing and later life. Moreover, if economic, political and cultural activity is becoming increasingly organised at the regional, rather than at the global or national, level then we might expect regional actors to be the most important actors in the production and reproduction of the conditions of ageing and later life. As regions gain greater economic and political coherence will they also emerge as the main policy makers in areas such as healthcare and retirement? In the cultural sphere one might also ask whether or not it is possible to identify regional identities in later life. Are there different American, European or Asian ways of ageing? We will return to empirically explore these issues in subsequent chapters.

The 'urge to merge' is nothing new and there are many historical examples of regional actors (Schulz et al 2001). Earlier forms, such as the European Coal and Steel Community (ECSC), were narrowly focused, state-led, 'top-down' initiatives. Moreover, these operated against the backdrop of a bipolar Cold War and, consequently, reflected its chief security concerns (Hettne 2001, Schulz et al 2001, Buzan and Wæver 2003). However, the nature of these organisations has changed over time and the more recent wave of regionalisation from the 1980s onwards is considered to be qualitatively different from its post war predecessors. It is a multifaceted, fluid, complex and dynamic set of processes (Hettne 2005, Warleigh-Lack 2006) and the new regions that have emerged, such as Mercosur in South America, are 'elusive entities, [with] undefined boundaries and newly invented concepts' (Schulz et al 2001). They are the result of the formal and informal actions of both state and non-state actors, such as markets, NGOs and liberation struggles, which can overlap, reinforce and even contradict each other (Marchand 2001, Beeson 2005). As Schultz and colleagues (2001) have noted this has often produced a tension between geographical, political, economic and social definitions of what counts as a 'region' which reflects the fact that these new regions are not reducible to any one particular factor.

These developments are also occurring within a different global system. The demise of the Soviet Union has meant that the new regionalism emerged in tandem with a shift to multi-polar world (Schulz et al 2001). While some see regionalisation as part of the wider project of globalisation (Hettne 2001, 2005, Schulz et al 2001, Donegan 2006), others see this as an antagonistic relationship.

> the foundation of a number of new regional trade blocs indicates regionalism is emerging with force as a strategic response to the pervasive and relentless global processes ... Regional trade integration has emerged once again as a viable way to shape and protect the nation state from the competitive pressures of globalization. (Robles 2001: 171)

These regions are also underpinned by the actions and activities of, formal and informal, economic actors. Key among these are the regional development banks, such as the European Bank for Reconstruction and Development (EBRD). Multinational companies (MNCs) are also important regional actors (Hettne 2001, Schulz et al 2001). Data on the direction of trade and, to a lesser extent, foreign direct investment (FDI) tend to show intraregional, rather than global, patterns (Stallings and Streeck 1995, Blomström et al 2000, Egger and Pfaffermayr 2004, Economic and Social Commission for Western Asia 2007). These findings are supported by Rugman's (2000, 2005) extensive studies of multinational corporations (MNCs) in which he argues that rather than a global economy FDI patterns revealed a 'triadic world economy' centred on the USA, the EU and Asia.

Political regionalisation, however, has not kept pace with economic development. Europe stands out as the most politically integrated region (Hettne 2001, Pinder and Usherwood 2007, Unwin 2007). However, the extent to which the EU operates as a supranational body, with its own powers, agenda and institutions, or as an inter-governmental organisation is hotly debated and has more recently become a source of tension (George and Bache 2001, Cini 2007, Pinder and Usherwood 2007). Although the degree of political integration in the EU is not matched elsewhere it has been an incentive and inspiration for the development of other regional bodies around the world (Hettne 2001). Finally, the social dimension of regionalisation appears to be the most underdeveloped of all. Despite various attempts to create 'Unity in Diversity', (the slogan used by both the EU and ASEAN), regional identities have not emerged.

Thus, from this perspective supranational regions can be seen as an alternative spatiality from either the global or the national. They have their own logics and actors and, as can be seen from the continued fallout from the Global Financial Crisis, each has dealt with the impact of global economic and political flows in different ways. As a result, it is important for us to assess the extent to which these regional bodies are useful for understanding the contemporary experience of ageing and later life. With the exception of work done around the EU's support for active ageing policies (Walker 2002, Foster and Walker 2015) there is relatively little gerontological research that has focused on the possible impact that these regional bodies might have on older people. It is therefore important to explore whether policies pursued in other regional bodies, such as ASEAN or the African Union, could also impact on older people in those areas.

Nationalism

If, as we argued in Chapter Two, modernist gerontological theories, such as the structured dependency approach, are wedded to a national time-space then any threat to the nation state ought to pose a radical challenge to the conceptualisation of later life. However, there are many writers who argue that the extent to which the nation state has been supplanted has been greatly exaggerated.

Held and McGrew (2003) identified two broad positions in opposition to the claim that there has been a fundamental reorganisation of social geography. The first of these they classify as the *Sceptics*, who, as their name suggests, question the extent or even existence of globalisation. The second group they call the *Transformationalists*, who generally accept many aspects of the globalisation theory but argue that the nation state has managed to adapt to this new politico-economic environment. Despite differences between these groups it is possible to identify a number of key arguments that are common. These positions share a historical critique of globalisation. Many of these authors are quick to point out that there is little that is novel or global about the present world economy. Globalisation has a long history (Frank 1967, Wallerstein 1979, Braudel 1993, Hirst and Thompson 2000, Jones 2000, Parry 2000, Braudel 2002) which has been interrupted by various periods of de-globalisation (Therborn 2000, Short 2001). Neither is the present period seen as necessarily the most globalised. Hirst and Thompson (2000) have argued that both the *belle époque* of the early 1900s and the period from the end of the Second World War to the beginning of the OPEC oil crises in the 1970s were both more globalised than the period at the end of the 20th century. This historical critique serves a number of purposes. First, it challenges the supposed novelty of globalisation. Second, it suggests that globalisation is neither linear nor inevitable. Finally, it demonstrates that nation states have survived and even thrived during earlier periods of globalisation.

Schwartz (2000) argues that modern states and modern markets developed together because states maintain and enforce the property rights essential for a market economy and encourage the globalisation of economic actors. However, the very success of nation states in monetising and 'marketising' their territories resulted in increasing amounts of market activity becoming domestically oriented. Thus states become both the originators and destinations of global economic activity. Viewed from these perspectives states are not opposed to globalisation but constitute, and are constituted by, the global system (Jessop 1994, Bauman 1998, Schwartz 2000, Short 2001). Following the 9/11 attacks in the USA, states have increased their capabilities in a number of areas, such as immigration (Sassen 2000, Neumayer 2006) and defence (Paul and Ripsman 2004). This has been made startling clear over the past few years so in response to the perceived growing 'migrant crises' throughout the world. Countries such as the US (McGreal 2011), Hungary (Thorpe 2015) and India (Hussain

2009) have constructed fences along their borders and this seems to be a process that is increasing as nation states become concerned at the ease with which people can cross their borders either to work or to commit acts of terror. Paradoxically rather than vanishing under a sea of globalisation the nation state is seen to be responding and adapting to the new geopolitical-economic realities (Piven and Cloward 2000, Tshuma 2000, Short 2001, Scholte 2005, Sassen 2006, Robinson 2008).

> notwithstanding the tendency for capital accumulation to produce a single world market, there are important counter-tendencies and other limits to globalization. Specific accumulation regimes and modes of regulation are typically constructed in specific social spaces and socio-temporal matrices. (Jessop 2003: 89)

These arguments are given empirical support from a range of studies which have failed to demonstrate any relationship between economic openness and social expenditure (Montanari 2001, Wolf 2002, Alderson 2004) or levels of taxation (Swank 1998, 2001, 2002). Moreover, although the image of the 'state under siege' is an emotive one, the facts seem to show little evidence that global factors have played a great part in welfare retrenchment in the advanced industrial economies (Pierson 1998, Clarke 2001, Hay 2001, Huber and Stephens 2001, Pierson 2001a, Schwartz 2001). Instead of globalisation forcing states to converge around a model of residual welfare provision there still remain national differences in public spending (Rhodes 1996, Schwartz 2001, Cox 2004, Powell and Barrientos 2004). A crucial issue for gerontologists has been whether or not these forces have led to downward pressure on the generosity of healthcare and/or pension systems, and whether nation states continue to determine their level of social spending on older people.

Perhaps the most celebrated (and probably the most critiqued) attempt to analyse these different national responses is Esping-Andersen's (1990) *Three Worlds of Welfare Capitalism*. Using the notion of 'de-commodification', defined as the extent to which an individual can survive without relying on the market, he identified three different 'welfare regimes'; the neoliberal/Anglo-Saxon model, the social democratic/Scandinavian model and the corporatist/Continental European model. Each of these regimes has responded differently to global economic pressures. States in the social democratic regime have relied on welfare induced employment while those following the corporatist model reduced labour supply, namely through early labour market exit schemes. Only in the neoliberal regime, typified by the UK and USA, has welfare retrenchment been a major policy goal. This has become even more evident in the period of austerity politics in Britain where welfare cutbacks and increased privatisation have become the watchwords of the current Conservative government. However, even here reductions in social expenditure have been achieved through passive alteration of the eligibility criteria (such as means testing) rather than the wholesale dismantling of benefits. Esping-Andersen (1990) argues that these regimes represent a 'frozen welfare state landscape'. Moreover, rather than being a disincentive for investment, (welfare) states provide series of public 'goods' for capital that would be prohibitively costly to provide privately, such as healthcare for the population or road building (Hay 2001, Benner 2003). Moreover, there are underlying historical and institutional reasons for these observed differences in the approach to welfare (Korpi 2001, Beyeler 2003). From an institutionalist perspective, welfare states are seen as rooted in political and social contexts which militate against their wholesale transformations (Cox 2004). Thus not only are these institutions deeply interconnected with other social institutions but they also establish path dependencies which 'create ... rules, constraints and incentives for future political actions' (Myles and Pierson 2001, p 312). Such issues are paramount when examining the potential impact of both economic and political pressures on the composition of pension systems. The mature pension systems in the advanced industrialised economies have developed over almost a century in some countries and for a considerable period in others. As such they might be expected to exert strong path dependencies that make them difficult to change.

However Busch (2010) argues that the Global Financial Crisis has had a dramatic effect on all forms of welfare systems across the globe. He argues that the crisis and the subsequent weaker growth that emerged from it have put welfare states in both the industrialised and developing countries under pressure. In Europe, cuts in services, as well as tax and contribution increases, are further entrenching the process of re-commodification which has characterised the reform of European welfare states for years. Moreover, he argues, contra Esping-Andersen, that there has been a high degree of convergence welfare reforms over the past two decades. This is especially so in regard to pension and labour market policies where change been radical, with existing structures being completely overhauled. In pension policy this has resulted in a range of policy initiatives including the introduction of the three pillar model, the transition from defined benefit schemes to defined contribution schemes, a relative cutback in services (re-commodification), and a tendency towards mixed financing (taxes/contributions). We will return to these issues in Chapters Four and Five.

Finally, the nation remains a major source of identity for most people. One obvious illustration of this is the continued growth of the number of nation states in the world. In 1900 there were 55 sovereign states compared to 191 in 2002 (Fukuyama 2004) and 195 in 2015. It is argued that the reason there is a desire for people to create their own nation state is because it is recognised as the unit of political legitimacy and authority throughout the world and a people without a state, such as the Kurds, have no means of political representation. National culture continues to remain the principal focus for most people (Smith 2003, Jackson 2004) and neither global nor regional identities appear to have achieved any purchase. Indeed we have seen a definite resurgence of nationalism across Europe and, in many countries a strong rejection of Europe and a pan-European identity (Roubini 2014). Nationalist and anti-EU parties such as Le Front National in France and the UK Independence Party (UKIP) in the UK have enjoyed growing popularity and, in many cases, this has translated into electoral success.

Localism

Seemingly at the opposite end of the spatial scale from the global is the local. Yet a number of writers point to the resurgence or emergence of the locality as a crucial space for the organisation of economic, political and social life. As noted in Chapter Two there has been a revival of gerontological interest in the importance of locality and community for older people. This is a very diverse field and covers issues from the built environment, differences between rural and urban ageing, ageing in place and retirement communities (Harper and Laws 1995, McHugh and Mings 1996, McHugh 2003, McHugh and Larson-Keagy 2005, Phillipson and Scharf 2005, Peace et al 2007, Phillipson 2007). This research agenda has been given an added impetus over the past few years with the WHO's promotion of Age Friendly Cities as a crucial site for ensuring the wellbeing of older people (World Health Organization 2007, Buffel et al 2012). Despite this range of approaches there is a shared belief among these writers that the local is an important and meaningful spatiality for ageing and later life.

According to Savage and colleagues (2005) early accounts of globalisation envisaged the death of locally based communities due to the increased fluidity and 'placeless-ness' of a hypermobile capital and communications technology. However, a different approach to the relationship between these two spatial logics soon emerged. In this account the local was not subordinate to or eroded by globalisation. Instead it was argued that the two form a mutually constitutive dynamic in which local forces actively shape globalisation and, in so doing, are themselves transformed. Hence Beck (2002) has argued that 'the global and the local do not exist as cultural polarities but as combined and mutually implicating principles'. This relationship has been described as glocalisation (Robertson 1995). However these attempts to resituate the local in the global have raised a number of conceptual issues about what constitutes the local (Danson 2007). As Savage and colleagues (2005) have observed, the local lacks a clear definition and is sometimes seen as synonymous with urban centres, such as cities, but at other times is taken to refer to the neighbourhood, the community, or even the home.

The main focus of this interest in localism has been, however, on economic activity. Academic interest in the importance of locally based industrial areas can be traced back to Marshall's work at the turn of the 20th century (Kim and Zhang 2008). But over the past 20 years these ideas have found new life in, what is loosely called, the 'new economic geography' (Storper 1997a, 1997b, Krugman 1998, Biggiero 2006). The relationship between the global and the local spatial logics which appears in this literature is complex. Yet it is possible to identify three key issues:

1. contrary to the view of a global economy, the empirical evidence reveals that investment and economic activity are unevenly distributed throughout the world (Storper 1997a, 1997b, Dicken et al 2001, Dicken 2007);
2. companies invest in specific localities not in nations *per se* (Ohmae 1990, Gordon and McCann 2000, Arita and McCann 2002); and
3. these localities possess particular resources that make them attractive for investment (Markusen 1996, 2007, McCann et al 2002, Eraydin and Armatli-Koroglu 2005, Dicken 2007).

This means that not only are huge swathes of the developing world excluded from investment, but so too are older industrial districts within advanced economies (Lash and Urry 1993, Hoogvelt 2001, Gupta and Subramanian 2008). Conversely while some places are left out, others, such as Silicon Valley, are sought out because they offer specific locational advantages (Dunning 2000, 2009, Dunning et al 2007). These attributes attract business and capture investment creating 'sticky places in slippery space' (Markusen 1996). Once these places become established there is 'very strong propensity for economic activities to agglomerate into *localised geographical clusters*' (Dicken 2007: 21).

Alongside these new technology-industrial districts, 'global cities', such as London, New York and Berlin, have emerged as key sites for the regulation and promotion of economic activity (Olds 1995, Pain 2008a). According to Sassen (1998, 2001) a focus on these global cities is an important corrective to the image of globalisation as ephemeral.

> The global economy materialises in a worldwide grid of strategic places … that cuts across national boundaries and across the old North-South divide. The national economy has become decomposed in to a variety of sub-national components which are more or less connected to the global economy. Global Cities have emerged as one of the key nodes in the global-local networks of flows of commerce, information and people. (Sassen 2004: 653).

Economically, politically and culturally these cities are seen to be more alike than the hinterlands that surround them. Increasingly they form a grid of strategic sites linked by a tangible and intangible economic relations (Sassen 1998, Pain 2008b). Indeed, national and local governments seek to create such mega-cities or economic regions in order to attract or capture resources. For example the Danish government recently announced a proposal to create 'Greater Copenhagen' by incorporating the southern Swedish region of Skåne to create a metropolis of around 3.8 million people (Crouch 2015). Similarly the UK government is proceeding with plans to increasingly devolve powers to new city regions across the country. The first of these agglomerations, centred around Manchester and dubbed the Northern Powerhouse, is expected to pool resources from a connected grid of cities in the north west of England to achieve greater economic competitiveness 'under the visible and accountable leadership of directly elected metro-mayors' (Cox and Hunter 2015).

Multiple spatialities

In this chapter we have considered arguments from a number of writers that one spatial logic, be it the global, the regional, the national, or indeed the local has become, or has remained, the principal scale for social organisation. However, in line with a number of other writers (Friedrichs 2001, Sassen 2006) we reject the notion that any spatial logic has primacy. At a very basic level it appears from the foregoing analyses that there is ample evidence to support the claims for existence or persistence of each spatial level. Thus, Friedrichs (2001) has argued that because globalisation theories are based on a totalising narrative in which the global eclipses all other spatial units, they are unable to account for the evidence that trends towards the seemingly contradictory processes of globalisation, fragmentation and sovereign statehood coexist. Indeed, we have already seen from the glocalisation literature how global and local (fragmentation) processes are deeply interconnected (Robertson 1995, Beck 1999). While the added complexity of this approach is to be welcomed, it remains problematic as it misses out potential interactions between the other spatial levels such as the national and the regional. For example a number of writers have demonstrated the links between supranational organisations and the growth of sub-national economic regions, such as the Greater Mekong River zone in South East Asia (Öjendal 2001, Dent 2008) or the Maputo Development Corridor in Southern Africa (Odén 2001). We have also seen that rather than new forms of local governance undermining the nation state, that the national and the local are highly interconnected through the creation of newly devolved city regions (Brenner 2004). From a different perspective many writers have been quick to point out that globalisation is not antithetical to the nation state, or vice versa, but that they can support each other. Taking this one step further Jayasuriya (2001, 2004) has argued that globalisation has transformed the internal architecture of the state. This has led to a new form of regulatory state that operates through the mechanisms of meta-governance which she calls the 'governance of governance'. Rather than seeing this in terms of a zero-sum game, she argues that this new form of governance collapses the binary distinction between the global and the national into a new relational structure. In this new regulatory regime state capacity is relational, instead of being invested in a particular actor, and operates through various sites of governance.

These in turn link to a dispersed network of regulatory resources and agents. Key actors in this new system of 'network governance' are the central banks which operate at the interface between global and domestic finance. This is broadly similar to Slaughter's (1997) argument that the state is not disappearing but 'it is disaggregating into its separate, functionally distinct parts'. These parts, such as the courts and the police, are being networked together with their transnational counterparts to create a 'dense web of relations that constitutes a new, trans-governmental order' (1997: 184). As these writers show the nation state itself, or parts thereof, have become an integral part of the global process making it problematic to clearly define where the national ends and the global begins. From this perspective, binary distinctions between the global and the national are no longer useful.

Just as the local and the global may be mutually constitutive so too can the regional and the local or the national and the global. Therefore, instead of relying on theories that try to impose a single spatiality as the only explanatory framework, the evidence for the coexistence of each of the different forms of space suggests that we need an approach that is open to the complex ways in which multiple spatialities interact. Looking at business activities Riain (2000) has argued that our theoretical and analytical models must simultaneously incorporate the local, national and global and the way they interact to (re)construct state–market relations. This approach treats social structures as *heterarchical* with different levels integrating in different ways in a structured but uneven process. Others have characterised the current situation as a 'neo-medieval world order' with present global conditions are similar to those which characterised medieval Europe with a number of different actors, from local warlords to the Pope, who sought but were unable to achieve dominance (Friedrichs 2001). As Sassen observes:

> In Europe the Middle Age was a period of complex interactions among particular forms of territorial fixity, the absence of exclusive territorial authority, the existence of multiple crisscrossing jurisdictions and the embedding of rights in classes of people rather than territorially exclusive units. (Sassen 2006: 32)

However, instead of the Church and the Holy Roman Empire, Friedrichs (2001) argues that today the world is held together by the antagonistic claims of the nation state system and transnational market economy. In contrast to the image of a more or less stable world order (re)constructed around a, dominant, spatial principle these writers are describing a system in flux where different spatial assemblages emerge and seek to gain supremacy. To borrow an analogy from the French Marxist Louis Althusser (1969) it might be better to think of the spatialisation of the modern world as a 'structure in dominance' which allows each spatial level, for example the global or the national, to have its own autonomy but also allows for an over determination of one particular level in particular circumstances.In this chapter we have argued that the current world order needs to be understood not as a single spatial logic but rather as a number of linked, overlapping processes constituting what could be seen as a 'structure in dominance'.

Following this conclusion, we are therefore able to look at how ageing and later life have been transformed at a number of different spatial levels. This will be the subject of the following chapters.

Part 2
Global landscapes of ageing

FOUR

Ageing, populations and health

Demography itself has become one of the key axes along which ageing has reconfigured the spatial and temporal regimes of later modernity. The uncertainty of the increases in life expectancy has become a constituent part of the ongoing problematic of reflexive modernisation and lays the foundation for understanding the extent to which population ageing is a global phenomenon. Furthermore, if as we have argued earlier, notions of time and space are intimately interconnected then, through changing our notions of time, the demographics of population ageing can impact on the reconstitution of space. This confluence between the processes of re-spatialisation, the shift away from the nation state as the key political actor, and scientific-medical developments that are reconfiguring the possibilities of health and longevity are seen to have led to a series of 'temporal world view paradoxes'.

> Nation-states' social policy making (e.g. pensions, health) now has to grapple with the historically unprecedented socio-demographic realities of ageing populations, and with the need for long-term intergenerational planning in a context in which public policy is simultaneously required to prioritize short-term adaptability in the face of an assumptively unpredictable future. (Roche 2003: 104)

This brings into being a whole host of other contingencies that go beyond purely demographic concerns. Given that old age has been synonymous with poor health for much of history then any break in this association would be crucial for opening up spaces for the realisation of alterative images and narratives of later life. So, although Appadurai (1996) leaves the issues of health and demography out of his model, we believe that they are crucial for understanding the contemporary spatial world order. Thus, following his formulation of the other 'scapes' we believe it is possible to identify what could be called the 'bioscape'. We see this as the uneven, shifting demographic landscape that encompasses not just fertility and mortality but extends to health, disease, illness and wellness, all of which have become more contingent. This concept of the bioscape forms a crucial component of our approach as it allows us to explore the global landscape of health for the ageing population and to see whether it is possible to identify areas of extreme good or poor health or whether older people around the world converging around a similar experience of health.

Ageing and later life have traditionally been understood in terms of the twin temporalities of mortality and morbidity. Biologists, such as Strehler (1962), view ageing as a universal phenomenon that occurs across all members of a species even if it is subject to some variation over timing and impact. It is seen as intrinsic, in that the causes must not depend on external factors, and progressive, insofar as the changes due to ageing must occur progressively during the latter part of the lifespan. Finally, ageing is presented as being deleterious to the individual's health and survival

The analogy between the natural cycle of growth, stasis and decay and the stages of life has been evident throughout recorded history (Shahar 2005, Thane 2005). Even as chronological age established itself as the standardised criteria for the categorisation of (old) age this distinction was still informed by ideas of health and functionality. Concern about the health of older people was a key component of modernist accounts of ageing. This was epitomised by the image of the 'worn out worker' as well as by the use of life tables of mortality to calculate pensions. As has already been noted, writers such as Estes (1980, 1986) and Townsend (1981) saw the emergence of the older person in modern society as not only an outcome of social policy but also a product of the medicalisation of old age, a process that they believed further disenfranchised older people. Paradoxically, by focusing on the poorest sections of the older population, both in terms of their health and their finances, many of these theories reinforced the association between ageing and illness. Health(iness) or its lack can be seen to constitute a critical dimension along which later life has been constructed.

However, changing patterns of health and life expectancy are forcing a re-evaluation of the simple association between older age and poor health (Higgs and Jones 2009). Later life is being reconstituted and reimagined along a new set of what can be called 'biotemporalities'. Time until death as a standard form of measuring the lives of older people has been replaced by more radical goals of extending healthy or disability free life expectancy. Significantly while life expectancy has improved across the most prosperous nations, so too has healthy and disability free life expectancy. For both cultural and critical gerontologists these changing health profiles underline the need to reevaluate earlier theories of ageing. Policy discourses have also shifted away from a focus on dependency to one which is constructed around healthy or positive ageing and which seeks to mobilise older people as a resource (Carmel et al 2007, Foster and Walker 2015). Similarly advances in biomedical sciences appear to hold out the possibility of reducing or even reversing the burden of ill health and disability in later life through new technologies and procedures (de Grey 2010, Rae et al 2010).

A grey globe?

Perhaps the clearest expression of these new bioscapes of later life can be seen in the global rise in life expectancy and the ageing of populations around the world. This is not just significant in demographic terms but is also important because it challenges conventional narratives of the life course. Although there remains a good deal of international variation in life expectancy, the number of countries in which people can expect to live into their 70s increased steadily throughout the latter part of the 20th century. The 'long-lived' club of nations is no longer restricted to Western Europe and North America but also includes members from all inhabited continents. As former UN General Secretary Kofi Annan warned 'major population shifts in the developing and developed countries' have made ageing a global policy issue (Borsch 2002). These sentiments are echoed even more strongly among those who predict a coming demographic and intergenerational crisis (see Restrepo and Rozental 1994, Wiener and Tilly 2002, Jackson and Howe 2003). However, the argument that population ageing is a global phenomenon is more often asserted than assessed. Furthermore, convergence theories overlook a great deal of heterogeneity that exists in the demographic profiles between and within world regions (Palacios 2002, Walker 2002). While there is some evidence of convergence we are far from the emergence of a global time-space of ageing. Instead, as O'Brien (2015) notes, there are significant historical and future differences exist in the timing, speed and level of population ageing as well as in the spatial distribution of older populations and the ageing of the older population itself. Hence (economic) geography still matters.

Analysis by the World Health Organization (2015) shows there is a clear association between the level of economic development within a country and the risks of death at different stages in the life course. In the low income countries the majority of deaths occur in infancy, after which the risk of dying is fairly evenly spread across the rest of life. In more developed countries improvements to public health systems reduces infant mortality which shifts the risk of dying away from childhood into adulthood. Finally, in the high income countries, such as those in Western Europe, North America and Japan, many of the diseases that might have previously resulted in death, such as cancer or heart disease, are now managed through medical technologies, shifting the risk of death even further along the life course such that most deaths occur in people over 70 years old. These findings show that where people are born and where they live has a huge impact on how long they are likely to live.

In order to assess whether we can truly talk about population ageing as a global phenomenon it is crucial to look at the whether the proportions of older people in the population have changed rather than talking about future possibilities, such as life expectancies, as if they are current realities. Data from the World Bank on the proportion of older people in the high, middle and low income countries, presented in Figure 4.1, show that far from being a global phenomenon population ageing is largely confined to the high and upper middle income countries. The variation in, rather than the similarity of, the demographic structures in these countries is what is most notable. While the proportion of those aged 65 years and older in the high income countries has doubled from around 8% in 1960 to 16% in 2013 there has been virtually no change in the lower middle income and low income countries. A similar picture of variation appears if we look at countries grouped in to geographic regions (Figure 4.2). Both East and West Europe and North America clearly stand out as the regions with the highest rates of population ageing. Conversely Sub-Saharan Africa and the Middle East have experienced hardly any increase in the proportions of those aged 65 and over. Even in East Asia and the Pacific region, where there has been a relatively rapid rate of population ageing, the proportion of older people in the population is the same in 2013 as it was in North America in 1960.

Thus, in purely demographic terms, we cannot talk about a population ageing as a global phenomenon. Contrary to what some commentators argue we do not see the emergence of one world in terms of low fertility and high life expectancy. International, and interregional differences persist for both these factors. Consequently, the evidence of converging population structures across the world is, at present, weak. However, in the absence of a global ageing population one should not assume that the experiences and expectations of later life are equally heterogeneous among the world's older people.

Figure 4.1: The proportion of the population aged 65 years and over in high, middle and low income countries, 1960, 1980 and 2013

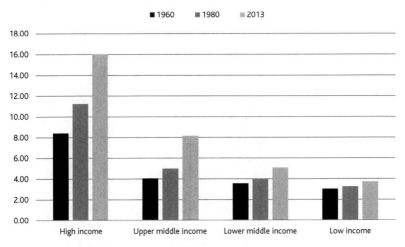

Source: (The United Nations Population Division's World Population Prospects 2015)

Figure 4.2: The proportion of the population aged 65 years and over by world regions, 1960, 1980 and 2013

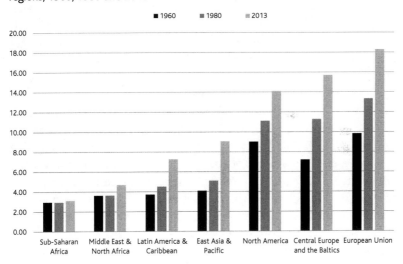

Source: (The United Nations Population Division's World Population Prospects 2015)

The health of the world's older people

The health of the world's older population has become a major policy concern and area of sustained research. This is motivated by concerns over the present and future viability of welfare systems to support ageing populations and is underpinned by a long-standing assumption that older age inevitably results in poor(er) health and thus higher costs. Crimmins (2004) identifies the argument that increased longevity might lead to higher rates of morbidity and/or disability as the 'failure of success' and situates it within a general set of theories that raise concerns about the impact of modern medicine on human ageing. Notable among these are the arguments that industrial societies have passed through a third (or fourth or even a fifth) epidemiological transition which, by eliminating many acute and occupational illnesses, has shifted the burden of disease away from infectious diseases and towards chronic conditions most often occurring in later life (Dubos 1965, Antonovsky 1968, Omran 1971, Olshansky and Ault 1986, Olshansky et al 1997, Smallman-Raynor and Phillips 1999).

However, these positions have become increasingly challenged. Some commentators have argued that linking industrialisation with chronic disease is based largely on the historically and culturally localised instances of increased risk of male coronary heart disease found in the USA and UK following the Second World War (Kaplan and Keil 1993). There is also evidence that the health of older people had been improving for a considerable time in parts of the industrialised world (Lanska and Mi 1993, Fogel 1994, Padiak 2005). This undermines the assumption that either increased life expectancy or population ageing will result in an unmanageable burden of ill health. Following on from this, and contrary to the 'expansion of morbidity' argument, some writers have proposed what has been termed the 'compression of morbidity' thesis (Fries 1984, 2000, 2002, 2005a, 2005b, Fries et al 1989). Simply stated the argument holds that, even with increasing longevity, the proportion of life that is spent in ill health will be concentrated into an ever shorter period prior to death. Data from a number of countries show that gains in healthy life expectancy (HLE) have been greater than gains in life expectancy which supports this thesis (Jeune and Brønnum-Hansen 2008, INSERM 2013, Office for National Statistics 2014). Finally, Manton (1982) has proposed a third model, the 'dynamic equilibrium model' which assumes that (population) ageing will result in a greater incidence of disease and chronic illness but that these will be less severe. Data from the USA (Crimmins 2004, Crimmins and Beltran-Sanchez 2011) and New

Zealand (Graham et al 2004) lend some support to this approach. What these latter two theories show is that health is becoming increasingly detached from age as these two temporalities, life expectancy and HLE, start to move at different paces. This rupture is creating a new 'contested terrain' about the meaning and nature of later life (Jones and Higgs 2010).

However, the majority of research on the health of older people is concentrated in the developed world. Yet older people in the developing world are often thought to have greater health problems and different health needs than those in the developed world. They are seen to suffer the double burden of infectious and non-infectious diseases, which is exacerbated by natural disasters and armed conflicts. Likewise, many older people living in rural communities in these countries are often unable to access or afford medical treatments. Limited resources and competing health priorities, such as AIDS or Ebola, means that Southern welfare states are often ill-equipped to deal with the challenges of an ageing population (Lloyd-Sherlock 2002b). Often the major source of care and financial assistance for older people in the developing world is the younger generation of the family. However urbanisation is believed to have attracted many younger people away from rural communities and their older relatives (Allen et al 2002). On the basis of these studies we can see that these bioscapes of ageing and later life are complex and dependent on a range of factors. However, it is crucial to directly assess whether there this any evidence of convergence in the state of health for the world's older people.

Spatial patterns of self-rated health in later life

Self-rated health is one of the most widely used indicators to measure health in the world. It is strongly related to both mortality and morbidity (Moller et al 1996, Idler and Benyamini 1997, Miilunpalo et al 1997, Regidor et al 2010) and it is collected in most social surveys. Studies from Europe (Bardage et al 2005, Vuorisalmi et al 2008) and the Caribbean (Zunzunegui et al 2009) show national variations in the levels of self-rated health among older people. However, although these studies are instructive, in order to fully assess the spatial patterning of health in later life it is crucial to take global perspective.

In line with these previous studies, Figure 4.3 shows that there is a great deal of international variation in how older people view their own health. Among the Western European countries, for example, there are notable differences between countries with around 28% of

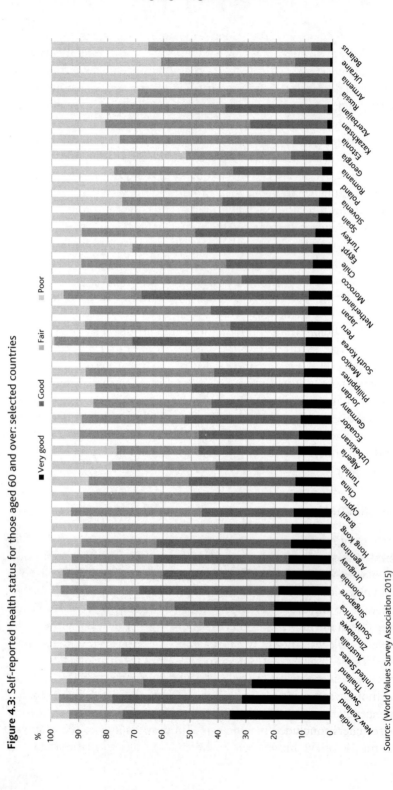

Figure 4.3: Self-reported health status for those aged 60 and over: selected countries

Source: (World Values Survey Association 2015)

older Swedes reporting very good health compared to under 10% of those in the Netherlands. The data also suggest that there is no simple association between the wealth, or indeed welfare structure, of a country and the perceived health of its older population. For example, we see a number of African countries, such as Zimbabwe and South Africa, where around one in five older people report being in very good health which is higher than countries like Singapore, Germany and Japan. Although these results could be explained by possible survivor effects among older people in these lower income countries or by cultural differences in the interpretation of what is meant by good or poor health, overall the results show that older age does not automatically result in perceived poorer health in many countries in the world. Of added importance for our argument these data also show that there is no simple correspondence between geographical location or national economic development and the self-perceived health of the older population.

The notable exception to this it is towards the bottom end of the spectrum which is exclusively made up of the former Soviet Union and Eastern Bloc countries. Almost none of the respondents from Belarus, Ukraine or Russia reported having very good health. Looking at the proportions reporting poor health reveals an even clearer picture of the relative position of these countries and an apparent bifurcation in the sample. Almost half of all older people in Georgia report being in poor health. This is followed by 46% in Armenia, 39% in Ukraine and 34% in Belarus.

Spatial patterns of disability and chronic illness in later life

Although the prevalence of poor health among the older population is a major research and policy focus, most of the research on the health of older people has tended to concentrate on functioning, (dis)ability and chronic illness. Some longitudinal research has suggested that the prevalence of severe disability may have declined over the last few decades in the high income countries (Hung et al 2011). For example, In the 1970s data from the National Health Interview Survey (NHIS) in the USA showed that increasing proportions of older adults classified themselves as having limitations in certain activities of daily living. Although some writers raised concerns over methodological and conceptual problems with these data (Wilson and Drury, 1984), many researchers concluded that the health of older people had deteriorated in the 1970s (Verbrugge 1984, Verbrugge et al 1989, Crimmins et al

1994). However, this trend appeared to change dramatically during the 1980s (Manton et al 1995, Waidmann et al 1995, Crimmins et al 1997, Freedman and Martin 1998, Waidmann and Manton 1998, Freedman et al 2007). More recently longitudinal research has suggested that the prevalence of severe disability may have declined over the last few decades in the high income countries (Hung et al 2011). While there was evidence that these findings tended to mask socioeconomic inequalities in the prevalence of disability (Manton et al 1995, Manton et al 1997, Schoeni et al 2005, Minkler et al 2006) and had some methodological shortcomings (Waidmann and Manton 1998, Schoeni et al 2001, Freedman et al 2004, Wolf et al 2005) a general consensus developed that 'overall the weight of evidence suggests large disability reductions' among older Americans (Schoeni et al 2001, Cutler 2001a, 2001b, Freedman et al 2002, Schoeni et al 2008).

However, the spatial patterning of disability in later life reveals a more complex picture of international variation. While most of the data supporting this argument have come from the USA, there are some studies from Europe and further afield which have shown similar trends. In the mid-1990s Bone (1995) published data on the rates of limiting long-standing illness in the older British population. Although she had expected to find increasing rates of dependency (an expansion of morbidity) she reported fairly stable trends over the two decades. These analyses have been updated and show that although there has been a rise in the proportions reporting a long-standing illness for both age groups (although more so for those aged 65–74 years) rates of limiting long-standing illness are stable across the period for both age groups (Hyde et al 2008). Similar patterns have been found in France (Robine et al 1998), Italy (Minicuci and Noale 2005), Australia (Mathers 1996), and the Caribbean (Reyes-Ortiz et al 2006). However, wider pan-European analyses have shown that the number of additional 'healthy life years' that one can expect from the age of 50 varies considerably between countries. In Estonia a 50 year old woman can look forward to around 11 years without a disability while her male counterpart can expect just 9 years. Conversely women and men in Denmark will have an average of 24 years of disability free life ahead of them. However, the findings appear to eschew any simple, economistic, explanation. There is no clear North–South or East–West divide with some former Communist countries, such as Slovenia, having a greater number of healthy life years than countries like Finland and Germany (Jagger et al 2008). This is supported by analysis of 12 high income countries from the OECD area which revealed a several distinct patterns (Balestat and Lafortune 2007). On the one hand the study found that rates of disability in later life were declining in five of the 12 countries studied (Denmark, Finland, Italy, the Netherlands and the United States), but on the other hand there was evidence of an increasing rate of severe disability in Belgium, Japan and Sweden and in Australia and Canada there had been no significant change at all. Lastly in France and the United Kingdom the picture was so complex that the authors were unable to reach any definitive conclusion on the direction of the trends in disability in these countries (Balestat and Lafortune 2007).

While the evidence from high income countries is confusing, the picture from low and middle income countries is even less clear. This is in part because data from these countries is largely absent. There are, however, some studies from China. Yet they show conflicting results with some claiming to demonstrate that active life expectancy has increased (Gu et al 2009) and disability rates have decreased between 1992 and 2002 (Peng et al 2010) while others seem to show significant increases in both physical and mental limitations from 1987 to 2006 (Zheng et al 2011).

Taken together these studies show that this is not simply a question of time, that is the number of healthy or disability free years, but also one of space and that there are wide international variations, even among the high income countries, in the levels and trends of disability in later life. This is equally evident when we look at measures of physical functioning. An analysis of international comparative data on grip strength from the Survey of Health, Ageing and Retirement in Europe (SHARE) and the Study on Global Ageing and Adult Health (SAGE), which covers India, Mexico, South Africa and Russia, shows high levels of international variation in grip strength, despite very similar age related patterns within countries, with older people in India and Mexico exhibiting much weaker grip strength at all ages than those in Europe (World Health Organization 2015).

Alongside functioning and disability, chronic illness is often used as a key indicator for the health of older people. There is a good deal of concern that, as populations age, the number and proportion of older people with chronic illnesses, such as cardiovascular disease, will rise and that this will put a strain on health services. Chronic illness is also sometimes seen as a more reliable, or objective, measure of health as it does not rely as much on individual perception. Unfortunately, getting reliable cross-national data on the rates of chronic illness among older people is often difficult (Kupari et al 1997). Hence, mortality patterns are often used as a proxy to provide an insight into the diseases that are important in later life. The Global Burden of Disease project uses data on cause-specific mortality to impute the average potential years of life an individual would be deprived of by specific diseases (Naghavi et al 2015). The data show that globally the greatest burden of disease in later life comes from non-communicable diseases, namely ischaemic heart disease, stroke and chronic obstructive pulmonary disease. However, this global picture masks considerable socioeconomic and geographic variation. In the low and middle income countries the impact of non-communicable diseases is greater and tends to be felt earlier in life than in the high income countries. Moreover, communicable diseases, such as malaria, are still a major risk to life throughout these areas creating a double burden of disease for many low and middle income countries. However, as the findings for the main causes of years lived with disability by country show, these economic patterns are overlaid and crosscut by geographical patterns. In Europe and North America back pain is the main cause of disability while in the Latin America and the Caribbean countries major depressive disorders are the most commonly reported main cause (Naghavi et al 2015).

Globalisation and health in later life

Thus far the empirical evidence appears to demonstrate the absence of a single, dominant spatial logic through which we can understand the patterning of health in later life. Rather we are confronted with a series of overlapping spatialities, from the global to the national. However, as we saw earlier, there are many who think that the ability of nation states to secure good health for their populations is being undermined by the spread of neoliberal globalisation (Greider 1998, Mishra 1999). Therefore, it is not surprising that a number of gerontological writers have also argued that improvements in health among the ageing populations in the advanced industrial countries are being threatened by cuts in spending and the increased privatisation of healthcare brought about by globalisation. As John Vincent has stated:

> Those excluded from markets, perhaps by old age, tend to do less well … [as] medical care is subject to the global market. In the West, healthcare is characterised as becoming increasingly expensive. Hence pressures to ration healthcare by price or age. (Vincent, 2003: 58)

Writers from this perspective often go further and argue that older people in the developing world will be denied even these advances as the demands of the global economy and neoliberal agenda effectively strangle any nascent healthcare regimes (Polivka 2001, Polivka and Borrayo 2002). Again quoting Vincent:

> The greatest gains in life expectancy at the cheapest cost are to be made in the developing world, but in global terms healthcare is rationed by price, and older people in these countries are those least likely to receive modern healthcare.
> (Vincent, 2003: 58)

To test these arguments, it is important to get a clear picture of how much individual countries spend on healthcare and whether there is any evidence of a 'race to the bottom'. To do this we need to look at a wide number of indicators such as the progressive intrusion of the private market into the healthcare provision for older people, the role of government policies, the growth of the pharmaceutical industry, as well as the overall amount spent on healthcare. These issues reflect some of the points raised by Carroll Estes (1980, 1986) in *The Aging Enterprise* and have been extended in the arguments advanced by Walker (2005) and by Estes and Phillipson (2002) on the marketisation and privatisation of healthcare services for older people. We can explore this by examining how much nation states spend on healthcare, the extent to which healthcare has become privatised and whether this has been affected by global factors. Again this will allow us to critically assess the extent to which we are witnessing the emergence of a global bioscape of ageing, based around a uniform approach to healthcare spending in all countries, or whether we can identify regional or national patterns of spending.

Global patterns of spending on healthcare

Figure 4.4 shows the amount that nation states spent on healthcare as a proportion of GDP in 2013. The data demonstrate that there is still a considerable degree of international variation in healthcare expenditure. There are a number of countries who spend proportionately little on healthcare, such as Pakistan and Turkmenistan. Conversely there are around 20 countries, such as the USA and France, where spending on healthcare is greater than 10% of GDP. This map clearly does not show a globalised bioscape of healthcare provision where different countries have similar levels of spending.

However, although we might not see a picture of global convergence in healthcare spending, there does appear to be some evidence of regional patterning or clusters of spending. South and East Asia (with

Figure 4.4: The amount that nation states spent on healthcare as a proportion of GDP, 2013

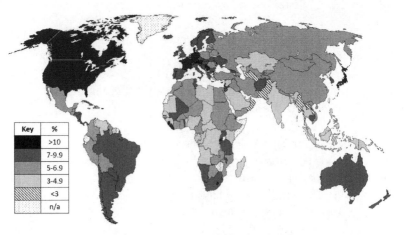

Key	%
	>10
	7-9.9
	5-6.9
	3-4.9
	<3
	n/a

Source: (World Health Organization Global Health Expenditure database 2015)

the exception of Japan) and Central Africa appear to be low spending regions. North America, Western Europe, Scandinavia and Australasia appear to be high spending areas. The former Soviet countries fall somewhere in between. However, the situation in Latin America, Southern Africa and Western Africa is more ambiguous with greater intra-regional variation. However, when we look at the actual statistics for each region the picture is somewhat different. Figure 4.5 shows the median values and the minimum and maximum amounts spent on healthcare for each of the World Bank geographic regions. North America, comprising Canada and the USA, stands out as a high spending region, yet there are not clear distinctions in spending in the other regions. Europe and Central Asia have a high average rate of healthcare spending (represented by the thick black bar in the middle of the rectangle) but there is also a large degree of variation within the region (represented by the lines running from the top and bottom of the rectangle).

While this may give us a global picture of healthcare spending these cross-sectional data do not tell us very much about trends over time. By examining the levels of spending from 1980 to 2013, in Figure 4.6, we can see quite clearly that there has been a general increase in the amount spent on healthcare as a proportion of GDP across a wide range of countries. Thus, rather than seeing a race to the bottom in terms of healthcare spending there has been a consistent trend towards higher levels of spending across both the high and middle income countries since 1980. This is further borne out when we look at patterns in

Figure 4.5: Regional differences in healthcare spending as a proportion of GDP, 2013

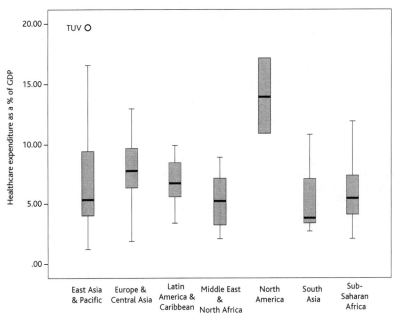

Source: (World Health Organization Global Health Expenditure database 2015)

spending across the major world regions (Figure 4.7). Although the time frame is shorter due to limited data the results are remarkably similar. In the high, middle and low income countries spending on healthcare has grown as a proportion of GDP since 1995. However, this picture also reveals the wide geographic and economic variations in healthcare spending. Although spending patterns are quite similar among the middle and low income countries, rising from around 4% of GDP to around 6% in each region, the gap between these regions and the high income countries is very noticeable. The amount spent on healthcare is around twice as great in the high income countries as in the other regions and this ratio has remained stable over the period.

The privatisation of healthcare

However, looking at the relative amounts that countries spend on healthcare is only part of the story. Many commentators have pointed to the growing market in health and healthcare as evidence of a broader neoliberal agenda for the development of a trade in services that have exposed hitherto nationally funded services, such as healthcare, to international competition (Holden 2005, Skala 2009).

international trade agreements increasingly serve as mechanisms to enforce the privatization, deregulation, and decentralization of health care and other services ... The goal of the GATS [General Agreement on Trade in Services], a WTO agreement that applies to all 148 WTO member nations, is to "progressively liberalize" all services. Basic GATS rules automatically apply to all services for all WTO members. (Shaffer and Brenner 2004: 467–73).

Figure 4.6: Trends in healthcare spending as a proportion of GDP, 1980–2013: selected countries

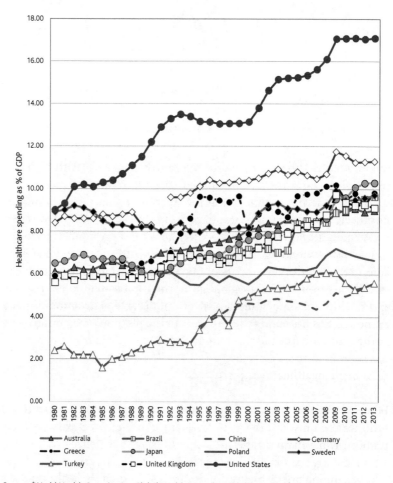

Source: (World Health Organization Global Health Expenditure database 2015)

Figure 4.7: Healthcare spending as a proportion of GDP, 1995, 2005 and 2013: selected countries

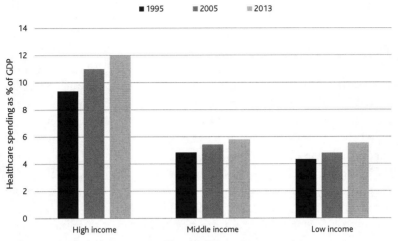

Source: (World Health Organization Global Health Expenditure database 2015)

A substantial body of work exists on the apparent shift from publically funded welfare in general, and healthcare in particular, towards greater reliance on the market among the advanced welfare states (Esping-Andersen 1990, Loader and Burrows 1994, Pierson 1994, 1998, 2001c, 2006, Huber and Stephens 2001). In the UK there has been a steady introduction of market mechanisms into the National Health Service. This started under the Thatcher and Major Conservative governments but accelerated with New Labour and 'the introduction of competitive contracting using cost-per-case currencies, more choice for patients where they will receive hospital treatment, and the freeing of NHS care providers from the direct political control of ministers' (Lewis and Gillam 2003: 77). The late 1990s and early part of this century saw further attempts to privatise Medicare in the US (Geyman 2004). Although this has been halted, and even partially reversed by Obama's Affordable Care Act, there are still constraints on a shift to a fully funded public healthcare system (McCanne 2009). Even Sweden has witnessed neoliberal healthcare reform under the centre-right government (Dahlgren 2008). A number of writers have raised concerns that it will be older people, who they see as most reliant on public healthcare, who will be most detrimentally affected by this. Bernard and Phillips (2000: 34) have argued that the

> changing policy agenda of the 1970s and 1980s which, for
> older people, has meant a breaking of the 'welfare compact'

between the generations; an emphasis on market solutions; the unregulated growth and expansion of the private and independent sectors; and the 'discovery' of informal carers.

They identified the NHS and Community Care Act (1990) as a key turning point in the policy approach to older people shifting away from the communitarian, state-led, provision of welfare to a new, market-led, reality. Similarly, from an American perspective Frank (2001) has argued that the increased privatisation of healthcare services in the USA has disempowered older people, due to their low incomes, and exposed them to 'fraud, profiteering, and poor or unaffordable services'.

To explore these issues, we have used World Bank data on the proportion of spending on healthcare in a country that is attributable to public, rather than private, spending (Figure 4.8). As with healthcare spending in general, there is a great deal of international variation in the extent to which countries are reliant on the private sector, given low levels of public spending, for the provision of healthcare. At the extreme end there is a very small number of countries where healthcare seems to be entirely dependent on private spending. In Haiti only 7% of spending on healthcare is from public sources. Alongside this there are countries like Sierra Leone (14%), Cambodia (20%) and Georgia (22%) where public expenditure accounts for less than a quarter of healthcare spending. Then there is a second tier of countries where public spending is greater than a quarter but remains less than a half of healthcare expenditure. This is a geographically varied group. There

Figure 4.8: The proportion of spending on healthcare from public sources, 2013

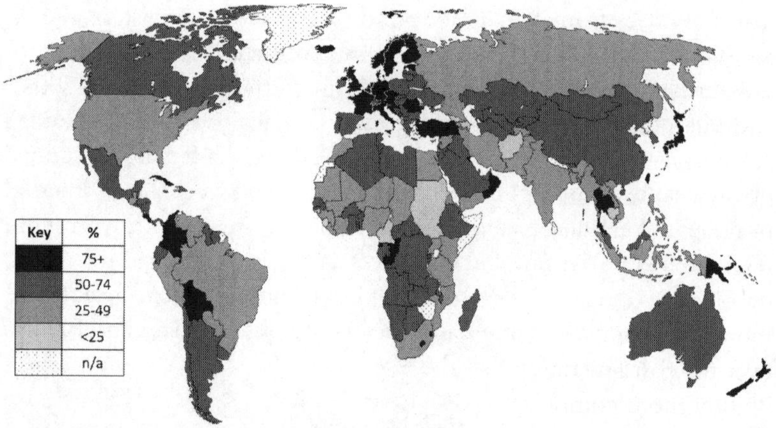

Source: (World Health Organization Global Health Expenditure database 2015)

appear to be some regional or sub-regional clusters, for example around West Africa and South Asia. However, this group also includes the USA (47%), Russia (48%), South Africa (48%) and Brazil (48%) which have very similar levels of public spending on healthcare. In the next group, where public spending accounts for between 50–74% of spending, there are appear to be some regional clusters. Levels of public expenditure are quite similar among a number of countries in Central and East Asia, such as Kazakhstan (53%), Uzbekistan (51%) and China (56%). Likewise, there appears to be a group in South West Africa comprising Namibia (60%), Angola (59%), Botswana (57%) and the Democratic Republic of Congo (53%). Alongside these a third cluster might be seen in the former Soviet economies of Eastern Europe comprising Ukraine (54%), Belarus (65%), Lithuania (67%), Latvia (62%), Bulgaria (59%) and Poland (70%). However, alongside these clusters are Portugal (65%), Switzerland (66%) and Spain (70%). Hence this is an internationally diverse group. Finally, there is a group where public expenditure accounts for 75% or more of total healthcare spending. Here again there is some evidence of regional clustering as the countries in this group are almost exclusively in Western and Northern Europe. Outside of these regions this is a much more geographically diverse group with countries such as Japan (82%), New Zealand (83%) and Cuba (93%).

To explore these possible interregional differences more carefully we present box plots for each of the World Bank regions (Figure 4.9). As with healthcare in general the data suggest that there are regional differences. The East Asia and Pacific region and Europe and Central Asia both have quite high average levels of public expenditure (represented by the horizontal black bar) while South Asia has a distinctly lower average. However, overall the picture is far from unambiguous. The wide intra-regional variations in expenditure, shown by the vertical black lines above and below the boxes, override any real interregional differences.

However, while these data are important for showing the range of interregional and international variation in the degree to which healthcare is publically financed, once again they tell us little about international variation in trends over time. In order to see whether states have converged around a neoliberal model of an increasingly more privatised healthcare sector we need to look at spending patterns over the past few decades. These data, shown in Figure 4.10, reveal a slightly more complex picture. International variation is still evident throughout almost three decades but there is some evidence of convergence among states. Yet, once again and contrary to the 'race to

Figure 4.9: Regional variations in the proportion of healthcare spending from public expenditure, 2013

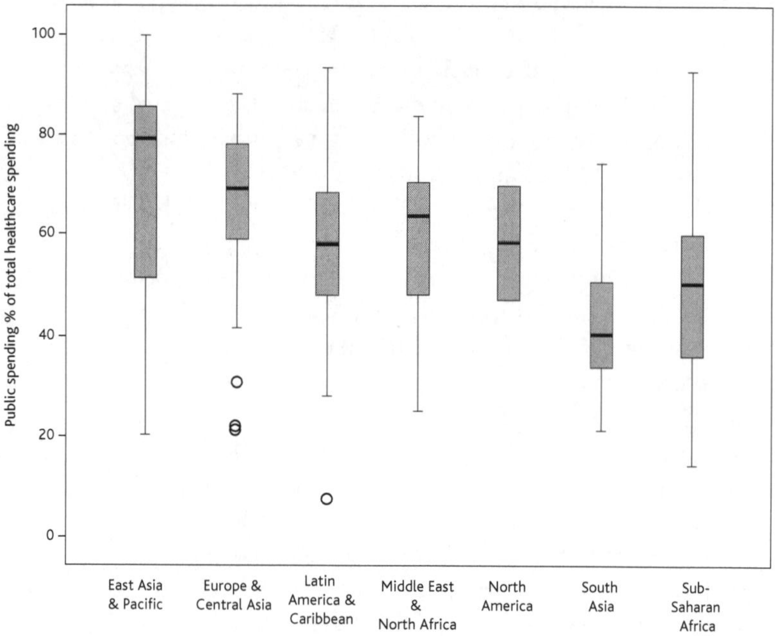

Source: (World Health Organization Global Health Expenditure database 2015)

the bottom' argument, this is not a uniformly downward trend in public spending. Rather there appears to be a 'race to the middle'; the data showing a trend towards convergence around the mean. Therefore, it can be concluded that although a number of high public spenders, such as Sweden, have reduced their spending, other less generous states, such as the USA, have actually increased the proportion of public spending on health. It is important, in the light of the arguments made by Polivka (2001) and Vincent (2003), that a number of the newly industrialised economies, like Brazil, have also increased the proportion of public spending on health over the period.

Globalisation and healthcare privatisation

Although the data suggest that one needs to be cautious about claims of a universal shift towards a residual welfare state, they do not directly demonstrate whether more economically globalised states have more privatised healthcare. In line with the general argument that exposure to (economic) globalisation has reduced the state's capacity to provide welfare services a number of writers have argued that this has led states to shift more and more of their healthcare services to the private sector

Figure 4.10: Trends in the proportion of public expenditure on healthcare, 1980–2013: selected countries

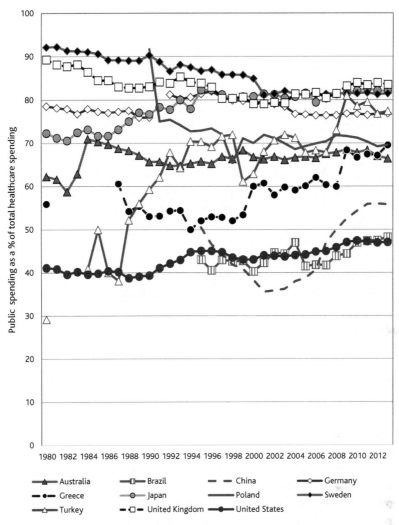

Source: (World Health Organization Global Health Expenditure database 2015)

(Allan and Scruggs, 2004; Burgoon, 2001; Garrett and Mitchell, 2001; Greider, 1998; Korpi and Palme, 2003; Strange, 1996). In contrast there are those who maintain that there is little evidence that economic openness is incompatible with publicly funded healthcare spending (Rieger and Leibfried 1998, Feo and Siqueira 2004, Navarro et al 2004, Bambra et al 2010)

The data presented in Figure 4.11 show the relationship between the extent to which a country is globalised, using the KOF Globalization

Index (Dreher 2006), and the amount spent on healthcare as a percentage of GDP in 2012. Higher values on the KOF Globalization Index mean that a country is more globalised, across economic, political and social dimensions. The first impression one gets from the data is that there is no clear relationship between the extent to which a country is more open to global flows and the amount it spends on healthcare. However, if a 'line of best fit' is drawn through the data points it becomes clear that there is in fact a positive, albeit weak, relationship between these two factors. Nevertheless, this contradicts the assumption that openness to globalisation will necessarily be accompanied by a reduction in spending on healthcare. In fact, high levels of spending and high levels of openness seem to be quite compatible. However, as we have seen with the figures for the US, this is only part of the story as these crude data on total spending on healthcare might mask quite different levels of public spending on healthcare. So, even though high levels of globalisation do not seem to have a negative impact on spending they might lead to a reduction in levels of public spending on healthcare. If this were the case, that globalisation led to increased privatisation of healthcare, then this would support the 'race to the bottom' argument espoused by writers such as Polivka (2001, Polivka and Borrayo 2002) and Vincent (2003). However, when we look at the data in Figure 4.12 we see a similar picture to the previous analyses. Although there is a lot of variation between the countries, once we draw our line of best fit, we can see a slight but, nonetheless, positive relationship between openness to global flows and high levels of public spending on healthcare. Taken together these data show that there is no necessary reduction in public spending on healthcare as countries become more open to globalisation. In fact, the opposite seems to be the case. This could be because global capital, for example, needs a healthy workforce and is therefore attracted to invest in countries which provide healthcare for their workforce, of all ages. However, whatever the reason, it does suggest that nation states still retain the ability to manage the amount they spend on healthcare.

Figure 4.11: The relationship between expenditure on health as a percentage of GDP and degree of globalisation, 2012

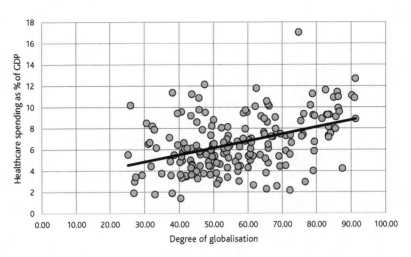

Sources: (Dreher 2006, World Health Organization Global Health Expenditure database 2015)

Figure 4.12: The relationship between public expenditure on health as a percentage of total healthcare spending and degree of globalisation, 2012

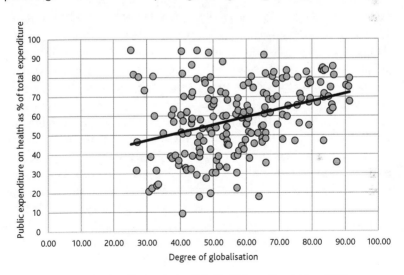

Sources: (Dreher 2006, World Health Organization Global Health Expenditure database 2015)

Conclusion

A number of conclusions can be drawn from the analyses presented in this chapter. First, it is clear that a new set of biotemporalities of ageing and later life have opened up. However, despite convergence along some of these temporal planes we are far from witnessing the emergence of a global time-space of ageing and later life. International and regional differences sit alongside these global trends. Similarly, there is limited evidence that global economic flows have had a major impact on the provision of healthcare for older people. Nonetheless, these new biotemporalities have created and are creating new sets of biospatialities through which health in later life is being realised. These spaces, and the actors that operate within them, comprise the local, national, regional and global and, we would argue, reflect the overlapping, multiple, heterarchical nature of a contemporary world order. At the global level, discussions about the demography of population ageing rest on a number of spatial dimensions. Key among these is that certain regions will not be able to cope with population ageing. However, as noted earlier, these discussions rest on a dual temporality. On the one hand, there is what might be seen as the individual temporality of life expectancy. It is clear that this is increasing and is shifting throughout most of the world. This is leading to instability around projects of ageing at the individual level. On the other hand, there is the slower temporality of population ageing. This has yet to establish itself at a global level and remains very much regionalised. For example, despite increases in life expectancy the African population is still relatively young.

The shift from mortality to longevity as a key biotemporality has been accompanied by an equally radical shift from morbidity to healthiness. The data show that later life is not uniformly a period of ill health. Ageing, or rather the acquisition of the status of old age, is no longer based on chronological age but is conceived of around the twin temporalities of natural versus normal ageing. The analyses suggest that in many parts of the world chronological age has become an increasingly unstable marker for where one is situated on the natural/normal trajectory of ageing. However, there are also some regional differences. The transition economies in Central and Eastern Europe are clearly identified by their older, modernist, experience of poor health in later life. It is perhaps no coincidence that this region also saw a reversal of life expectancy in the 1990s.

The absence of a global time-space of demography and health in later life is reflected in the weak relationship between global economic forces and public spending on health. The data here lend greater support to welfare regime theory than those who predicted a race to the bottom. Even when looking at the privatisation of healthcare the data show more of a race to the middle. When viewed from the higher income countries it looks like a shift away from public welfare. However, within the less developed economies there has been an increase in public spending on health.

FIVE

Time and money in
later life

Economic issues form a key dimension for both globalisation and social gerontology. As noted in Chapter Three, globalisation is often seen as an essentially economic phenomenon. Throughout this book we have contended that economic processes represent only one aspect of globalisation, albeit an important one, and that they need to be understood as interacting with other levels or 'scapes'. We have also pointed out in Chapter Two, that old(er) age has often been conflated with retirement and/or poverty and therefore it is important to examine the different ways in which economics and later life interact in the contemporary world.

As we have noted, the institutionalisation of the life course during the period of first modernity meant that retirement became the dominant temporality through which old age was understood. Alongside this the creation of state retirement pensions meant that the nation state became the dominant spatial actor through which retirement and economic 'sufficiency' in later life was organised. Consequently, modernist social gerontology has been focused upon the nation state as a welfare state. However, both these temporal and spatial assumptions have been subject to a sustained challenge. From the late 1980s through to the early 2000s, rates of early labour market exit (LME) successively 'de-standardised' retirement throughout most of the advanced industrialised economies (Kohli and Rein 1991, Henkens and Tazelaar 1994, 1997, Maule 1995, van Dalen and Henkens 2002, Guillemard 2003). This undermined the connection between ageing and retirement as well as the connection between retirement and state pensions. In the UK this process had been supported by an increasing reliance on occupational and private pensions which further de-institutionalised retirement and created opportunities for certain groups of workers to leave the labour market early with a relatively high degree of financial security. But it has also made income in later life far more contingent and dependent upon the global economy (Blackburn 2002). Early labour market exit also became a feature of many other pension systems where a combination of economic restructuring and previously established generous pension entitlements made it attractive for older workers to retire rather than continue to work (Ebbinghaus 2006). However, over the past five to ten years a number of governments in the high income economies throughout the OECD area have sought to reverse this trend and have enacted policies to extend working lives (Keese 2006, Kasneci 2007). As Ekerdt (2010) states: 'The trend toward earlier retirement is history'. Exit routes have been closed, benefit levels are lower, and the duration of these benefits has shortened. These reforms have taken place within a macroeconomic context of increasing job and pension insecurity and an erosion of trust in governing institutions (Hershey et al 2010). The shift from an early exit culture (De Vroom 2004, Ebbinghaus 2006) to a culture in which extended labour force participation by older adults is expected (Henkens and Schippers 2012) raises many questions about how current and future generations of older adults are managing and will manage their late careers (Phillipson 2013b). Older workers, who are expected to work much longer than they had envisioned, are challenged to find ways to remain productive. Individuals who lose their jobs because of unemployment or disability are challenged to find new employment under the looming risk of poverty if they do not succeed. Finally employers also face challenges to offer opportunities to attain that goal (Phillipson 2015).

Thus in the second decade of the 21st century a new phase in the de-standardisation of the life course is occurring across the most prosperous nations. In the previous phase, from the 1990s to the 2000s, there was a simultaneous decoupling of exit from the labour market and state pension age through a proliferation of different pathways to early retirement. However, the reversal of these early exit routes as part of the drive for 'active ageing' policies has seen labour market participation rates return to, or even surpass, those experienced in the 1990s (OECD 2015). Yet these policies have not re-established a standardised retirement. Instead they have created an increasingly complex set of new labour market positions as older workers have been encouraged to remain in employment through a multiplicity of new routes, given names such as bridge jobs, un-retirement, partial retirement, blended careers, encore careers, and so on. However, it is important to bear in mind that this situation is relatively particularised and that in the global South the dominant discourse is still focused on the right of older workers to retire, leave work and have access to state pensions (Lloyd-Sherlock 2002b, 2010).

Therefore, the key dimensions along which one can judge whether we are moving towards a global financial time-space of ageing and later life would be the extent to which one can identify a global convergence around labour market participation rates, retirement age, financial circumstances and pension policies.

The labour market position of older people around the world

Modernist social gerontology of the structured dependency or political economy schools of thought have, in the main, treated retirement as a product of the needs of the state or of capitalism with the result that retirement was often seen a 'personal tragedy' for older people (Townsend 1963, 1981, Estes 1980, Phillipson 1982, 1990). However, changes in work and pension provision have transformed retirement. Gilleard and Higgs (2000, 2005) have observed retirement is often a sought after status for many. No longer is it necessarily accompanied by poverty or ill health and it can be seen to have attained the status as a valued cultural good. Moreover, the more differentiated patterns of LME have disrupted the modernist life course and its implicit structuring (Kohli and Rein 1991). In the West this has made the identification of later life as a state of welfare dependency in the shape of state pensions much more problematic and has been part of the justification for the increases to pension age being implemented in many different countries (Blair 2014). These developments have made economic activity rates among older people a major policy issue in recent decades. However much less is known about the economic activity of older workers in the developing world (Allen et al 2002) and whether or not they are converging across the world or whether international or interregional differences contradict such a conclusion.

The data in Figure 5.1 extend the analyses by Kohli and Rein (1991) on the economic activity rates for those aged 55–64 to 2013. First, although data are not available for all countries, it is clear that there is not a similar global experience of employment in later life around the world. Instead there is a great deal of variability in older people's connection to the labour market depending on the country in which they live. While there may be little evidence for a global convergence of late life working there does appear to be evidence for some relatively distinct geographical clusters. Southern, Eastern and Western Europe are marked out as relatively low employment regimes. The exceptions to this rule are countries such as Germany and Holland which emerge as a separate group exhibiting somewhat higher employment rates than their continental neighbours. Alongside these countries, the Nordic nations appear to represent even higher employment regimes for older people. The UK and Ireland occupy a mid-point between these clusters with around 50–60% labour market participation (LMP) rates. Outside Europe, Canada and the USA clearly group together with 60% of older people in employment in their respective countries. Latin America appears to be made up of more of a patchwork of different regimes, some high and some low, without a clear north–south, east–west or linguistic differentiation. Conversely East and South East Asia and Australasia are almost exclusively high employment regimes where over 70% of older people are in work in these regions. This is also the case in West Africa which has some of the highest employment rates for older people in the world.

Figure 5.1: Employment rates for those aged 55–64, 2012/13

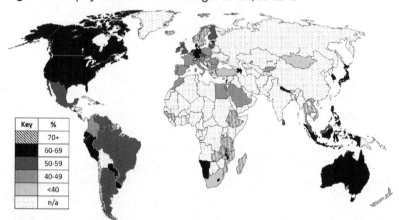

Source: (International Labour Organization 2015)

There is, however, relatively little data on the employment situation of older people in much of the developing world. In the absence of data from labour force surveys it has been necessary to rely on self-reported accounts to examine the labour market status of older people from a more global perspective. Subjective accounts also allow us to explore how older people think about their labour market status across a wide range of countries. As with the data in Figure 5.1, the data presented in Figure 5.2 show that older people around the world cannot be said to share a similar labour market experience. There are a number of countries in which older people are much more likely to report being in work until later in life than in others. However, it is not the case that these countries are all located in the middle or lower income bands. Although half of all those aged 60 and over in the Philippines are still working and around a third are still working in countries such as India, Malaysia and Colombia. Conversely there are a number of countries where it is normal for the majority of older people to see themselves as retired, such as Germany (80%) and Australia (66%). However, alongside this pattern of international variation, there does appear to be some evidence of a regional cluster. The former Soviet countries in Europe and Central Asia are predominantly clustered at the top end of the scale with older people in these countries having the highest rates of retirement. It is possible that this is a product of former labour market and retirement policies created under Soviet rule.

Work and retirement in a global era

Although these cross-national comparisons are a useful point of departure when considering the global employment situation of older people, they do not tell us what effects, if any, globalisation has had on work and retirement in later life. As noted earlier, theorists argue that improvements in the speed and capacity of global transportation, as well as the proliferation of information and communication technologies, has allowed businesses to relocate substantial elements of their productive capacity in other countries (Fröbel et al 1981, Dicken 2007). As a result of developments in sub-assembly practices alongside the growth of a skilled, but still relatively cheap, labour force in countries like China it has been assumed that this has had the greatest effect on the manufacturing sector in the advanced industrial economies (Greider 1998, Klein 2001). As discussed earlier the degree and extent to which capital is truly 'footloose' has been questioned. Significantly, little or no work has looked at how or whether these new risks affect older workers (Blossfeld et al 2006, McKelvey 2009). This is surprising given the volume of work on LMP rates in later life and the fact that most older, male workers are concentrated in more traditional manufacturing jobs (Yeandle 2003). It would be expected that countries with a high level of FDI, which indicates that the economy is open to both inward and outward global flows, would have relatively low LMP rates for older (male) workers.

Many writers have argued that in order to attract FDI governments have enacted laws to repress trades' unions, deregulate the labour market and keep wages low (Greider 1998, Piven and Cloward 2000, Myles and Pierson 2001, Schwartz 2001, Pierson 2006): all of which are seen to have deleterious effects on job security and economic wellbeing (Standing 1997, Rama 2003, Scheve and Slaughter 2004). However, it is less clear how FDI might affect the LMP rates of older workers. Older workers tend to be relatively more expensive than younger

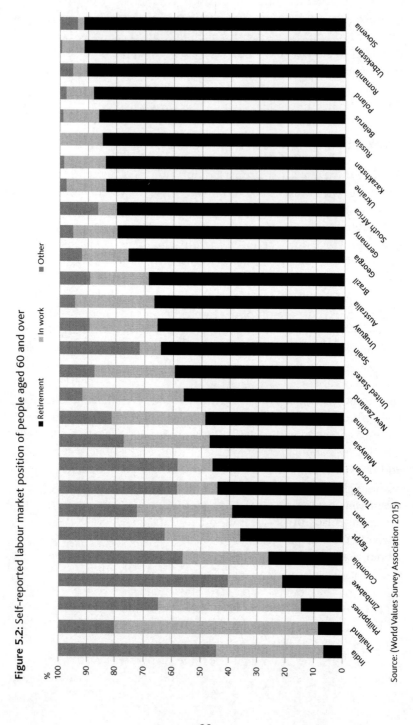

Figure 5.2: Self-reported labour market position of people aged 60 and over

Source: (World Values Survey Association 2015)

workers (Annual Survey of Hours and Earnings 2010) and are also often perceived to be less capable of adapting to new technologies (Hansson et al 1997, Borghans and ter Weel 2002). If this is the case then companies ought to have a preference for younger workers and therefore either lay off older workers, if they acquire existing firms in the host country, or only seek to employ young workers if they establish new 'greenfield' sites, potentially undercutting more established domestic firms which might be more likely to employ older workers. Either or both of these outcomes would have a negative impact on the LMP rates of older workers in the host country. Alternatively, investing companies might either create new employment opportunities for older workers, as part of a general expansion of jobs, or perhaps actively seek to retain older workers and benefit from their experience of working within the firm and the local economy. In either of these cases one would expect to see a positive effect on older workers' employment.

By combining the data on employment rates with data on the extent to which a country is economically globalised it is possible to assess whether such relationships exist. We have used the economic globalisation subscale from the KOF Globalization Index for these analyses (Dreher 2006). This is a multidimensional measure that covers actual flows, such as trade, FDI and remittances, and restrictions on flows, such as tariff rates and capital account restrictions. As men and women in many countries have different employment patterns (Wahrendorf 2015) we have performed the analyses separately by sex. Figure 5.3 shows that there is a reasonably strong negative relationship between the degree of economic openness and LMP rates for older men. This means that economies that are more economically globalised are also those who which have lower rates of male employment in later life. The results for the relationship between economic globalisation and female employment rates (Figure 5.4) are less clear. The data points are widely scattered across the graph with no discernible pattern. This is borne out when we include a line of best fit which is almost flat, indicating a lack of any notable relationship between the two. Taken together these results suggest that older male workers face particular labour market risks in a global economy.

Figure5.3: The relationship between employment rates for men aged 55–64 and the degree of economic globalisation, 2012: selected countries

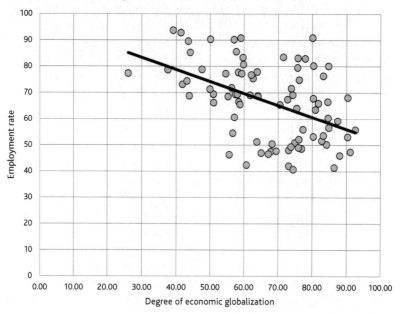

Sources: (Dreher 2006, International Labour Organization 2015)

Figure 5.4: The relationship between employment rates for women aged 55-64 and the degree of economic globalisation, 2012: selected countries

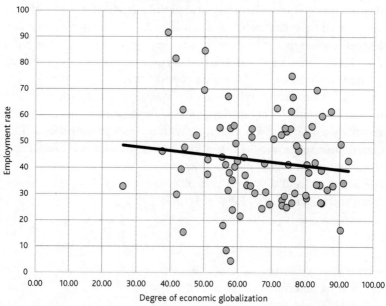

Sources: (Dreher 2006, International Labour Organization 2015)

The financial circumstances of older people

In general, older people in the advanced industrial economies have benefitted from the general increase in economic wellbeing in these countries over the past three decades (OECD 2001, 2007, 2013, Casey and Yamada 2002). This has led to a considerable change in poverty levels in retirement both in the USA and Western Europe.

> During most of history to be old was to be poor. This is certainly no longer the case in the United States. On average the elderly appear to be at least as well off as the non-elderly and possibly better off. (Hurd 1989: 663)

Though little systematic longitudinal work exists on the nature of pre- and post-retirement income (Barker and Hancock 2000) what work has been done indicates an increasing equivalence in net incomes between the two (Casey and Yamada 2002, Hungerford 2003, Hills and Stewart 2005, Department of Work and Pensions 2006, Middleton et al 2007). This transformation has largely been due to the growth of occupational pensions and, in the UK, the fact that many purchased their council houses (Forrest and Leather 1998, Department of Work and Pensions 2006). It is also the case that pensioner incomes in countries such as the UK have risen faster than those of other, particularly younger, groups (Belfield et al 2014).

However, these findings have been challenged. A report by Age UK, the UKs largest organisation for older people, estimated that in 2011/12 1.6 million older people were in relative poverty, defined as having incomes below 60% median income after housing costs. In addition, nearly a million pensioners were in severe poverty and 800,000 older people reported that they could not afford the things that most people regard as necessities (Norton and West 2014). These figures corroborate earlier findings from the British Household Panel Survey which consistently found retirees in the lowest income quintile (Bardasi et al 2002) although this seems to have changed in more recent years (Jenkins 2015). However, wealth and income are different concepts with some households being income poor but asset rich. Thus, using their definition of 'core poor', Dorling and colleagues (2007) identify a fall in the percentage of single pensioner households in core poverty in the UK. Furthermore it has been estimated that one fifth of income poor pensioners hold housing equity in excess of £100,000 per household (Dixon and Margo 2006). Some scholars suggest that, as incomes become more transitory and subject to short term volatility, then expenditure is a better measure of household welfare as it measures 'permanent income', but more research is needed in this area (Blundell and Preston 1998).

It is important to note that the general improvement in financial circumstances has been accompanied with greater inequality among the older population (Hills 2004, Förster and D'Ercole 2005, Chou et al 2006) as several groups, namely women and ethnic minorities, have missed out on the growth in occupational pensions (Ginn and Arber 2001, Calasanti 2003, Ginn 2004, Turner et al 2004). Likewise, those who retire due to poor health are also more likely to have lower retirement income and savings (McDonald and Donahue 2000). To this we could add those in the lowest paid jobs. Data from the Family Expenditure Survey has shown that state pension accounts for a greater proportion of total income, almost 100%, for those in the lowest income quintile compared to those in the highest income quintile where it is around one quarter (Department of Work and Pensions 2007).

Across the European Union, while income inequality in later life remains an issue (and has come to the top of the political agenda in countries such as Greece) it has been noted that the effects of the economic crises from 2008 onwards have not had any widespread consequences for pensioners in most EU even though there has been considerable institutional change (Vis et al 2011, Hallerberg 2013, Grech 2015). As Grech (2015: 49) writes:

> the financial crisis did not result in a substantial weakening of pension entitlements. Even in stressed countries, pension wealth appears to be higher, while replacement rates for women improved. Pension entitlements fell in just seven countries, with the largest falls in Greece and Luxembourg. Meanwhile, five of the most populous nations boosted pension generosity.

That there may be a transformed situation in years to come is a moot point, particularly in relation to Mediterranean countries, but it does not seem to be the case that there has been an increase in relative poverty among older people in the EU and indeed Grech argues that the opposite seems to be the case.

Finally, it is important not just to concentrate on the income and wealth dynamics of older people in the West but to examine whether these trends in financial circumstances is being repeated around the world. There is, once again, a real lack of comparative international data on the financial circumstances of older people in the developing world.

This is arguably due to the relatively underdeveloped government statistics collected within these countries, especially outside of urban areas, and the widespread belief that it is more important to focus on the rates and determinants of poverty among younger age groups in these regions (Lloyd-Sherlock 2010). An example of this is that none of the UN's earlier Millennium Development Goals referred to the financial wellbeing of older people (Pearson et al 2008). The reasons behind this are of course debatable. What is important here, however, is that oversights such as these make it difficult to get an accurate global picture of the financial circumstances of older people. In the absence of any large-scale surveys of the 'objective' financial status of older people in these countries, it is necessary to use subjective assessments of satisfaction with one's household financial situation. Looking at these data (Figure 5.5) it is clear that older people around the world do not share a common experience of dissatisfaction with their financial situation. Just by comparing the average level of satisfaction across the countries it is clear that in a number of countries, such as Brazil, Australia, Peru, Poland and Tunisia, older people are generally happy with their financial position. Conversely older people in countries such as the USA and Ukraine are generally dissatisfied with their financial position. These data defy any attempts to come up with simplistic accounts regarding the financial status of older people based on assumptions about the presence or absence of factors connected to welfare system types.

Three worlds into one? Globalisation and pensions

While any impact of globalisation on the employment or employability of older workers is likely to have an effect on their economic wellbeing, the majority of arguments regarding the potential negative impact of globalisation on older people centres on the constraints that are supposedly exerted on the state's ability to provide welfare (Polivka 2001, Estes and Phillipson 2002, Vincent 2003). As discussed in Chapter Three, there is a substantial volume of research on whether or not globalisation has led, or is leading, to a reduction in welfare spending. However, there is relatively little work that has focused specifically on older people or pensions.

An important first step to redress this is to look at amount that different countries spend on supporting older people. If we are seeing a 'race to the bottom' then we should see very similar and very low levels of expenditure on old age benefits across a wide range of countries. In order to explore this we have used data to look at the amount of

Figure 5.5: Reported income satisfaction amongst those aged 60 and over, 2013: selected countries

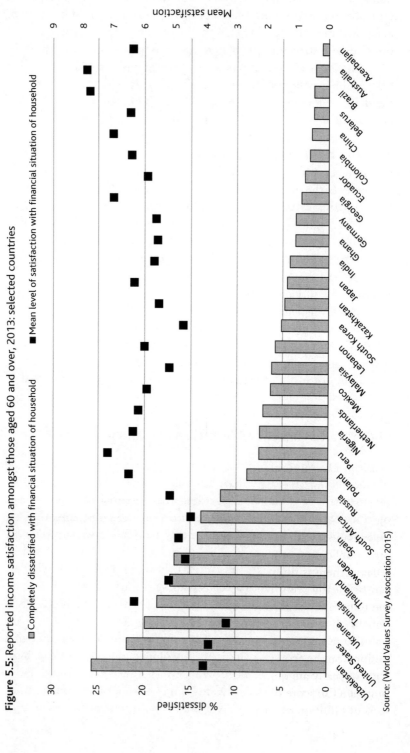

■ Completely dissatisfied with financial situation of household
■ Mean level of satisfaction with financial situation of household

Source: (World Values Survey Association 2015)

public expenditure spent on old age, expressed as a percentage of GDP, across the OECD countries (Adema et al 2011). From these data, presented in Figure 5.6, we can see that there is a wide range of international variability in the relative amounts that governments in the OECD countries spend on old age benefits. At one extreme there are a number of countries such as Mexico, the Republic of Korea and Chile that spend relatively little on old age benefits. Conversely there are a number of much more generous countries where spending on these benefits exceeds the equivalent of 10% of GDP. This includes countries such as Japan, Finland, France and Italy. The second feature of these data is that there are no clear geographic or economic patterns to the positioning of countries along this scale. Neither does the relative position on such a scale seem to be influenced by the size of the economy with the effect that larger economies might spend relatively less as a proportion of GDP. Germany has the largest economy in Europe yet spends relatively more than countries such as Belgium and the Netherlands. So, although the data we are using are too restrictive to allow for an analysis of regional patterns on a truly global scale, the degree of international variation and the absence of any clear pattern strongly suggest that no such regional groupings actually exist. Moreover, we would also conclude that we are not witnessing a global race to the bottom around a residual welfare model.

While these data do provide an important corrective to the argument that we are seeing the emergence of a homogenous global financescape of old age benefits, they actually tell us little about the actual impact or otherwise of global economic flows on public spending on later life. To address this issue, the data in Figure 5.7 examine the relationship between economic globalisation, measured using the KOF subscale (Dreher 2006) and the amount of public expenditure spent on old age, in terms of pensions and other forms of old age benefits across the OECD countries. Against the argument that greater economic globalisation will exert negative pressure on the ability of states to fund public pensions, these data show that, for the OECD countries at least, there is no real relationship between these two factors. This can be clearly seen by looking at the line of best fit, represented by the thick black line, which runs almost horizontally through the data points. To illustrate this further, we can compare the amount spent on old age benefits between countries that occupy roughly the same position on the economic globalisation scale. For example, both France and Germany are quite similar in their degree of economic openness (with a KOF score of around 66), yet France spends the equivalent of 12% of GDP on old age benefits compared to 9% in Germany. This

Figure 5.6: Public expenditure on old age benefits as a percentage of GDP, 2011: OECD countries

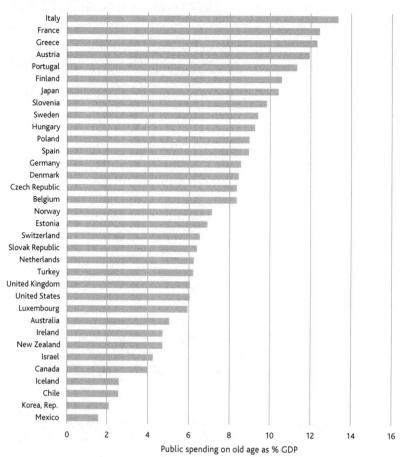

Source: (OECD 2015)

strongly suggests that, far from being bulldozed by the inexorable tide of globalisation, national governments still retain a degree of control over their social expenditure on later life. These results are far more consistent with those of writers like Huber and Stephens (2001), Schwartz (2001) and Esping-Andersen (1990) than those of the global pessimists such as Daly (2001) and Yeates (2001).

The data do seem to lend support to the general argument that economic openness is not necessarily related to more or less generous old age benefits and there appears to be little evidence of distinct regional or welfare regime clusters. For example, countries that are usually seen to share similar welfare characteristics, geographical location, or both, differ markedly in terms of the relative amounts they devote to financing later life. Yet these analyses are still rather broad. By referring to the OECD's (2013) *Pensions at a Glance*, it is possible to quantify several important dimensions of the structure of the pension package in each member state. The report provides data on the contribution that various components of the pension system make to the overall potential resource transfer to pensions under the mandatory provision.

Figure 5.7: The relationship between economic globalization and public spending on old age benefits, 2011: OECD countries

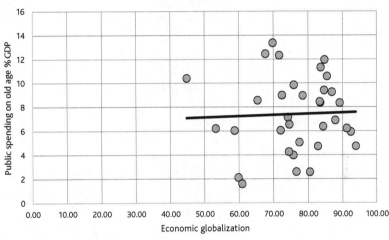

Source:(Dreher 2006, OECD 2015)

Pension systems can also be classified along a continuum from 'pure-basic' to 'pure-insurance' (OECD 2007, 2013). Pure-basic systems are considered to be much more redistributive as they pay the same flat rate amount to all those who are entitled regardless of how much they earned before retirement and any other sources of income that they may receive in retirement. Thus the value of the pension is independent of lifetime earnings and the replacement rate is inversely related to income. At the other end of the scale are pure-insurance schemes under which the replacement rate is directly related to earnings over the lifetime or for a specified number of years depending formula used to calculate benefits.

These poles represent 'ideal' types and few pension systems are either completely pure-basic or pure-insurance. Most systems exhibit a mix of the two and therefore appear someway along the continuum away from either extreme. However, using this model the OECD (2013) has constructed an 'index of progressivity' which measures the relative contribution of basic versus insurance components in each member state's mandatory pension system.[1] The index is based on a Gini coefficient that calculates the distribution of the pension between the two poles. From this, the progressivity index is calculated as 100 minus the ratio of the Gini coefficient of pension entitlements divided by the Gini coefficient of earnings. It is important to emphasise that this is not a measure of income inequality in later life but of the 'progressivity' of each pension system. Thus a pure-basic scheme would score 100% while a pure-insurance scheme would score zero. Moreover, the OECD notes that a high score is not necessarily 'better' than a low score or vice versa. Countries with a high score simply have different objectives than countries with a low score.

The results of the OECD (2013) analyses show that there is a wide range in Gini coefficients and, by extension, the progressivity of the pension benefit formulas throughout the OECD. Countries such as Ireland, New Zealand and South Africa which conform to a pure-basic model score the highest, 100%, while others with a much greater insurance component are less progressive. For example, there are eight countries, including the Netherlands, Turkey and Finland, where the index is less than 10%. However, there is little evidence of any regional similarity or welfare regime clusters. As the report notes, the Anglophone countries tend to score higher on the progressivity index. Indeed, Ireland, New Zealand, South Africa, Canada, the UK and Australia make up six of the top ten most progressive counties ranging from 100% to 73%. However, the USA is distinct from this group with only 43%. Differences are even more marked between the Scandinavian or social democratic welfare states. Similarly, high variation is evident among the continental or conservative welfare states such as Belgium (61%), France (31%) and the Netherlands (4%). The Southern European states are also quite diverse, for example Greece scores 39%, Spain 24% and Portugal -1%. Outside of the OECD there is a similarly varied picture. Although India (33%), China (25%) and Russia (24%) are all quite close, countries such as Brazil, Indonesia and Saudi Arabia are much less progressive. Again these figures contradict the image of a unified, global, financescape of pension provision.

---

[1] As the report's authors make clear it is important not to overlook the fact that many countries also have extensive private occupational and personal pension provision. They go on to note that were these systems included in the calculations the distribution of pensioners' incomes would doubtless be wider.

It is clear that some countries aim to and are able to pursue more progressive pension systems whereas others have a greater reliance on insurance-based pensions.

Given this variation and what is already known about the different levels of economic openness among the OECD member states one might, prima facia, conclude that there is no evidence of a 'race to the bottom' in terms of welfare provision for older people. However, the report does not explicitly test the degree to which the economic globalisation might impact on the progressivity of pension provision in these countries. However, it is important to assess rather than assume this by looking at the relationship between the KOF economic globalisation subscale and the OECD data above. As we may suspect, there is no discernible relationship between the degree of economic openness and the level of pension progressivity among these countries presented in Figure 5.8. Again this appears to be another challenge to the argument that (economic) globalisation is forcing welfare states to coalesce around a model of residual welfare expenditure. Instead, it appears that national governments still have some power to determine the nature of their pension systems and that in many cases they are able to combine progressive pensions with an economically open economy. Correspondingly, we would contend that there is nothing inevitable about exposure to economic globalisation and welfare retrenchment.

Figure 5.8: The relationship between economic globalisation and pension progressivity, 2013: OECD and selected non-OECD countries

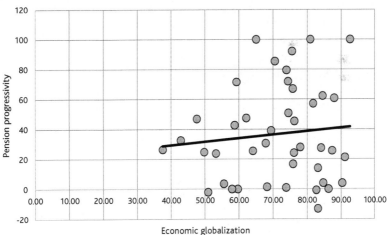

Source: (Dreher 2006, OECD 2013)

Conclusion

In reviewing the analyses in this chapter a number of points have become evident. New temporalities of ageing and later life have opened up around work and retirement but there is little evidence of an emerging global economic time-space of ageing and later life. Neither do global economic flows seem to have much of a direct impact on the economic circumstances of older people. International and regional variations in work and income point to the importance of non-global political and economic structures for older people. As with the analyses on the health of the world's older population, the picture that emerges is of a complex multi-layered reality.

The analyses of LME confirm much of what is already known about the older workers in Europe and North America. As with the data from the previous chapter, they point to an increasingly fluid set of temporalities around ageing and later life. In many countries LME is occurring early and through a variety of pathways. Thus leaving the workforce has become largely divorced from state retirement age or the receipt of a state pension. Although many OECD countries are now acting to reverse the trends of early LME most governments have not aimed to set new definitive limits for retirement but, have rather sought, to open up a more flexible time-space of retirement. The Austrian government's 'retirement corridor' and the end of the mandatory retirement age in the UK are good examples of this. These developments make retirement a more individualised and personal event. However, there are a number of risks attached to this in terms of receiving higher or possibly lower pensions. The shift to lifetime earnings as a way of assessing pension eligibility is yet another example of this variability. This change too does not attempt to fix a standard age, as those who start work earlier could possibly retire earlier, but it does make this decision more conditional upon differential financial returns. Thus starting work at an earlier age might mean starting on a lower wage and therefore accruing a smaller pension across the life course. Not completing the required years necessary for eligibility may also mean having a reduced income in later life.

There is some evidence of regional patterning of the financescapes of ageing and later life. Western, Southern, Central and Eastern Europe countries appear as relatively low employment regimes. Conversely Northern Europe, North America, East Asia and parts of Latin America are high employment regimes. In a number of countries, such as Mexico, people appear to work beyond the official retirement age. The OECD data lend some qualified support to the influence of welfare regime type has on employment rates in later life. Certainly, the self-reported data suggest that high levels of employment in later life outside of the high income economies might be due to necessity rather than to choice as many older workers might find themselves reliant on 'informal labour markets'. Hence in the absence of formal or universal pension systems older people may need to work until poor health prevents them from continuing. This is reminiscent of the experience of a pre-modern, rather than late modern, time-space of ageing.

The global pattern of income in later life is one of differences rather than similarities between countries. In a number of European and North American countries later life has become less associated with poverty or the risk of poverty. Throughout the OECD area, older people's incomes grew faster than the population's between the mid-1990s and the late 2000s (OECD 2013). Elsewhere, however, poverty and the risk of poverty still blight the lives of older people. In Europe this is most evident in the Mediterranean countries, such as Cyprus, and in many of the transition economies. Unlike in Western Europe, early LME in Southern and Central and Eastern Europe is not accompanied by levels of financial security but is dominated by the (modernist) experience of poverty and deprivation in later life. However, older people's self-reported financial status does not necessarily reflect this. For example, Danes and Australians rate themselves alongside Latvians and Ukrainians in the lowest income quintile. Likewise, there are counter-intuitive patterns in self-reported satisfaction with income. This suggests that objective measures of poverty and subjective feelings of impoverishment might have very different impacts on older people.

Turning to globalisation there is limited evidence that economic global factors have an impact on the financial wellbeing of older people. Rather this lends support to the argument that national welfare structures act as potential buffers against the risks of globalisation. In addition, it could be that MNCs look to invest in stable markets and countries with good infrastructure and these countries also happen to be those with a more interventionist (welfare) state. In addition, there is no real evidence of a race to the bottom in welfare spending or on the relative generosity of pension packages. Instead there is still wide variation in spending, in general and for old age in particular, and in the composition of pension income. What we are left with, as has been true in other chapters, is a much more mixed picture of the relationship between globalisation and later life. There have been undoubted changes, both positive and negative, but there are not the clear patterns of the relationship between the imputed consequences of a globalised capitalism and the position of older people that some writers within social gerontology have expected. This is in part because the financescape of later life operates and interacts with a number of different temporal and spatial levels; no one being reducible to the others. This has meant that we see a series of seeming paradoxes particularly in relation to the longest lived welfare states where not only has the position for older improved over the past few decades, but that retrenchment and austerity appear to have had relatively smaller effects than had been anticipated. For those in the developing welfare states the issues might be different but are mainly ones of degree as witnessed in Latin America and South East Asia. The general lessons that could be learned from this overview are that we must treat ageing and later life as having escaped the confines of a residual category of social policy and accept it as a full player in the interplay of the different levels of contemporary global society. Failure to do this ignores reality and possibly deepens the difficulties of global ageing.

SIX

The cultures of ageing and later life

In the preceding chapters we have looked at what we have termed the bioscapes and the financescapes of ageing and later life. This chapter explores the ways in which belonging and identity are produced and reproduced along what can be called the ethnoscapes of ageing and later life. Appadurai (1996) defines the ethnoscape as 'the landscape of persons who constitute the shifting world in which we live: tourists, immigrants, refugees, exiles, guest workers and other moving groups'. As noted in Chapter Two, a key issue in both cultural and critical gerontology has been the creation of (new) identities in later life. Writers from both perspectives recognise that the earlier, modernist nation state based sources of identity for later life have been undermined and challenged (Wilson 1997, Phillipson 1998, Gilleard and Higgs 2000, Powell and Longino 2002). For Appadurai (1996) two of the key challenges to the nation state are the global mobility of peoples and of signs. These challenges raise a number of questions for social gerontology. What do the ethnoscapes of later life look like? To what extent are older people part of these new mobilities, in terms of travel and migration? Has the third age become a free floating global signifier, or do national or regional differences regarding identity and mobility continue to construct old age?

The previous two chapters have demonstrated that the key coordinates that have traditionally been used to identify old age, such as health and retirement, have become relatively unstable and are now much more fluid than they once were. Older people can no longer be regarded as uniformly ill, disabled or poor. The institutional arrangements that produced and were reproduced by these earlier experiences of ageing have themselves been transformed. Welfare systems, pensions in particular, have become less stable as they respond to demographic and cultural changes and as they themselves become part of the shift to late modernity. This suggests that there are number of new temporal vistas along which ageing occurs. These have shifted from the stable, linear trajectories of classical or high modernity to the more fluid reversible and conditional temporalities of late, reflexive or second modernity.

If there is an emergent phase of the life course opening up in which the older definitions of later life no longer pertain then what, if anything, will provide the material and cultural basis for new identities and lifestyles. Gilleard and Higgs (2000, 2005, 2011) have argued that we need to look to the cultures promoted by the third age to contextualise contemporary later life. For them a third age habitus is produced and reproduced through the dynamics of consumer practices that coincide with a generational habitus. The present and soon-to-be cohorts of retirees, in the UK and USA at least, participated in the creation of consumer culture in the 1960s and 1970s. The retirees of today and tomorrow, they point out, were the teenagers of yesteryear and approach 'old age' from a very different perspective than their parents. For Gilleard and Higgs the cultural field of ageing is now determined by the cultural dispositions of the post war cohorts for whom choice and consumption are key motifs in their positioning in the social world. In this way they argue that many of the most prosperous nations are not witnessing the emergence of a new life stage but rather a transformation of the cultural and social coordinates of later life. Moreover, through the generational dispositions of the teenagers who have grown old the very distinctions between age groups are being eroded and flattened in the pursuit of 'ageless selves' for whom age is literally a number. This challenges and throws into confusion more conventional assumptions about age, seniority and social role; particularly those established through social policy and the welfare state. Many other writers, however, contend that there are other, equally salient, sources of identity in later life. Some draw attention to the role of the older people within the family (Askham et al 2007) or the importance of community (Phillipson and Scharf 2005, Peace et al 2007, Phillipson 2007).

However, this tells us relatively little about how identities in later life are formed or how older people themselves think about ageing in a global context. We must therefore be cautious about reading off identities in later life from changes in the socio-demographics of ageing. As Appadurai (1996) notes, these scapes, the economic and the cultural, can be deeply disjunctive. Therefore, it is necessary to explore in more detail how older people themselves think about ageing and old age and whether new coordinates for identities in later life are emerging.

A global third age?

Despite its popularity the concept of the third age remains contested. Laslett (1987, 1996) argued that one could classify 'third age' societies based on a simple demographic calculation, which he termed the 'third age indicator' (3AI). This was based on there being a at least a 50% chance that a person of aged 25 years would live to 70 years, 10% or more of the whole population being over age 65 and GDP per capita being above US$10,000. When these conditions were met, he argued, there would be critical mass of older people to transform the nature and expectations of later life. While this may represent a useful start in thinking about the global spread of the conditions for the realisation of a third age, it tells us little about how older people themselves feel about or experience later life. Gilleard and Higgs (2000, 2005, 2007, 2011), dissatisfied with Laslett's demographic determinism, have, as we have seen, argued that the third age represents an emergent social and cultural space in the life course. This definition pre-supposes that awareness and participation in the third age is a reflexive, agentic process in which older people produce and reproduce (new) meanings and identities in later life. A key component of this is the emergence of a social and cultural field between the end of work and what could be said to constitute the condition of old age. Taking this argument as a point of departure, the first step is to see whether there is evidence for this new temporality and, then, to assess the extent to which this is evident throughout the world.

Data from the English Longitudinal Study of Ageing (ELSA) lend some support to this argument (Figure 6.1). Respondents were asked at what age they thought middle age ended and at what age they thought old age started (Demakakos et al 2004). For all age groups over 50 years old these ages were not coterminous. What is even more striking though is that as the age of the respondent increased so did the age at which they put the start of old age, while the end of middle age remained relatively constant at around 62 years. One interpretation of this is that while middle age could be seen as a relatively fixed social and cultural location, old age was becoming something that was possibly identified as 'unsuccessful ageing' (Higgs and Gilleard 2015).

Table 6.1 supports this finding with cross-national data. Respondents from 23 European countries were asked at what age they considered men and women to become old and what age they thought was the ideal age of retirement for each sex. There are wide international variations in the age at which men and women age thought to become old as well as differences in the ideal age of retirement. It is also notable that in no country is the ideal age of retirement synonymous with the start of old age. For women this gap is largest in Ireland, some 28 years, and is the smallest in Spain, just 2 years. For men this is longest in France, 19 years, and is shortest in Cyprus, only 6 years.

Figure 6.1: Perceived age at which middle age ends and at which old age begins

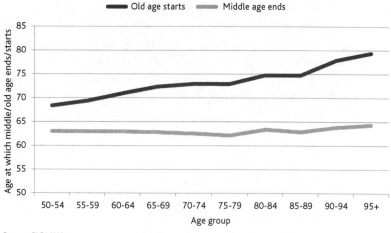

Source: ELSA W1

Thus, if old age is not set by any chronological marker or by the cessation of working life, what, if anything, has moved in to occupy this space opened up by the end of middle age and the onset of old age? How stable are other coordinates such as health or familial relations? As can be seen from the data in Table 6.2 the majority of those aged 60 years and over in Europe do not consider physical frailty to be a defining characteristic of being old. Similarly, very low proportions of older people define old age in generational[1] terms. Only in Bulgaria do half of the population say that one becomes old on the birth of one's grandchildren. In most countries only around a third or fewer of the respondents believe that once you become a grandparent you ought to be considered as old. Finally, one can see that respondents were more likely to associate being in need of care with being old. Around two thirds of respondents in France, Denmark and Bulgaria agreed with this statement and in most of the other countries it was between one third and half of the respondents. The exceptions to this were Spain and Sweden, for both sexes, and in Austria, for men, where only around a quarter felt that to be considered old it was important to be cared for by others.

These data suggest that chronological age, in later life at least, has become a very unstable measure of a person's health, labour market position or social activity. Instead it must compete against an ever growing number of other temporal schemes, such as emotional age

[1]   This refers to generations in the kinship sense (Kertzer 1983).

104

Table 6.1 Mean age at which men and women are considered to have become old and mean ideal age at which men and women ought to retire amongst those aged 60 years and over in Europe: 2006/7.

	Women		Men	
	Become old	Ideal retirement age	Become old	Ideal retirement age
Austria	64.78	53.04	62.02	53.05
Belgium	65.24	48.80	64.97	53.28
Bulgaria	59.73	52.83	62.17	53.22
Switzerland	54.55	40.14	56.83	49.86
Cyprus	49.39	45.70	55.17	49.33
Germany	58.27	52.42	60.14	52.86
Denmark	60.65	50.15	60.26	52.18
Estonia	65.92	51.93	65.94	55.94
Spain	56.04	54.11	60.66	49.48
Finland	66.10	46.68	64.15	49.44
France	72.38	49.74	72.84	54.33
UK	65.31	48.45	65.43	52.31
Hungary	58.89	52.05	61.04	52.10
Ireland	66.32	38.63	65.50	49.85
Netherlands	68.55	51.05	67.56	53.57
Norway	70.04	54.20	72.10	55.96
Poland	62.44	51.92	63.86	49.49
Portugal	64.58	47.34	65.25	48.95
Russian Fed.	57.45	51.74	61.43	52.56
Sweden	59.33	51.42	61.90	52.79
Slovenia	56.69	46.87	57.35	49.12
Slovakia	64.69	47.64	62.42	51.17
Ukraine	55.58	48.64	60.72	49.04

Source: (European Social Survey 2006)

(Bain 1945), biological age (Jackson et al 2003, Belsky et al 2015), functional age (Sharkey 1987, Graham et al 1999) and cognitive age (Barak and Gould 1985, Barak 1987). It has been argued that these alternative measures give a much more accurate indication of an individual's health and wellbeing. There is some evidence that subjective age is an internationally meaningful concept (Barak 2009). But there are also cross-national and gender differences in ideal age and subjective age (Uotinen 1998). ELSA data, presented in Figure 6.2, allow us to look at this in a UK context. The data show a remarkable degree of homogeneity for both these 'ages'. Even people in their 80s reported that they felt more like they were in their mid-40s and would like to be somewhere in their late 30s.

Alternatively, one could examine the importance that older people attach to age. Data from the International Social Survey Program (ISSP), presented in Figure 6.3, permit this for a wide range of countries. Respondents were asked what the most important factor was for their sense of identity. We restricted the analyses to those

Table 6.2 Characteristics which are thought to be important for identifying older men and women amongst those aged 60 years and over in Europe: 2006/7

	For a woman to be considered old is it important to be...			For a man to be considered old is it important to be...		
	physically frail	a grand-mother	cared for by others	physically frail	a grand-father	cared for by others
Austria	11.98	23.86	35.38	10.43	17.16	26.19
Belgium	38.53	25.11	50.68	40.71	25.00	54.63
Bulgaria	40.86	50.00	69.02	45.65	50.54	67.03
Switzerland	38.43	18.75	43.31	32.13	14.48	42.73
Germany	48.11	18.97	52.75	46.97	20.10	51.57
Denmark	63.23	24.44	63.16	65.65	28.33	70.43
Estonia	31.05	21.56	42.66	33.64	22.17	41.94
Spain	23.63	24.27	29.71	18.26	17.70	23.53
Finland	19.80	24.24	43.77	26.52	30.28	51.25
France	43.84	26.58	66.52	48.57	29.86	71.56
UK	18.10	14.97	34.74	24.75	17.67	36.31
Hungary	38.31	14.43	41.21	35.06	12.39	36.75
Ireland	16.06	14.50	38.58	22.49	13.15	40.55
Netherlands	18.10	14.41	32.14	15.45	14.04	29.06
Norway	18.72	17.24	36.95	25.76	16.00	45.00
Poland	30.90	35.14	38.12	27.81	36.26	36.59
Portugal	47.99	45.04	52.99	48.23	39.69	56.39
Russian Fed.	46.48	17.10	45.15	38.56	14.34	40.17
Sweden	15.04	5.02	24.44	21.57	6.44	25.68
Slovenia	18.97	19.29	35.75	24.28	19.13	34.08
Slovakia	26.26	14.13	33.15	28.00	18.64	32.00
Ukraine	40.24	18.80	37.61	37.35	26.07	41.39

Source: (European Social Survey 2006)

Figure 6.2: Figure 6.2: Mean subjective age and mean desired age for those aged 60 years and over in 5-year age bands living in England, 2004

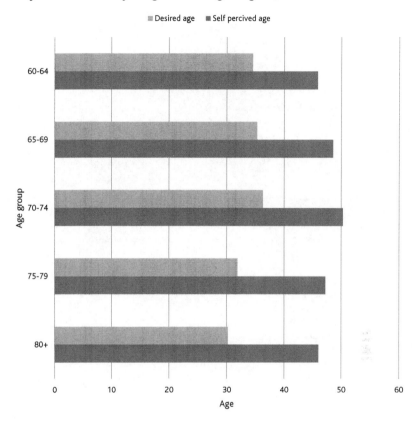

Source: ELSA W2

aged 60 and over. The results show two things. First, that there is a reasonable degree of international variation attached to the importance of age among the world's older population. Second, that despite this variation only a minority of older people in any country said that their age was the most important source for their identity. In the vast majority of countries fewer than 10% of those asked said that their age was important for their sense of identity. Moreover, the data do not provide any evidence for regional clusters or the emergence of a global convergence around a certain level of age identification. Instead the level of international variation in the results suggests that the degree to which older people feel age is important for their sense of identity is highly dependent on the country in which they live.

Figure 6.3: Proportion of those aged 60 and over who say that their age is the most important source for their identity

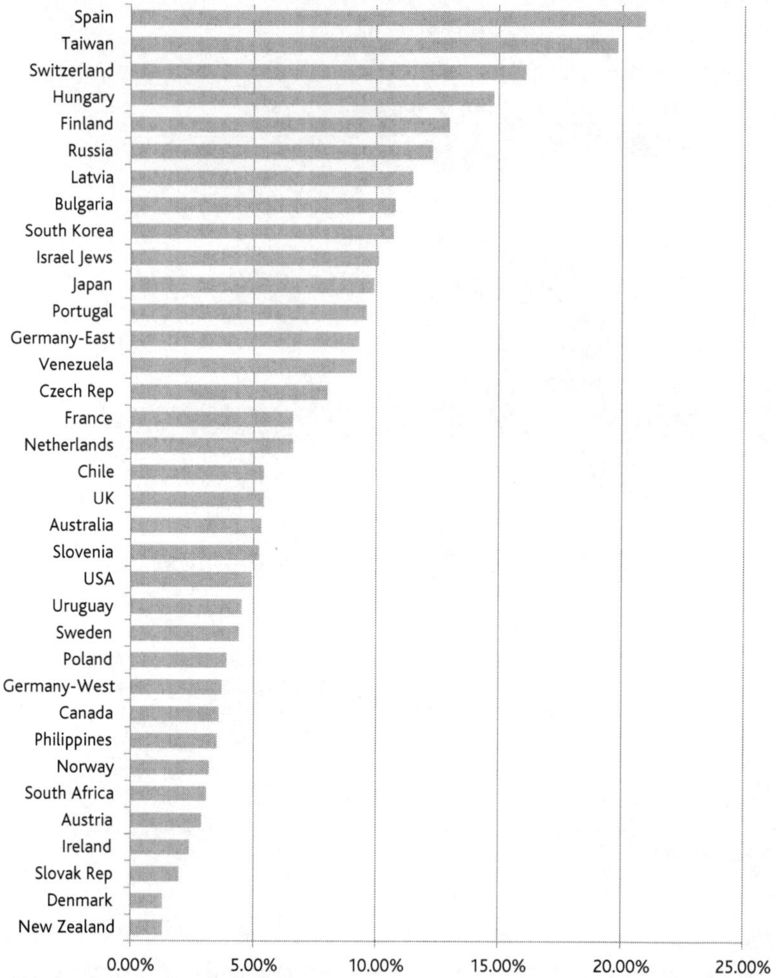

Source: (ISSP Research Group 2015)

Consumerism and identity in later life

A central argument in cultural gerontology is that consumption has become a key site for the construction of identities in later life (Gilleard 1996, Gilleard and Higgs 2000, 2005, 2011, 2015, Gilleard et al 2005, Hyde et al 2009, Twigg and Martin 2015). However, apart from a few notable exceptions consumer behaviour has been largely overlooked within gerontology. Older consumers have been similarly neglected within marketing and consumer studies (Greco 1993). As Burt and Gabbott (1995) noted this is due to a perceived lack of spending power in later life as well as the negative attitudes and stereotyped perceptions of the poor health of older people. These factors are compounded by the preoccupation of marketers with young, wealthy and more 'exciting' consumer groups. But this is beginning to change. As noted earlier, Gilleard and Higgs (1996, 2000, 2002, 2005, 2005, 2007, 2010) have long argued for the importance of consumption for the creation of identities in the third age. From their perspective it is important not just to look at the consumption in terms of the shopping patterns of older people, but to go beyond this and examine its role in the formation of a generational habitus of those now entering later life. Whereas older people were once at the margins of a consumer society, they are now increasingly drawn into the cultural processes of consumer capitalism. Consumption is seen to open up a new set of possible sites for the construction of alternative identities for older people from which they can reject or resist the (state) imposed categorisation of the poor, sick pensioner (Wilson 1997, Gilleard and Higgs 2000, 2005, Powell and Longino 2002). In line with these arguments a number of other writers have begun to critically explore how older people, mostly women, use clothing and beauty products to negotiate ageing identities (Twigg 2007, Clarke and Griffin 2008, Clarke et al 2009, Muise and Desmarais 2010, Hurd Clarke and Bennett 2015). It should, however, be reiterated that some writers have questioned the extent to which consumer practices have penetrated into later life (Falkingham and Victor 1991, Vincent 2003, Biggs 2004, Fox 2005).

There has also been a growing awareness among marketers that population ageing presents opportunities and challenges. Thirty years ago, Greco (1986) noted that retailers should be interested in this market not only due to the sheer number of older people, but also because they have high levels of disposable income. As Sawchuck (1995) has observed, a number of companies, especially in the USA, began to see the potential to turn the grey market into gold. She identifies this 'alchemical trope' as 'one of the major discursive regularities in contemporary marketing literature'. In order to achieve this marketers and advertisers started to use much more positive images of older people to sell goods to this emerging market. Although this is still a relatively small area of research, the common conclusion is that (older) age is a very poor indicator of consumption or shopping behaviour (Lumpkin 1984, Mertz and Stephens 1986, Barak 1987, Moschis 1994, Carrigan and Szmigin 2000, Szmigin and Carrigan 2001a, 2001b, Nam et al 2007, Moschis 2009).

However, while these studies are an important corrective to the mutual neglect of consumption and later life they are limited by a number of factors. First, they tend to focus on single items, such as food or clothing, or single sites, such as particular shopping malls. Consequently, they tend to involve relatively small, convenience, samples from which it is difficult to generalise. Second, and perhaps more importantly for the argument being pursed here, they are overwhelmingly carried out in either the USA or the UK. It has been argued that although the third age has the potential to become a global construct it has yet to gain full expression outside of the developed world.

> A global future for a third age is still some way off. Whether and how it might be realized within the existing structure of the world economy is a question requiring a considerably broader analysis ... For the moment we must content ourselves with treating the third age as a phenomenon of the 'Westernized' life course, one that has been conceived and delivered against the historical backdrop of modernity. (Gilleard and Higgs 2005: 4–5)

Others have questioned the applicability of Western concepts such as successful ageing (Lamb and Myers 1999, Chung and Park 2008) and the third age (Fox 2005) to the experience of later life for those in the developing world. However, there is a small, but growing, number of Asian studies on consumption in later life (Chou et al 2006, Cheung and Leung 2007, Fon Sim and Phillips 2007, Fon Sim et al 2008, Ying and Yao 2010). Thus it is important to explore these issues 'globally'.

To redress these issues, it is necessary to examine the patterns of spending on leisure and consumer goods and services from a wide range of countries. In line with earlier work (see Jones et al 2008, Higgs et al 2009, Hyde et al 2009), we will first report on findings on the proportion of total expenditure spent on cultural consumption using published data from several national income and expenditure surveys. However, as these surveys are used to calculate each country's Retail Price Index the categories used are not always the same. Thus broadly comparable categories which cover spending on leisure, recreation, entertainment and culture have been used. Following this, spending on travel and tourism is analysed given its relevance to the debate on globalisation.

Data from a range of household budget surveys and expenditure and income surveys reveal that the extent to which older people are engaged in cultural consumption varies between countries. Following Jones and colleagues (2008), we have taken the amount spent on recreation, leisure and/or entertainment as a proportion of total expenditure as an indicator of engagement in cultural consumption. This ensures that figures are comparable between age groups and across countries. Using this measure, we can identify two clusters or groups of countries: high-cultural consumption countries and low-cultural consumption countries. Older people in the first cluster spend, on average, as much or more on recreation and culture as a proportion of their total expenditure as those in the other age groups. By contrast, in the second cluster the older age group has very low or even the lowest levels of engagement of all the age groups.

The first cluster of countries comprises a number of countries from Western Europe, the USA, Australia and Japan. The data for the UK, shown in Figure 6.4, are quite typical of the countries in this group. Here we can see a clear increase in the proportion of total household expenditure that was spent on recreation and culture as we move up the age groups from those under 30, for whom this accounted for about 8% of total spending, to those aged 65–74 who have the highest level spending at just under 18% of total expenditure. Even though this falls quite dramatically among the over-75s they still spend a greater proportion on these activities than those aged 30–49 years. They are very much in line with the earlier findings Jones and colleagues (2008) and give us clear evidence of this baby boom cohort engaging in third age consumer practices (Gilleard and Higgs 2000). This is not restricted to the UK. Australian data (Australian Bureau of Statistics 2011) show a similar pattern with the relative amounts spent on recreation rising steadily with age. In the USA, although the variation across the age groups is not as stark as in the UK or Australia, those aged 65–74 years are also those most engaged with consumer leisure consumption. However, the figures show the same drop in spending for the older, 75+, age group as is evident in the UK data (Office for National Statistics 2015a). The data for the countries in this cluster from outside of the English speaking world show a slightly different, more evenly distributed, pattern. In these countries older people appear to participate in cultural consumption as much as younger people. For example, the figures from the 2014 Japanese 'Family Income and Expenditure Survey' show very little variation in the relative amounts spent on recreation and culture between the different age groups (Japanese Statistics Bureau 2014). The pattern is the same in Norway, where there is hardly any difference across the entire age range (Statistics Norway 2013). Finally, in this group, the figures for Finland are somewhat different again. Although there is a similarly low level of variation between the age groups there is a shallow 'inverted-U' trend with those in the youngest and the oldest age groups having the lowest levels of relative spending. Thus, among those aged 65–74 years average expenditure on recreation and culture as a proportion of total expenditure is the same as for those aged 55–64 and those aged 35–44. However, the 75+ years age group has the lowest level of relative spending on these activities (Official Statistics of Finland 2014).

The story for the second group is quite different. Here there is relatively little evidence of engagement in cultural consumption in later life. This is clearly demonstrated by the data from the Lithuanian Household Budget Survey in 2012, shown in Figure 6.5. The picture here is almost the reverse of what we have seen for the UK. Instead of a clear increase with age, we see a steep fall in the relative amounts spent on recreational and cultural activities with each successive age group. The other two countries in this group are Taiwan (National Statistics Taiwan 2014) and Singapore (Department of Statistics Singapore 2013). Here we do not see the same steady decline across the age groups. Instead the figures for both countries show a U-shaped pattern up to the age of 64, after which there is a rather precipitous drop in spending on recreation among those aged 65 and over. In both countries this group devotes the lowest proportion of its spending on these activities. This is in line with other studies that have identified a developing 'silver market' in many Asian countries (Fon Sim and Phillips 2007, Fon Sim et al 2008, Ying and Yao 2010). However, this seems to be directed at younger cohorts who are just entering later life. This is interesting as both of these Asian countries experienced a large post war baby boom, like the USA and the UK, and these boomers are now entering retirement (BBC 2006, Committee on Ageing Issues, 2006; Soong 2011).

These analyses suggest a number of things. First, that in many countries, the younger cohorts of older people are not divorced from the general levels engagement in cultural and/or recreational activities. In fact, in a number of countries, like the USA, UK and Australia, they devote a higher proportion of their total expenditure to such pursuits than younger age groups. That this is a function of lower incomes seems unlikely when one takes into account the data from Chapter Five on the relative income positions of older people in these countries. Thus there is real evidence of an emerging 'global' third age centred on engagement in consumer culture. However, there are also 'regional' differences in consumption behaviour. The data from Lithuania in particular suggest that older people are still marginalised from this consumer culture. It would be impossible to

Figure 6.4: Proportion of total household expenditure spent on recreation and culture by age group of the reference person, 2014: UK

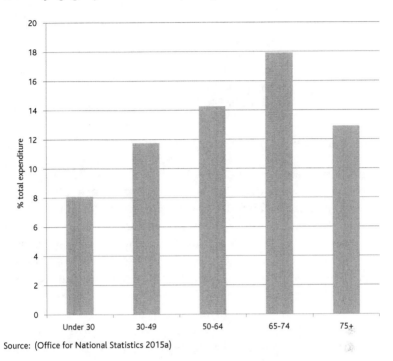

Source: (Office for National Statistics 2015a)

Figure 6.5: Proportion of total household expenditure spent on recreation and culture Lithuania by age group of the reference person, 2012: Lithuania

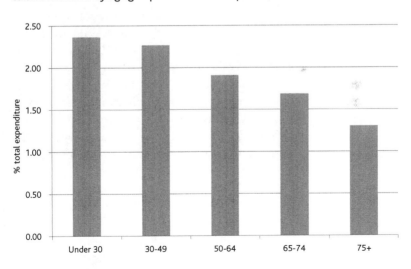

Source: (Statistics Lithuania 2013)

generalise from a single country but the findings do fit with the data on the health and financial wellbeing of older people in this region. It must be remembered that these older cohorts had grown up during Soviet rule and were therefore much less exposed to capitalist consumer culture in their youth. Finally, however, a common feature for almost all countries, except Australia and Japan, is the relatively sharp break in cultural consumption between the younger- and older-old cohorts. This pattern appears most clearly in Singapore and Taiwan.

Travel and tourism trends in later life

The sheer number of people travelling around the world for business and pleasure as well as the ease and speed with which they can do so are often seen as the most compelling evidence for globalisation. International tourist arrivals have grown, virtually uninterrupted, from 25 million in 1950 to 880 million today. This is expected to grow to 1.6 billion by 2020. Moreover, it is a hugely important source of revenue. In 2009 the income generated by inbound tourism exceeded US$1 trillion (UNWTO 2010). Travel and transport, it is often repeated, have shrunk the distance between places thus making it an increasingly small world. However, many writers have pointed to the social divisions in access to these new forms of mobility. Those who are prevented from engaging in and enjoying the benefits of these new mobilities are seen as the new poor, marginalised for their sedentary behaviour, while a new mobile global elite move effortlessly around the world (Bauman 1998, Urry 2000, Russell 2003, Sheller and Urry 2006). However, relatively few studies have looked at the role in which (older) age might play in these mobilities (Hyde 2015). As with consumption in general, tourism and later life seems to fall between the respective stools of gerontology and tourism research. It is possible that researchers on either side think that later life is a time for stability not mobility, or that due to problems in getting travel insurance, older people slowly withdraw from (foreign) travel as they age. But this would ignore the steady growth in companies like Saga in the UK who aim to capture this growing market of older tourists. Those studies that do exist identify older consumers as the fastest growing group of tourists and observe that there are increasing attempts by travel companies to attract their business (Morgan et al 2001, Mak et al 2005, Sedgley et al 2011).

Data from the International Passenger Survey (IPS) in the UK have been used to explore these issues. The data in Figure 6.6 show that the majority of older British tourist visits are concentrated in a relatively small number of countries worldwide. The vast majority take place in neighbouring European countries. Spain stands out as the main destination receiving over 1.8 million visits in 2014. However, France is also a major destination with just over a million visits. Outside Europe the USA is by far and away the most common destination with 297,000 visits. This is followed by Turkey, Australia, India and Canada. The pattern then is highly regionalised rather than globalised. European countries, particularly Mediterranean countries, are the prime destinations for older British tourists. There is little evidence of extensive travel to Central and Eastern Europe or to Scandinavia. Outside Europe, English speaking countries, such as the USA and Australia, are popular destinations. The exceptions to this are Turkey and India. This is interesting as it suggests that a number of global dynamics are potentially emerging. Perhaps the growth of cheap flights has encouraged a growing number of older travellers to seek destinations outside of the EU. However, it is possible that the data for India are picking up predominately family visits rather than tourism *per se*. Although it is not possible to directly test this with the data that are publically available it does suggest that older Britons of Indian descent, were born here after the influx of Commonwealth citizens after the Second World War, are now making trips back to India perhaps to visit family or potentially to prepare for an eventual permanent return.

An examination of recent trends (Figure 6.7) shows that the number of tourist visits per year taken by older age groups in the UK has grown at a much faster rate than that for the population as a whole. Compared to 2000 the number of visits taken by those aged between 55 and 64 was over 40% higher in 2008 and by 2014 remained 20% higher. For those aged 65 and over the number of annual visits taken abroad in 2014 was 60% higher than it was in 2000. This compares with much lower growth rates for all age groups. The amount of international travel taken by all ages was only 5% greater in 2014 than it was in 2000. So although these older groups had a lower starting point, in terms of the absolute number of visits these figures confirm that that 'grey tourism' is a growing market segment in the UK.

The data in Figure 6.8 show a similar pattern for the origins of older foreign tourists to the UK to that of the destinations that British tourists visit abroad. For the most part older tourists coming to the UK are still concentrated in European and English speaking counties. The key difference however is that the USA now ranks as the main source of tourism. In 2014 older Americans made nearly 300,000 visits to the UK. They were followed by the French and the Irish with just under

Figure 6.6: Top 20 most visited international tourist destinations by older British tourists, 2014 (thousands of visits)

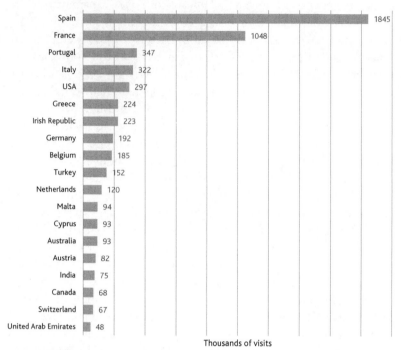

Thousands of visits

Source: (Office for National Statistics 2015b)

a quarter of a million visits each. Canadians, Australians, Indians, New Zealanders and South Africans were also among the top 20 nationalities that visited the UK. Thus travel to the UK appears to be somewhat more global than travel from the UK insofar as non-European countries feature more prominently. However, these are still overwhelmingly from the English speaking world.

The time-series data for visits to the UK from overseas travellers show a similar pattern to that for travel by older Britons (Figure 6.9). Visits to the UK have increased for both of the older cohorts at a greater than average rate. Although visits fell for all age groups from 2000 to 2001, those aged 55–64 grew steadily thereafter. From 2000 to 2014 the number of visits to the UK from those aged 55 to 64 rose by over 50%. However, the increase was even more dramatic for those aged 65 and over. By 2014 this group were making 75% more trips to the UK than they did in 2000. This compares to only a 36% rise for all the age groups combined. Hence it is not just older Britons who have become more mobile and who are increasingly engaged in foreign travel. Older people living abroad are increasingly coming to the UK as part of a set of global flows of older tourists around the world.

Figure 6.7: Tourism travel trends for UK citizens aged 55–64, 65 and over and for all age groups, 2000–14 (2000 = 100)

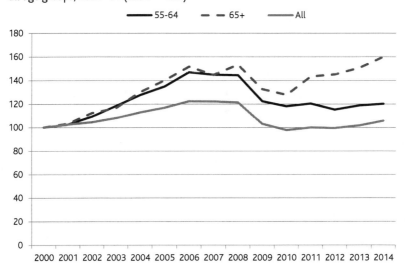

Source: (Office for National Statistics 2015b)

Figure 6.8: Top 20 worldwide origins of tourists to the UK, 2014 (thousands of visits)

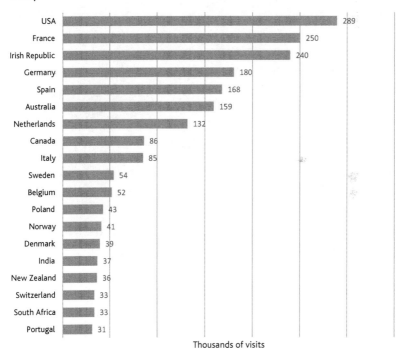

Source: (Office for National Statistics 2015b)

Figure 6.9: Tourism travel trends for overseas citizens visiting the UK aged 55–64, 65 and over and for all age groups, 2000–14 (2000 = 100)

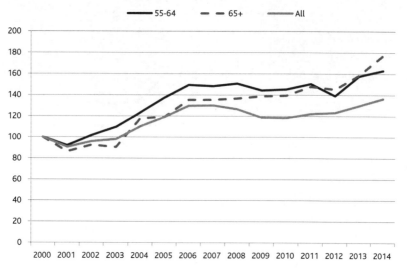

Source: (Office for National Statistics 2015b)

However, these statistics only tell part of the story. Travel and tourism forms an increasingly important part of the self-identity or sense of personhood for older people who are engaged in these practices. For some travel is important for maintaining a youthful identity which has allowed them to resist being stereotyped as an 'old fogey' while for others travel offers the opportunity to create new narratives about identity in later life through doing things they have not done before (Desforges 2000). White and White's (2004) ethnographic study of 45 older long-term travellers in the Australian outback echoes this. They found that travel provided a 'transition' between endings, for example changed family circumstances either through bereavement or the 'empty nest', the (anticipated) end of good health or retirement, and new beginnings.

Living arrangements of older people around the world

The data presented so far show that there is evidence of an emerging 'third age', a new cultural space in which new identities for later life are potentially being fashioned through consumption and leisure. However, it is important not to overlook other possible sources of identity for older people and how they might operate in these new temporalities. One key source of identity and a persistent topic of research in gerontology is the household/family.

Despite the fact that many of the tenets of modernisation and ageing theory have been questioned and often fail to stand up to empirical enquiry, interest in and concern about the living arrangements of older people have proved to be remarkably enduring features of much gerontological research. However, there is a dual discourse on the living arrangements of older people around the world. In the advanced welfare economies of Europe and North America the focus is in on supporting independent living in later life, as opposed to the institutionalisation of older people, conversely when looking at the developing world commentators express increasing concern about the deterioration of traditional, multigenerational family structures. This reflects the fact that the family is often the main, if not the sole, provider of welfare for older people in low income countries (Aldous 1962, Nyangweso 1998, Mba 2007).

These concerns rehearse, albeit on a global scale, the post war debates about the family that took place in North America and Europe. Famously Parsons (1955, 1971) argued that, by creating a new set of social structures, industrialisation had made the need for extended family structures redundant. According to his functionalist account the nuclear family formation, with its specialised (gendered) division of labour and through its role as primary socialiser, became the dominant family type because it fitted best into these new institutional arrangements. Following his teleological approach this change was viewed as unequivocally good for society and its members. These arguments have been criticised on ideological and theoretical grounds by feminist researchers who have drawn attention to the dysfunctional imbalance of power and resources between spouses that this view endorses (Oakley 1974). However, these views were also criticised on historical and empirical grounds by a number of writers who cautioned against such idyllic notions of a past 'golden age' of the extended family (Hareven 1994, Askham et al 2007). Instead, given the consequences of high mortality rates and low life expectancy nuclear families have been the norm for centuries in the West (Laslett and Wall 1972, Laslett 1977, Hareven 1994). Yet other writers have pointed instead to the persistence of extended family types throughout the modern period (Young and Willmott 1957, Litwak 1959, Anderson 1971, Devine 1992).

The evidence is also equivocal when looking at the living arrangements of older people on an international scale. On the one hand there are those who argue that the living arrangements for older people around the world are converging around a Western model of living independently or alone. Data from the only global 'survey' of information on the living arrangements of older people tends to support this view (UN 2004). So too do a number of national studies in Asia (Thornton and Fricke 1987, Albert and Cattell 1994, Knodel and Debavalya 1997, Raymo and Kaneda 2003). An and colleagues (2008) argue that post war modernisation in South Korea has led to 'the rapid transition from the traditional expanded family to the Westernised nuclear family' which has undermined the traditional forms of kinship-based social support and is having a detrimental effect on the wellbeing of older Korean women in particular. Similarly Fan (2007) argues that the Confucian ethic of filial obligation in China has collapsed and points to a growing number of suicides among older people in Hong Kong as evidence of 'the miserable fate of aged persons in the ill process of modernisation'. Similar, although somewhat less dramatic, evidence comes from a number of studies in Africa. Qualitative research in both Kenya and Ghana reveal that both older and younger adults feel that there has been a decline in the support available to older people due to the break-up of traditional family formations (Nyangweso 1998, Aboderin 2004a).

There also appears to be equally convincing evidence that national and regional differences in the living arrangements of older people persist. Thus, although the UN report cited above concluded that a growing number of older people throughout the world were living alone, they still found that around three quarters of older people in less developed countries lived with either a child or grandchild (UN 2004). A similar picture is evident from the Demographic and Health Surveys carried out in 43 developing countries. These show that, although older people are more likely to live alone than other age groups, most older people do not live alone. The study also revealed a great deal of regional variation in the living arrangements of older people. Living in a large household and with young children was most prevalent in Africa while co-residence with adult children was most common in Asia and least common in Africa. Being co-resident with sons is found to be more common in Asia and Africa (where co-residence occurs) while co-residence with daughters was more common in Latin America. Furthermore, the study found, contrary to the modernisation and ageing theory, that neither urbanisation nor GNP level had any significant effects on living arrangements in the developing world (Bongaarts and Zimmer 2001, 2002). These findings are supported by studies in both Africa (Kimuna 2005, Mba 2007) and Asia (Chan 1997, Ofstedal et al 1999, Knight and Traphagan 2003) which show the persistence of traditional family formations. Moreover, a number of writers argue that rather than being antithetical to industrialisation, (modified) extended family formations have been actively encouraged by the state in some Asian countries as a way to manage rapid modernisation (Ha 2007). An example of this is the rise of *nisetai-jūtaka*, 'two household family homes', in Japan which has been supported by the state to promote intergenerational living to deal with the perceived burden of providing care for both older people and children (Brown 2003). Finally, a number of writers argue that the focus on independent living in Europe masks intra-regional variation. Living independently or alone in later life is much more characteristic of Northern European countries while multigenerational living still remains common in Southern and Eastern Europe (De Vos and Sandefur 2002, Tomassini et al 2004).

However, while the foregoing literature is crucial for determining the material living arrangements of older people, they tell us little about how older people feel about family. To address this, data from the ISSP on what older people felt was most important for their sense of identity were used. In almost all countries older people reported that their family or marital status was the most important source of identity. However, as the data in Figure 6.10 show, there are wide international differences. Sixty-five percent of older Danes see family status as the main source of their identity. At the other end of the spectrum only 5% of those in Taiwan felt that it was important. However, as with the earlier results for age identity, it is difficult to identify any regional patterns. Denmark and Finland are at opposite ends of the scale. Spain and Portugal are separated by 17 percentage points. The possible exception to this is Latin America. Chile, Uruguay and Venezuela are all relatively closely clustered. What is remarkable, however, is that a number of countries which have high levels of independent living, such as Sweden, also have high levels of family identity. Conversely a number of Asian countries, such as Taiwan and Japan, where filial obligation is supposed to be strong have weak family identity.

Socio-spatialities of belonging in later life

Alongside family and kinship networks, community and the residential environment are also considered to be important in later life (Phillipson and Scharf 2005, Peace et al 2007, Phillipson 2007). Where one lives has been shown to impact on the health (Cagney et al 2005, Subramanian et al 2006, Wight et al 2008, Andrade et al 2010, Beard and Petitot 2010, Ferreira et al 2010, Parra et al 2010), wellbeing (Breeze et al 2005, Scharf and Gierveld 2008, Wight et al 2011) and mortality of older people (Roux et al 2004, Wight et al 2010). However, while

Figure 6.10: Percentage of those aged 60 and over who report that their family or marital status is the most important source of identity

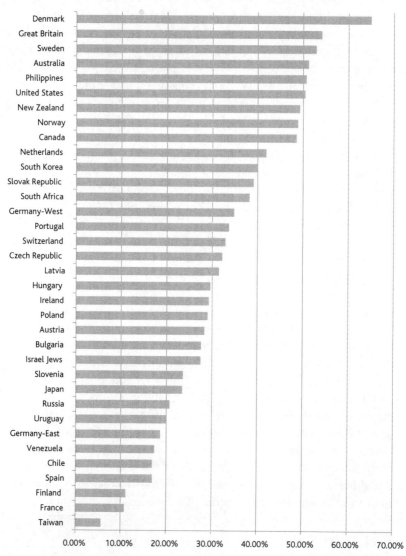

Source: (ISSP Research Group 2015)

these studies are important and demonstrate the impact that place has on the lives of older people the focus here is on a more general topography of attachment and the salience, or otherwise, of place for identities in later life.

It has often been assumed that place holds a special importance for older people. As Gilleard and Higgs (2005: 101) note,

> If the study of cohorts and generations emphasizes historical contingency in the social and cultural ordering of the life course, the study of communities, by contrast, emphasizes the 'grounding' of the life cycle within the constancies of place and person. Whereas cohorts qualify and particularize identity, community roots it.

Community is seen as particularly important given the tendency for rates of residential mobility to decline with age (Kim 2011). It was generally believed that older people overwhelmingly prefer to age in place, particularly in their single family homes (Folts and Muir 2002, Department for Communities and Local Government 2008) and that they only move following serious health or financial problems (Golant 1975, Clark and White 1990, Streib 2002). Thus older people are likely to have spent a longer proportion of their lives in the place where they have aged. As a result, it is argued they tend to be more attached to their communities and have more developed locally based social networks (Phillipson et al 1999, Bernard et al 2001). This can be seen in Townsend's (1963) seminal study that mapped the thick connections between kin, class and community for older people in East London. Furthermore, as Easthope (2009: 71) argues, '[p]lace also situates time through the concretisation of memory'. Hence one would expect the local area to be of greater importance for older people as they will have accumulated more memories in these places. However, this can have negative as well as positive effects. The onset of poor mental health (Brittain et al 2010), fear of crime (Ferreira et al 2010) and loss of private or public transport (Janevic et al 2004) can all limit the ability of some older people to travel far from their home. Some older people, especially those in more deprived neighbourhoods or rural areas, are also at risk of social exclusion (Phillipson and Scharf 2005, Social Exclusion Unit 2005, Phillipson 2007, Scharf and Bartlam 2008). Nonetheless, for better or worse, older people who have lived all or most of their lives in the same place ought to have a higher sense of area identification than younger residents who have moved in more recently and/or who are more able to leave.

However, it has been argued that, over the last century, there has been a shift from place-based (prescribed) identities to more mobile (acquired) identities (see Easthope 2009).

> In our times of "liquid" modernity ... not just the individual placements in society, but the places to which the individuals may gain access and in which they may wish to settle are melting fast and can hardly serve as targets for life projects. (Bauman 2001: 146)

> [C]ommunities of the Global Age generally have no local centre ... where there are localised bases for community then they serve predominantly a special category of people, the retired and elderly, those with learning difficulties ... If we want to characterize these relationships between people living in the same area under globalized conditions, it might be best called disconnected contiguity. (Albrow 1996: 156–7)

For Appadurai (1996) and Bhabha (1994) the flux of people, signs and signifiers that characterises late modernity has led to the emergence of novel, post-colonial spaces. These flows are believed to have fundamentally upset the here/now, then/there, self/other binaries of modernist theorising about identity. Instead what emerges is the hybrid, the in-between, the border dweller. For Gilleard and Higgs (2005) all of this has led to the demise of 'communities of propinquity' which afforded relatively stable sites for the maintenance of identity in later life.

> As globalization promotes further belonging of social identities and the continuing destabilization of the institutional organisation of time and space ... A globalizing market and a globalizing culture threatened to steamroller through the boundaries of the 'old' communities. (Gilleard and Higgs 2005: 122–7)

As the number of older people caught up in and creating these flows increases so to do the possibilities for the negotiation of new identities in later life. Key among these movements is migration. There is now a substantial literature on migration in later life (see the edited book by Karl and Torres, 2016, for state of the art research on this). The majority of these studies have explored the extent of and reasons for migration among different groups of older people. The data point to an increase in both permanent and seasonal, or 'snowbird', retirement migration (Longino and Bradley 2003, Wolf and Longino 2005). However, older people are still less likely to move than younger age groups (Kim 2011) and some suggest that this growth might reverse with changes in pensions and retirement (Haas and Serow 2002). The studies also show that younger-old migrants tend to move in search of better amenities, generally to rural or coastal locations. In contrast older-old migrants tend to move towards more urban areas, to be closer to kin, following a major health problem (Litwak and Longino 1987, Sunil et al 2007, Bradley et al 2008, Wilmoth 2010, Bradley 2011, Kim 2011). A smaller number of studies have looked at the relationship between identity and place among retirement migrants. Ethnographic studies of seasonal migrants to the Arizona Sun Belt show that identities are not static, located in either here or there, but are made on the move (McHugh and Mings 1996, McHugh 2000a, 2000b, 2003, McHugh and Larson-Keagy 2005). Thus mobility not stability is crucial for the identity of this group. Similarly in a study of permanent retirement migrants Cloutier-Fisher and Harvey (2009: 246) found that

> there exists a zone between the home and community, that can be viewed as a geographic space comprised of overlapping and interwoven personal, social and physical domains ... Consequently, for younger in-migrants the boundary between home and community blurs into one larger, symbolic entity experienced as 'home'.

These studies illustrate the complexity and potential multiplicity of socio-spatial attachment in later life.

However, almost all of these studies focus on intra-national mobility and the vast majority come from the USA or the UK. There is a relative dearth of studies on international migration in later life (Warnes 2006, Chou 2007, Raymer et al 2007, Sunil et al 2007). Those studies that do exist generally show that, while there is a growing number of international destinations for retirement migrants (Howard 2008), most tend to be concentrated in a relatively small number of established destinations. Studies of British and Swedish retirement migrants show that many regularly return to the same coastal regions in Southern Europe (Warnes et al 1999, King et al 2000, Gustafson 2001, 2002, 2008). Similarly, US retirement migration to Mexico tends to be concentrated in a few key areas (Sunil et al 2007, Topmiller et al 2010). However, the older migrant population also includes migrants from the developing world to the developed world, both those who migrated when they were younger and have aged in those societies and those who migrated when they were already older. Here the lack of data is even more acute. What studies there are suggest that these communities face problems of social exclusion, often due to language issues, which leads to different forms of attachment which are both more local, with co-ethnics, and more global, with the wider transnational ethnic or religious community (Torres 2001, Warnes et al 2004, Lewis 2009).

Residential location of older people around the world

A number of writers have noted that there is relatively little research done on the residential location of older people outside of Europe and North America (Ferreira et al 2010, Parra et al 2010). In order to explore whether there is any international or regional variation in the residential location of older people data on where older people live have been taken from the ISSP survey (Figure 6.11). These data are self-reported so they need to be treated with some degree of caution as what people in one country might define as a town or a small city might be seen as a country village in another context. This issue notwithstanding the data give an important indication of where older people live in different countries, at different levels of economic development, throughout the world.

It is immediately apparent that there are wide international differences in the proportion of those aged 60 and over who live in urban areas. Around half of the older population in South Africa, Chile, and Russia live in big cities. This finding takes on special importance when considered alongside Lloyd-Sherlock's (1997, 2002a) research on the living arrangements of poorer older people in Buenos Aires and São Paulo. He notes that many of the shanty towns or favelas that have grown up around the major metropolitan areas in Latin America are experiencing population ageing. This is because of limited opportunities for return migration among people who moved to the city for work during their youth. Thus there is concern that increasing numbers of older people in developing countries will be ageing in place in areas with limited access to basic amenities. One suspects that similar patterns might become evident in parts of Africa in the coming decades as the number of people living in slums has grown considerably and is predicted to continue to grow (United Nations Human Settlements Programme 2003, Davis 2006).

An examination of the data reveals some interesting patterns. In those countries with high concentrations of older people in urban areas there is appears to be a real polarisation between urban and rural areas. For example, in South Africa almost all of those who do not live in the big cities live in rural areas such as country villages or farms. In other countries there is a much more identifiable segment of older people living in suburban areas. For example, in the USA over half

Figure 6.11: Residential locations of those aged 60 years and over, 2012: selected countries

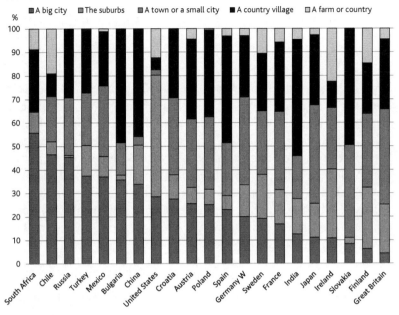

Source: (ISSP Research Group 2015)

of those aged 60 and over live in the suburbs or outskirts of a major city. Most of the West European nations such as Sweden or the UK also have relatively large concentrations of older people in these areas. This reflects the history of suburban development in these countries (Clapson 2003). However, there are also high proportions of older people in the UK and Sweden who live in small towns. This trends fits with the evidence on counter-urban migration in later life particularly to costal or seaside areas that occurs in these countries (Cloke 1985, Boyle 1994, Warnes 2006). When one looks at either Southern or Central and Eastern Europe there is a general shift to more rural forms of living. For example, over 40% of older people in Spain, Slovakia and Bulgaria live in country villages. Similarly, China also has a large proportion of the older population who live in the country. Finally, a few countries such as the USA and Sweden stand out as only countries where a significant proportion of older people report living on a farm or having a home in the country. This is especially the case in Ireland where 23% percent of older people report living in such rural locations.

Migration and ageing

As has already been noted, there has been a growing interest in retirement migration. However, many of the studies that have been undertaken on this topic rely on very small and often self-selected, snowball, samples. To assess the extent of migration in later life in large-scale nationally representative survey data from SHARE and the World Values Survey (WVS) have been used. In SHARE respondents were asked whether they regularly spent time in another residence and, if so, whether this was in a foreign country. These data were used to capture the temporary or seasonal type of retirement migration where older people split their time between two or more residences throughout the year. Just over a half of 1% of the sample (0.6%) said that they regularly spent time in another residence outside of the county. Unfortunately, these figures are too small to allow any meaningful breakdown by individual country.

In order to look at more permanent migration in later life we used WVS data from a wide range of countries from around the world. These analyses take on an added sense of meaning given the current focus on international migration. At the time of writing Europe is in the midst of a 'migration crisis'. Hundreds of thousands of people fleeing war, civil unrest and poverty in the Middle East, Africa and Central Asia are trying to enter Europe in the hope of finding safety and security. This has put a strain on the political leadership and institutional structures of Europe as, initially at least, few countries were willing to accept them. This eventually changed with countries such as Germany and Finland opening their borders as a result of the huge numbers of refugees landing in Southern Europe.

However, the picture that emerges from these analyses (Figure 6.12) is one of stability rather than mobility in later life. In spite of the academic and media attention on retirement migration the data appear to show that migration in later life is not a widespread global phenomenon. However, it needs to be noted that these data are from 2013 and therefore will not capture the most recent surge in migration noted above. Overall the proportion of those aged over 60 years who reported being born abroad in 2013 is low, only 8%. Yet this masks a good deal of international variation. In a number of countries, such as South Korea, Chile and South Africa, rates of late life migration in the country are close to zero. However, there are countries where a relatively high proportion of older people have migrated into the country.

For example, 8% of older people in Sweden and in the USA see themselves as migrants. This rises to 12% in Germany and 17% in New Zealand. This might be a product of the *gastarbieter* policy in the former in which workers from Turkey, in particular, were invited to come to the country for work but were denied full citizenship rights. It is likely that a number of these guest workers have remained in Germany, ageing in place, rather than returning to their home countries. Conversely the relatively high rates in New Zealand might be the product of retirement migration. As King and colleagues (2000) note the English speaking countries of North America and Australasia have traditionally been popular destinations for British retirees. Above these figures a number of the former Soviet countries report even higher proportions of older migrants, ranging from 18% in Ukraine to 27% in Estonia. This too could be a product of the Soviet era policy of relocating large number of people of working age to various parts of the Soviet Union to meet the demand for labour as well as the more subtle policy of Russification

Figure 6.12: Proportion of older people who consider themselves to be migrants in their current country of residence, 2013: selected countries

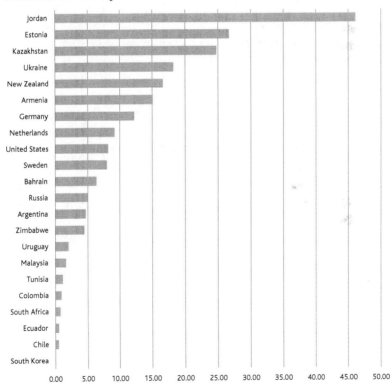

Source: (World Values Survey Association 2015)

of the Soviet states through the migration of ethnic Russians to these states. Finally, Jordan stands out as an extreme example. Nearly half of all those older people surveyed reported that they were migrants. As with Germany Jordan has a history of bringing in guest workers to boost its domestic labour force. Hence it is possible that a number of these older migrants came to work in the country and then stayed on. However, rates of foreign born workers in the country have been falling due to economic pressures since the 2008 global crisis. More apposite might be the fact that Jordan has become a major destination for the millions who are fleeing unrest in the Middle East. Since the start of the civil war in neighbouring Syria nearly 425,000 Syrian nationals have fled to Jordan. Even though UN statistics show that 80% of these are aged 40 years or younger it is very likely that large numbers of older people have also fled over the border to Jordan (Migration Policy Team 2013). In both Germany and the former Soviet bloc countries the higher levels of older migrants are likely to be historical products as current generations of older people who migrated to these countries when they were younger have aged in place. While the proportion of older migrants in New Zealand and Jordan may be due to people moving to these countries later in life, the reasons behind individual decisions can be seen to be polar opposites in these different locations. Consequently, it is important to differentiate between those who can choose to migrate in later life and those who are forced to do so. Again this points to the absence of a common global experience of this most 'global' of conditions. Contrary to the image of the footloose retirement migrant, older people are not in general caught up in a series of global ethnoscapes of migration. Rates of migration are generally low and even then a substantial proportion can be attributed to younger migrants who have aged in place. Furthermore, those who are on the move in later life represent a heterogeneous group with widely different experiences and expectations.

Conclusion

The data presented in this chapter lend further support to the argument that there has been a radical transformation in the temporal foundations of ageing and late life. Perhaps because these data are based on the subjective accounts of older people themselves they exemplify the new, complex, temporalities of later life more so than the data on demography, health or labour market position. The modernist temporality of chronological age which clearly demarcated and underpinned the different segments of the life course has given way to a much more fluid set of late modern temporalities around subjective, desired and cognitive age. Nor is this phenomenon restricted to the advanced industrialised economies of the global North. In almost all the countries for which data have been presented there is a clear gap opening up between the end of working life and the perceived start of old age. This appears to be strong evidence of the emergence of a 'global' space in which the third age can take root. This is the first time that this phenomenon has been presented for large-scale cross-national representative data.

The analyses also lend some support to the argument, discussed in Chapter Two, that the shift to late or second modernity has rendered problematic the fixed and stable reference points that people relied on in the past to form their identities and to 'know their place'. In most of the countries for which data were available the relationship between the traditional identifiers of old age, such as retirement and poor health, and the status of old age has become disconnected. Both chronological age and the status of 'old age' have become more malleable and older people are actively engaged in distancing themselves from these identifiers. It is clear from looking at how older people in many different countries talk about old age that there is a clear rejection of old age as a source of identity. As Gilleard and Higgs (2007: 26) have previously argued, in relation to older people in the USA and the UK, old age is 'the signifier of material and symbolic bankruptcy, [it] is simply not a choice'. What appears to be true for these cohorts in the West appears true for many older people around the world. However, such temporalities eschew any simple spatial fix. The age at which old age is assumed to begin in some countries is the same as the age of ideal retirement in others. So, although there is evidence of an emerging global third age, the length and timing of this new stage in the life course are very much conditioned by the national context. These findings we would contend clearly illustrate the overlapping spatial and temporal logics figurative of a multi-scalar world.

The analyses also provide evidence that new coordinates have emerged for the construction and maintenance of meaning and identities in later life. The data on spending patterns add further support to the argument coming from cultural gerontology that consumerism has expanded to occupy the sociocultural space created by the disconnection between subjective age and chronological age. The results show that in a number of countries in North America, Europe and Asia that older people are actively engaged in cultural consumption. However, in many cases this is bifurcated between older and younger cohorts. They are also crosscut by gender and national differences. Nonetheless these findings lend considerable support to Gilleard and Higgs' (2000, 2005) argument for a 'cultures of ageing' approach that, in the context of rapidly expanding consumer capitalism, identities based on non-participation in consumerism are considerably less desirable and that old age itself often has a negative value. Outside of these more affluent regions however, older people in for instance the former Eastern Bloc countries show little engagement with consumerism. They grew up under a very different set of sociocultural circumstances than their Western peers. Unlike British and American teenagers they had only limited and sporadic exposure to consumerism, for example the experiments with 'Goulash Communism' in Hungary (Kovrig 1986). Equally the pace and nature of the 'shock treatment' of economic reform placed the older population in very straitened circumstances where the valued status of the pensioner was no longer protected (Gilleard and Higgs 2009).

Alongside consumerism other sources of identity remain or have become important. The results for the salience of both family relationships and attachment to place for identities in later life reveal the complex and seemingly contradictory nature of these sources of identity in late modernity. Despite increasing levels of independent living in Europe family remains a major source of identity for many older people. Perversely, in countries which are perceived to be very family-centric, such as those in East Asia, few people said that it was important. These findings act as an important corrective to arguments that there are fundamental cultural differences in the status of older people within the family in Asia compared to Europe. As has been noted in some Asian countries, such as Japan, the state has been a key actor in the production and reproduction of these cultural norms through such activities as housing policy.

The socio-spatial levels of belonging also present a confusing picture. On the one hand there is evidence that, contrary to the arguments common in cultural gerontology, the local community is important for older people in many countries. On the other hand, very few older people say that where they live is an important source of identity in later life. Methodological reasons must account for part of the explanation for this apparent contradiction. The data are taken from two different studies and from different countries. Nonetheless, both studies are nationally representative and there are a number of countries that are common to each study. Thus methodological factors cannot be the sole explanation. Rather this suggests that notions of place have become fluid as signs, symbols and people increasingly move through them. There is certainly evidence that older people are becoming much more internationally mobile through tourism and travel. Although these analyses were restricted to the UK they show increasing numbers of older people moving through its borders. However, patterns of travel and of retirement migration do not spread out in some form of Brownian motion. Instead they are highly regionalised. Where they are not they tend to follow longer historical relations between countries of origin and countries of destination. However, this growth in international travel does not seem to have led to a more globalised or regionalised sense of attachment. What all this adds up to, once again, appears to be a complex set of overlapping, sometimes coordinated, sometimes contradictory set of spatialities. That this does not represent a clear demonstration of the simplified processes of a hegemonic globalisation is precisely the point, as is the awareness that a major source of this complex picture is the changing lives and experiences of older people themselves who seem to be removing themselves from the residual status that they have generally occupied in most thinking about their situation.

SEVEN

Politics, place and ageing

In this chapter we explore the spatiality of Appadurai's final 'scape', that of the ideoscape. This is important because any understanding of the relationship between globalisation and ageing needs also to address the political dimensions that are specific to each polity. Topics such as the rise of the 'grey planet' or the restructuring of politics around generational inequity or conflict need to be seen as having their own specificity and context rather than being products of a relatively unreflexive approach to globalisation where old age is treated as a unitary category producing either greater dependency or negative societal outcomes. The concept of the ideoscape therefore represents how the nation state's power is one form of global flow and refers to both prevailing dominant discourses operating within the nation as well as existing and emergent counter-discourses that seek to challenge or question that status quo. Appadurai (1996: 36 emphasis in original) defines ideoscapes as:

> concatenations of images, ... [which] are often directly political and frequently have to do with the ideologies of states and the counter-ideologies of movements explicitly oriented to capturing state power or a piece of it. These ideoscapes are composed of elements of the Enlightenment world view, which consists of a chain of ideas, terms and images including *freedom, welfare, rights, sovereignty, representation* and the master term *democracy*.

However, they are not just simple extensions of a hegemonic capitalism. As he points out contemporary ideoscapes are much more complicated. Consequently,

> the diaspora of these terms and images across the world, especially since the nineteenth century, has loosened the internal coherence that held them together in a Euro-American master narrative and provided instead a loosely structured syncopation of politics, in which different nation states, as part of their evolution, have organised their

> political cultures around different keywords. (Appadurai, 1996: 36)

Moreover, and of particular importance for our argument, he believes that these ideoscapes operate across a number of 'scalar dynamics' in which actors operating at the national and local levels risk, and resist, being absorbed in the 'imagined communities' of higher scales.

Appadurai's image of actors coming together to promote a core set of beliefs over those of other actors or groups resonates with the idea of an 'epistemic community'. Although, as Meyer and Molyneus-Hodgson (2010) note, the concept of the epistemic community can be traced back to the 1960s and 1970s (see Holzner 1968, Holzner and Marx 1979) it was popularised by international relations theorist Peter M. Haas (1989, 1992). He argued that an epistemic community had the following characteristics:

1. a shared set of normative and principled beliefs which provide a value-based rationale for the social action of community members;
2. shared causal beliefs, which are derived from their analysis of practices leading or contributing to a central set of problems in their domain and which then serve as the basis for elucidating the multiples linkages between possible policy actions and desired outcomes;
3. shared notions of validity – that is, intersubjective, internally defined criteria for weighting and validating knowledge in the domain of their expertise; and
4. common policy enterprise – that is, a set of common practices associated with a set of problems to which their professional competence is directed, presumably out of the conviction that human welfare will be enhanced as a consequence. (Haas 1992: 3)

From this perspective epistemic communities are not merely concerned with producing policies. Instead, they are concerned with producing knowledge about particular social issues and, perhaps more importantly, they seek to determine what constitutes valid or legitimate knowledge about that issue. For example, certain groups might lobby to ensure that only knowledge generated through certain means, such as randomised-controlled experiments, should be taken as the basis for making funding or policy decisions. Epistemic communities can be composed of a range of different actors, such as international non-governmental organisations (INGOs), supra-state organisations, multinational banks, academics, what Berger (2002) refers to as the 'faculty club', national government departments and private companies (Haas 1992, Deacon 2007). From our reading and analyses, we have identified three epistemic communities that have emerged around the issues of ageing and later life: 1) the anti-ageing enterprise; 2) the new pension orthodoxy; and 3) the active ageing epistemic community. These communities are focused respectively on issues around the health, pensions and labour market activity of older people. Following Appadurai's definition each of these epistemic communities can be seen to be pursuing their own ideoscape and attempting to incorporate actors across a range of spatial levels to secure their own vision of how to address population ageing.

The anti-ageing enterprise

The first of these epistemic communities that we identify is the 'anti-ageing enterprise'. The actors in this community are bound together by a shared belief in and commitment to the use of medico-technical practices to combat or reverse the ageing process. The increase in number and range of pharmaceutical, cosmetic and cosmeceutical[1] products has been discussed in Chapter Two. These products form a crucial part of the late modern time-space of later life. They are produced by and in turn reproduce the multiple, indeterminate, cyclical notions ageing by deploying metaphors of renewal, recycling and regeneration (Gilleard and Higgs 2013).

> [The] re-engineering of the body, regenerative medicine is the most accomplished manifestation of contemporary biopolitics ... regenerative medicine is rooted in the modern biomedical deconstruction of death, which underlies the contemporary technoscientific fantasy of indefinitely extending longevity. (Lafontaine 2009: 53)

Our goal here is not to assess whether anti-ageing technologies represent new emancipatory opportunities for older people or whether they constitute a consumerist driven form of 'false consciousness' which denies the essence of ageing. These arguments have been rehearsed elsewhere (Gilleard and Higgs 2005, Vincent 2006, 2007, Vincent et al 2008, Higgs and Jones 2009). Instead we aim to look at the spatial logics through which these new technologies are deployed. Using this model it is possible to identify an emergent anti-ageing enterprise.

[1] Cosmeceuticals are cosmetic products that are said to have medical properties.

This is nebulous, multifaceted and encompasses a wide range of different actors. It is not driven purely by 'social' welfare institutions as in the Aging Enterprise (see Estes 1980) but neither is it a purely a market or consumer driven group. Rather we would contend it is a broad but loose alliance of both private and public actors operating across all spatial levels. As Figure 7.1 shows these include cosmetics and cosmeceutical companies, cosmetic surgeons, global healthcare destinations, pharmaceutical companies and anti-ageing medical practitioners. Despite the diversity (and even hostility) between these different actors they share an increasingly common discourse and vision for ageing and later life.

Figure 7.1: The components of an emerging global anti-ageing epistemic community

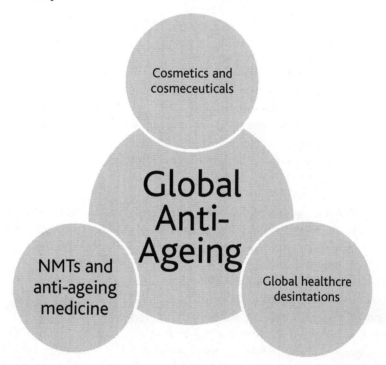

Cosmetics and cosmeceuticals

The sheer scale and rapid rate of growth of the market for anti-ageing cosmetics attests to the cultural salience of these new biotemporalities and gives an indication of some of the key actors in this emergent epistemic community. Global sales of topical and injectable cosmeceutical products amounted to nearly US$31.7 billion in 2011. This is projected to reach US$45.6 billion in 2017 (Agheyisi 2013). By 2011 there were over 400 suppliers and manufacturers of cosmeceutical products in the US alone, and the industry was estimated to grow by a further 7.4% by 2012 and be worth US$9.2 billion (Brandt et al 2011). European markets show similar patterns. France had the largest cosmetic and skin care market worth around US$2.8 billion in 2007. Within this the anti-ageing market comprised US$1.04 billion worth of sales. The UK cosmetics market was valued at £8.38 million in 2014 (Cosmetic, Toiletry & Perfumery Association, 2016). This compares to the European cosmetics market which was worth EUR 72.5 billion in 2014, making it one of the largest cosmetics and personal care markets in the world and more than the United States and Chinese markets combined (Cosmetics Europe, 2014). Industry analysts are unanimous on the reason for these figures. According to a senior beauty and personal care product analyst at Mintel:

> Anti-aging won't fall to the recession. Looking young is extremely important to many women, especially Baby Boomers, and it's not an issue they're willing to compromise on because of tightened budgets. Many women see anti-aging skincare as a reasonably priced investment in their appearance and well-being. (Cosmetic Design 2010)

As these markets have grown so too have consumers' expectations regarding the ability of products to arrest or reverse (the signs of) ageing. This is, in part, driving greater cooperation between cosmetics producers and the scientific and pharmaceutical industry to create ever more apparently sophisticated and expensive products. This merging of cosmetics with biotic and/or pharmaceutical ingredients led to the emergence of cosmeceuticals. Choi and Berson (2006: 163) define a cosmeceutical as 'a cosmetic product that exerts a pharmaceutical therapeutic benefit but not necessarily a biologic therapeutic benefit'. Many of the anti-ageing products such as Olay's *Regenerist*, Nivea's *DNAage* and Estee Lauder's *Creme de la Mer* which have driven the performance of the beauty industry are typical of these cosmeceuticals. USA and Western European sales of cosmeceutical ingredients related only to anti-ageing claims totalled approximately US$130–150 million in 2005. Of which, skincare cosmeceuticals account for 80% of the US and European market (Brandt et al 2011). This is a highly differentiated market with mass consumer products making up 72% of total sales in 2010, while the premium segment accounted for the remaining 28%

(Łopaciuk, and Łoboda, 2013). Hence this cosmeceutical market is opening up a commercialised space which promises the realisation of these new temporalities. Coupland (2009: 39) argues that it is in the 'interests of market forces in consumer culture to promote fear and insecurity about ageing appearance and to provide aspirational models of possible age-less futures'. Through the deployment of scientific terminology these products claim to be able to retard or even reverse the ageing process. They share a common discourse on the undesirability and the reversibility of the signs of ageing. The product description for NIVEA VISAGE DNAge CELL RENEWAL is typical of this. It lists, among its other ingredients, 'Folic Acid, an essential vitamin renowned for stimulating cell renewal ... Creatine, a micro peptide, that triggers collagen production ... [and] SPF 12 with enhanced levels of UVA filters, which helps protect skin cell's DNA against external damages'. In turn it promises that the benefits of regular use are:

- Increased cell renewal from within
- Noticeably firmer, younger-looking skin
- A fresh and glowing complexion.

This is not just a Western market. Asia, Eastern Europe and Latin America have seen significant growth. The cosmetic market in China alone grew by over 10% per year from the mid-1990s to early 2000s (Kumar 2005) and emerging markets, such as China, were anticipated to account for 13% of global anti-ageing sales by 2013 (Brandt et al 2011). It is clear that the major cosmetics companies are looking to expand into a number of emerging markets outside of Europe and North America. L'Oreal decided to open a number of research and innovation hubs in countries like China, India and Brazil to attempt to capture a billion new customers over the coming years (Cosmetic Design 2010). This is driven by the ageing of the populations in these countries as well as the saturation of mature markets in Europe and North America, increased competition and the rising costs of research and development (Brandt et al 2011).

Although this is fast becoming a 'global' business the beauty industry is dominated by a handful of huge MNCs such as Estee Lauder, Nivea and Olay: overall the top 20 producers account for around 73% of the global market (Kumar 2005). However, these commercial giants are increasingly entering into partnerships with smaller bio-tech and drug companies who are seeking to enter the less well-regulated cosmeceutical market (Heymann 1997, Nasto 2007). Rising R&D costs and the growing overlap in technology and information has also led to an increasing number of mergers in this field (Curran et al 2010). These developments are creating a nebulous network of interconnected companies which is beginning to emerge as a key, commercial, component of an embryonic global anti-ageing enterprise.

However, this is not yet a unified global market. Rather there are series of different regulatory regimes throughout the world that delimit national or regional markets. Despite, or perhaps because of, their proliferation cosmeceuticals remain poorly defined, in relation to both cosmetics and pharmaceuticals (Heymann 1997, Millikan 2001, Choi and Berson 2006, Draelos 2009). As Morganti and Paglialunga (2008: 392) observed, there are three different EU directives regulating cosmetics, drugs and medical devices which potentially cover cosmeceuticals. Interestingly they identify '[t]he activity at the level of the epidermis or dermis [as] the borderline for dermatological or cosmetic products'. Hence a cosmetic product should not penetrate the skin. This is the field of pharmaceuticals. However, they argue that this boundary is increasingly porous and ambiguous. The Japanese market too is a myriad of different regimes. Although the Japanese government recognises cosmeceuticals as a category, whether a product is considered as a pharmaceutical or a cosmeceutical is determined by a series of lists of ingredients. Perhaps most surprising, given the size of the market in this country, is the fact that the US government, through the auspices of the Food and Drug Administration (FDA), does not recognise cosmeceuticals as distinct category (Heymann 1997, Choi and Berson 2006, Brandt et al 2011). This is not simply a semantic issue.

> The cosmetic/drug distinction has considerable implications for the cosmetics industry because of the difference in regulation between cosmetics and drugs, most notably the lack of any requirement of premarket review for cosmetic products. A decision that [cosmeceutical ingredients] are to be regulated as drugs could force manufacturers to pull available products from the market and submit extensive tests as to the products' safety and effectiveness for FDA approval, clearly an undesirable result for the industry. (Heymann 1997: 2)

Thus a critical issue for these companies is the creation of a market-friendly global regulatory regime. This is becoming a key focal point for a host of actors involved in this industry. As a number of senior managers for Proctor & Gamble argued at the beginning of this century:

> ... global cosmetic harmonization of the regulations that control these products is a priority for our business. To put it very simply, the goal of global cosmetic regulatory harmonization is to be able to quickly develop and sell new cosmetic products around the world. (Lindenschmidt et al 2001: 237)

Moreover, their model for a global regulatory regime is constructed very much around neoliberal principles in which companies are mainly responsible for regulating their products through what is called that 'post-market surveillance'. This effectively means that no premarket approval should be required and that any problems with the product will be detected through consumer complaints and dealt with, if and when, these are established. Advocates of such a regime argue that both national health authorities and local producers stand in way of achieving this harmonisation. In order to overcome these barriers they argue that it is necessary to:

> develop allies amongst key government officials ... Develop a broad industry alliance (both local and regional) ... Education of government officials on the proper approaches to risk assessment and risk management of cosmetic products and ingredients ... Establish a strong working relationship with the authorities responsible for trade and economy who [support] free trade agreements ... Organise regional/global harmonisation events (Lindenschmidt et al, 2001: 239).

Evidence is emerging that these activities are already leading to the consolidation of such networks which could see it emerge as a major component of any future global anti-ageing enterprise. There are also a number of regional and global lobbying groups that represent the industry. For example Colipa, the European Cosmetics Association, successfully lobbied the EU for the inclusion of cosmetics in the EU REACH Directive on chemicals (Halliday 2005). In 1998 industry leaders produced the Florence Principles which set out their vision for a global regulatory regime. This has been mirrored at the governmental level through the Cosmetics Harmonization and International Cooperation (CHIC) project. This has been a quadripartite meeting between the governments of the USA, EU, Japan and Canada with a view to the alignment of cosmetic regulations. Many have also celebrated what is seen as the greatest deregulation of the cosmetics and cosmeceutical market in contemporary times as the ASEAN countries move from having ten separate regulatory regimes to a single 'Mutual Recognition' cosmetic system. The ASEAN Harmonized Cosmetic Regulatory Scheme was signed on 2 September 2003 creating a single cosmetics market of over 500 million people (ASEAN Cosmetics 2007). This means that all countries in the region now have an EU-like cosmetic regulatory system that requires no premarket approval in any member state.

Cosmetic surgery, new medical technologies and medical tourism

At the far end of the anti-ageing industry are surgical and non-surgical interventions, such as Botox. The evidence suggests that, as with the cosmeceutical market, these procedures too have witnessed a rapid and massive growth over the past decades. It must be noted, however, that the majority of these data come from the United States. Nonetheless, according to the American Society for Aesthetic Plastic Surgery (ASAPS) (2006, 2009) from 1997 to 2009 there was almost a 150% increase in the total number of cosmetic procedures in the USA. In 2009 alone Americans spent almost US$10.5 billion on cosmetic procedures. However, these figures mask a change in the balance between surgical and non-surgical procedures as surgical procedures increased by 50% while non-surgical procedures increased by 231% and made up well over 80% of all procedures by 2009. The ASAPS predicted that demand for facelifts and other (non-surgical) facial rejuvenation surgery will increase (ASAPS 2009). This has been confirmed for both the US and UK such where a link with the economy's performance has also been noticed (Nassab and Harris 2013).

There is an increasingly global dimension to this market as people travel abroad for treatments (Banerjee et al 2015). This phenomenon, which has been called medical or cosmetic tourism, forms an emerging circuit in the present global bioeconomy in which the ageing body itself becomes a form of bio-capital.

> Globalisation has led to an increased acceptance of outsourcing in the provision of key goods and services to the UK population as a whole. In parallel, the increased availability of cheap flights abroad has removed a key financial barrier for those seeking aesthetic surgery abroad, a phenomenon labelled as 'cosmetic tourism'. (Jeevan and Armstrong 2008: 1)

One must be cautious when using data on medical or cosmetic tourism. There are no definitive figures on the number of people involved as it is often private and often occurs as part of general holidays. However, what data there are suggest that this is a widespread and fast growing activity. Balaban and Marano (2010) noted that it is a 'world-wide, multi-billion dollar phenomenon that is expected to grow substantially over the next 5–10 years' and give figures of between 600,000 and 750,000 medical tourists each year. Carrera and Lunt (2010) gave similar global estimates. They go on to say, in relation to the UK, that

> Figures are sketchy, however, with the number in the United Kingdom estimated at about 50,000 in 2008, according to figures provided by industry, and said to be set to grow by 25 percent in the following 6 to 12 months. Of these 50,000 medical tourists, the estimates indicated 20,000 dental, 14,500 cosmetic, and 9,000 elective (including hip, knee, and eye surgery), with a further 5,000 undergoing fertility treatments. (Carrera and Lunt 2010: 476)

These medical tourists are catered for by an emerging global network of locations that includes India, Malaysia, Singapore, Thailand, the Philippines, South Africa, Argentina, Brazil, Costa Rica, Cuba, Mexico and Dubai (Carrera and Lunt 2010). As Ramerez de Arellano (2007) observes there has been a growth in cross-border travel by Americans to Mexican border towns to purchase cheaper medicines and dental care. In Asia the Singaporean government is one of many that have explicitly identified medical tourism as a growth area. In 2006 410,000 tourists went to Singapore to use healthcare services and the government aimed to increase this to 1 million by 2012. In order to promote itself as a key 'Wellness Tourism Destination' it has included *SingaporeMedicine*, a multi-agency government initiative, as part of its 'Uniquely Singapore' tourism marketing strategy (Woodman 2007, Lee 2010). Moreover the Singaporean government has described the UK's ageing population as 'a great potential to be tapped into' (Shipiro 2008). However, it faces growing competition in Asia from Thailand and India who are also seeking to capture this growing market. Bumrungrad Hospital in Bangkok attracts patients from 150 countries and foreign patients account for 50% of its clientele. It has interpreters for 26 languages and a ward specifically for Japanese patients. Like Singapore the Indian government aims to 'encourage the supply of services to patients of foreign origin on payment' through its National Health Policy (Ramerez de Arellano 2007, Terry 2007, Shetty 2010).

More radically Eto and Mahujchariyawong (2015) explicitly call for the development of long stay care health tourism funded by both public and private sectors as a way of promoting development in poorer parts of South East Asia.

Despite this impressionistic evidence this movement might not be as large a global phenomenon as is often assumed. Results of a Eurobarometer survey on the use of and attitudes towards cross-border health services in the EU show that only around 3% of respondents over 55 years (the oldest age group they show) have travelled to another EU member state to receive medical treatment. Moreover, the older age group were the least likely to say that they would be willing to travel abroad for treatment (The Gallup Organisation 2007). Nor is this as unregulated a space as might be supposed. A lot of what known in this still very under-researched area has tended to either come from the USA or focus on one or two global destination hubs. This gives the impression of highly mobile individual consumers who make a choice from a range of (competitive) locations within the developing world. However, UK data from the British Association of Plastic, Reconstructive and Aesthetic Surgeons (BAPRAS) show that there is a more regional, European pattern for British medical tourism. In a survey of their members they found that countries in Eastern Europe were the top destinations for patients who went abroad for cosmetic surgery. This was closely followed by Western Europe while Asian countries only accounted for 11% of destinations (Jeevan and Armstrong 2008). Carrera and Lunt (2010: 470) suggest that this regionalised pattern occurs because European medical tourism 'takes place against a backdrop of the enlargement of the European Union and a deepening of its regulatory reach'. They distinguish between two types of medical tourist: the citizen and the consumer. Whereas US citizens tend to be more consumer-oriented, EU citizens see medical tourism as an entitlement, supported by EU and national laws, as well as a commercial exchange. This is underpinned by the recently adopted EU directive on cross-border healthcare as part of its Renewed Social Agenda programme. As well as seeking better coordination of healthcare among member states, especially around technology and 'e-Health', a key policy is the guarantee that '[p]atients have the right to seek healthcare abroad and be reimbursed up to what they would have received at home' (http://europa.eu). However, it would be a mistake to counter-pose a highly regulated European market for medical tourism with a de-regulated market in Asia or elsewhere. As has already been noted, national governments, such as Singapore, are key actors in the establishment of these global healthcare hubs. Moreover, hospitals seeking to attract foreign patients will often seek approval by the health authorities in those countries where their (potential) customers come from. Both the USA and the UK have accreditation schemes for foreign healthcare providers. In the USA these are the Joint Commission International (JCI) and HealthCare Tourism International while in the UK it is the United Kingdom Accreditation Forum (UKAF).

Anti-ageing medicine

Perhaps the key component of this emergent epistemic community comprises a range of actors involved in what is generally termed 'anti-ageing medicine'. This is a contentious and rather nebulous term. It covers a wide range of techniques and approaches from homeopathy through to biotechnology (Binstock et al 2006, Mykytyn 2006, 2010, Vincent et al 2008). Some practitioners also include cosmetic or aesthetic procedures as part of their practice while others reject these as part of proper anti-ageing medicine which they see as working on the 'inside' rather than the outside of the body. In order to distance themselves from what they see as a pejorative use of the term anti-ageing medicine and to establish their scientific credentials, certain groups of practitioners have adopted alternative labels, such as preventative medicine, age management medicine, wellness medicine and regenerative or rejuvenation medicine (Fishman et al 2008). Vincent (2006) identified four types of anti-ageing medicine: i) symptom alleviation; ii) life expectancy extension; iii) lifespan extension; and iv) abolition (that is immortality). However, he argues that all four share a common biomedical approach which sees ageing as a disease to be cured. Likewise Mykytyn (2010) and Fishman and colleagues (2010) have observed that, despite the diversity of practices and the various attempts to create and maintain (professional) boundaries between different groups, they share a common belief that ageing is a painful, negative process that can and should be arrested or even reversed. Fishman and colleagues (2010) cite the mission statement of the American Academy of Anti-Ageing Medicine (A4M) as evidence.

> A4M believes that the disabilities associated with normal aging are caused by physiological dysfunction which in many cases are ameliorable to medical treatment, such that the human life span can be increased, and the quality of one's life improved as one grows chronologically older.

Fishman et al (2010: 30) argue that this is indicative of the movement in biomedicine 'away from the classification of diseases towards the construction of an ever-improvable self'. For a number of authors this reaches its zenith in regenerative medicine (Cooper 2006, Lafontaine 2009).

> Encompassing the whole range of regenerative biotechnologies, from growth factors to tissue engineering and stem cells, the field of regenerative medicine is currently being promoted as a solution to the many crises of old age … Regenerative medicine is also being touted as a means of promoting productivity growth in the pharmaceutical sector. (Cooper 2006: 9)

These technologies and the ideas behind them are seen to elide with the neoliberal economic approach to population ageing as advocated by the World Bank (which will be discussed in more detail below), as well as broader attempts to create more bio-based economies (see Lorenz and Zinke 2005). In short they can be viewed as part of the new contested terrain of ageing (Jones and Higgs 2010).

Binstock (2003) and Mykytyn (2010) both give good histories of the development and consolidation of the anti-ageing medicine community in the USA and its running battles with the National Institute for Health (NIH) to establish its credibility. Both show how over time anti-ageing medicine has moved from the fringes to establish itself as a 'medical specialism' with a clearly identifiable professional body (A4M), annual conferences, anti-ageing internships and fellowship and its own peer reviewed journal. Yet, while these analyses provide a crucial historical perspective, the spatial focus is narrowly focused on the USA. However, there are a growing number of anti-ageing medicine practitioners and organisations around the world. These are represented by a number of regional and global associations, such as the European Society of Anti-Aging Medicine (ESAAM), the World Anti-Aging Academy of Medicine (WAAAM) and the World Society Interdisciplinary of Anti-Aging Medicine (WOSIAM). These bodies explicitly seek to advance the ideas and practices of anti-ageing medicine throughout the world. As the WOSIAM and WAAAM mission statements make clear:

> The World Society Interdisciplinary of Anti-Aging Medicine (WOSIAM) has quickly become the World Fastest growing Anti-Aging Medicine Society, to federate international physicians and Scientific Societies. The main

goal ... is to promote anti-aging medicine through research
and educational events for physicians and the general public'
(WOSIAM 2009)

The World Anti-Aging Academy of Medicine (WAAAM)
is a member-based society dedicated to the protection and
preservation of the health of the public, and the advancement
of education and research in the clinical specialties of anti-
aging and regenerative medicine. (WAAAM 2010)

The global spread of these networks is presented in Figures 7.2 and
7.3. These show the concentrations of WOSIAM members in each
country around the world. This is truly global insofar as all continents
are represented.

Overall there are WOSIAM members in 50 countries. However,
the concentrations are highest in North America, Latin America and
Western Europe and lowest in Asia and Africa. Brazil has the highest
number of members with 18, France and the USA both have seven
members while the majority of countries that have a member have
only one member. A review of the professions given by the members,
which range from GP to endocrinologist to plastic surgeon, reflects the
diversity of anti-ageing medicine. Similarly, the list of the 96 affiliated
member organisations of the WAAAM also gives a good illustration
of the geographic coverage of these networks. Asia, the Americas and
Europe are all well represented by both national and regional bodies.

Figure 7.2: Map of WOSIAM members

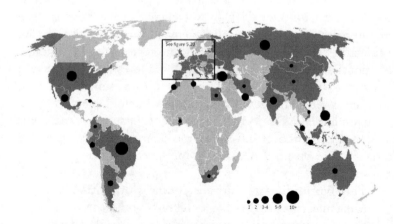

Source:(WOSIAM 2009)

Figure 7.3: Map of WOSIAM members in Europe

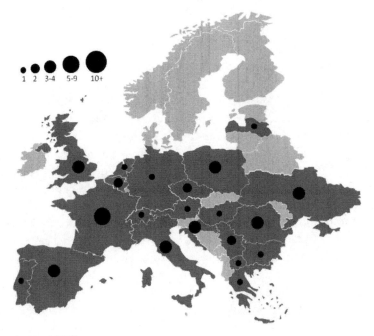

Source:(WOSIAM 2009)

However, unlike the WOSIAM there are no African representatives. Still this is a globally coordinated community with a shared ideology about and approach to ageing. A common discourse, a key component of an epistemic community, is clearly evident when reviewing the individual websites of the members. Almost all groups depict ageing as something which is harmful and that should and can be avoided.

> We [Sociedad Española de Medicina Antienvejecimiento y Longevidad] can define the anti-aging medicine as a comprehensive, preventive and curative, that from the study of natural aging, removes harmful factors that cause premature aging, proposes a system of life in health promotion, and applying corrective techniques and organic aesthetic signs of bodily decay. (www.semal.org/en.html)

> 'In the last ten years, the dynamic of medical research in the area of prevention has contributed to a rapid development of the medicine of longevity...Benefiting from technological progress, the medicine of longevity has developed high-performance methods for the early detection, prevention

and treatment of illnesses associated with aging. The holistic medical concept of the Ana Aslan International Academy of Aging [in Romania] is based on a cutting-edge, integrative and personalised medical approach, capable of leading to high-performance assessment and monitoring of the patient' (Ana Aslan International Foundation, 2010).

These ideas are actively promoted through a series of annual anti-ageing conferences, speaking tours and journals, both web-based and published. However, these organisations are not on the fringes of the debates on healthcare and ageing. They are increasingly engaged with and being engaged by governments and policy makers, particularly outside of Europe and North America. As the earlier data on the health and life expectancy of older people in countries such as China, India and South Africa show this is creating a new time-space for ageing and later life in these countries which is being rapidly occupied by the ideas and actors of anti-ageing medicine. As JAAM observes: 'health maintenance of the elderly has become a national issue in Japan' and that there has been a shift towards 'preventative medicine' in the government's overall approach to healthcare. Thus it argues that it is perfectly poised to advance anti-ageing methods and ideas in to mainstream medicine (JAAM 2010). China is seen as an emerging and potentially huge market for anti-ageing medicine. Another group, World Anti-Aging, point to the (relatively) recent and rapid epidemiological and nutritional transition that has occurred in China, the growing number of wealthy Chinese and recent government healthcare reforms as reasons for the need to promote anti-ageing ideas in the country. They argue that

> World Anti-Aging™ (W.A.) has identified this need that China has for integrative health care known as anti-aging medicine. Anti-aging medicine, also known as regenerative medicine, makes it possible to slow, stop and substantially reverse the physical deterioration and diseases which are commonly considered "natural" aging. Such progress allows not just for improved looks and an extended existence, but for the enjoyment of optimum wellness and quality of life. (World Anti-Aging 2010)

In order to capture this market they have established training academies for anti-ageing medicine and invested in stem cell research.

The W.A. Academy trains and certifies doctors across China to administer W.A. stem cells and anti-aging treatments. It will also host physician seminars, anti-aging conferences, and send doctors around the globe to research new anti-aging technologies. (World Anti-Aging 2010)

Again, it is important not to overstate the degree of coherence within this community. Clearly there is competition among the groups to capture markets and members. This, in and of itself, does not militate against the establishment of an epistemic community. What is lacking, and what is crucial for such a community, is a common solution to the perceived problems of ageing. As might be expected from the range of activities that fall under anti-ageing medicine (Fishman et al 2008), this is still a very protean, nebulous community which is composed of groups and individuals with very different approaches to anti-ageing. At one end of the spectrum are those who are very much focused on the cosmetic and aesthetic dimensions of anti-ageing, such as dermatological treatments, Botox and cosmetic surgery. This group is in many ways more similar in its discourse and methods to the large multinational cosmeceutical companies discussed earlier. Somewhere in the middle of this spectrum are what might be called lifestyle approaches which focus on exercise, diet and spa therapies. These are very much grounded in an alternative therapy approach which shuns the use of 'artificial' pharmaceutical products in favour of natural remedies. Finally, at the far end are those who have a much more biomedical approach, largely around the expected advances in stem cell and genetic research. Thus the divisions that Fishman observes within the American community are just as evident at the global level. Added to this are different approaches to or relationships with government and health authorities in the pursuit and promotion of anti-ageing medicine. This is neatly illustrated by Figure 7.4 (adapted from the JAAM website) in which Japanese and American approaches are contrasted.

Figure 7.4: American and Japanese approaches to anti-ageing medicine contrasted

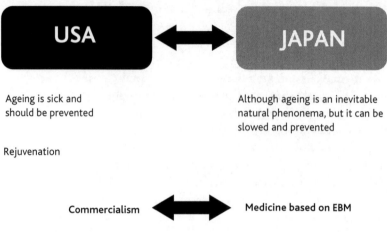

Source: (JAAM 2010)

The global politics of pension reform and the new pension orthodoxy

The second epistemic community that can be identified in the literature has emerged around neoliberal approaches to reforming pension systems around the world. As we saw in Chapter Five, there is little evidence that global economic flows have a significant impact on pension provision within nation states. However, a number of writers have argued that global political, rather than economic, forces have led to pension reform (Ervik 2005, Orenstein 2005, Ervik et al 2006, Deacon 2007). Pension policy has become a hotly contested field which involves numerous global actors and Müller (2003) identifies the dominant epistemic community in the present debate on pension policy as that which is centred around a commitment to and the promotion of the 'new pension orthodoxy'. Figure 7.5 illustrates the components of this epistemic community.

The 'new pension orthodoxy'

The initial impetus for the 'new pension orthodoxy' came from a small group of academics based around Milton Freidman and Fredrick Hayek and their theories of monetarist economics. As Müller (2003) notes this group had seen itself as engaged in a 'guerrilla war against social security' in the USA for some time. However, the military coup in Chile which ousted the Socialist Party's President Salvador Allende provided an opportunity to put those ideas into practice. A group of Chilean economists, often dubbed the 'Chicago Boys', who had been working alongside Freidman were invited to take up positions in and around the military government (Orenstein 2005). Although Chile had in fact been the first country in Latin America to institute an old age social security programme in 1924, by the 1970s it was argued that this was beginning to break down (Andrews 2006). However, rather than attempt to repair the existing pay-as-you-go (PAYG) system the government, influenced by the Chicago Boys, completely overhauled the system. It was dismantled and replaced with a pre-funded individual account system based on mandatory contributions and managed by one of a number of pension funds (Andrews 2006, Deacon 2007). This became known as the Chilean model. However, despite the apparent success of this reform the model did not meet with immediate international adoption. Orenstein (2003) explains the slow diffusion of these reforms as a result of Chile's status as a

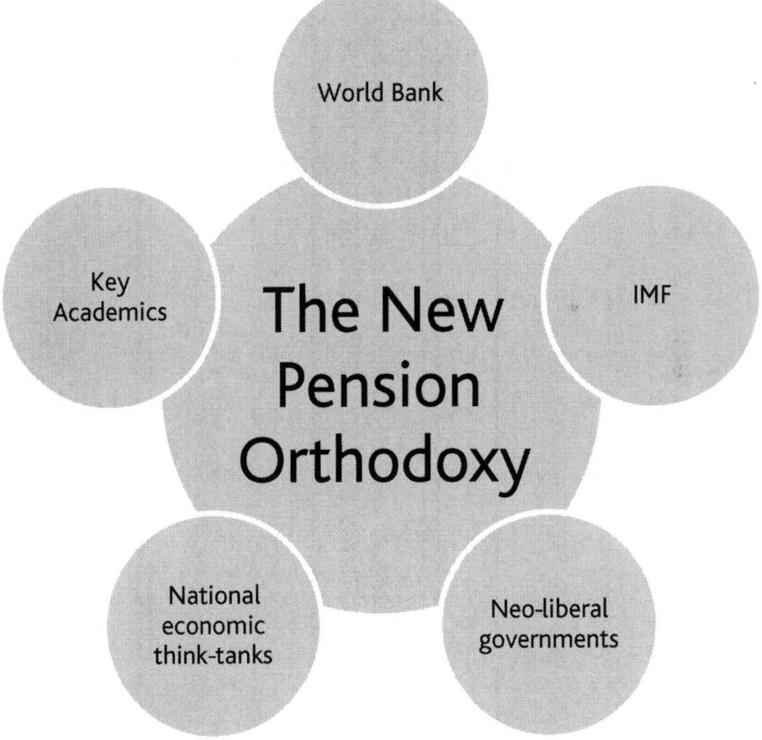

Figure 7.5: The key components of the New Pension Orthodoxy epistemic community

'semi-peripheral middle income country' within the global economy. However, it did become something of a regional role model for other Latin American governments seeking to reform their pension systems. Although none went as far as their neighbour in dismantling their old age security systems, Chile provided both expertise to and experience for these governments (Müller 2003). But it was the adoption and slight adaption of this model by the World Bank (hereafter the Bank) in the early 1990s that thrust the multi-pillar model of pension reform into the international limelight (Orenstein 2003).

Although economists working at the Bank had been exploring a range of reform options for the transition economies during the early part of the decade (see Fox 1994) their grand vision for pension reform was set out in the, now infamous, 1994 publication *Averting the Old Age Crisis* (hereafter *Averting*). Here the Bank set out its arguments for a three pillar model. The principal justification for a move away from existing, formal and informal,[2] systems of old age security was that population ageing, notably in the developing world, had rendered such systems unsustainable (World Bank 1994). James (1996) argued that the historical conditions that led to the creation of PAYG systems in the developed world no longer existed and, therefore, such schemes were not a viable for governments in the developing world. PAYG systems were portrayed as both inefficient and iniquitous by permitting early LME and failing to fairly redistribute income over the life course or between generations. A key argument in the attack on PAYG systems is that they are actuarially unfair. Because benefits are not linked to contributions under PAYG implicit intra-generational redistribution takes place which benefits retirees from low paying jobs. However, the Bank argued that this was not the case due to socioeconomic differences in life expectancy which meant that the 'lifetime rich' benefitted at the expense of the 'lifetime poor'. Furthermore, because present cohorts of retirees are funded by present cohorts of workers, increasing dependency ratios are likely to place a high economic burden younger generations of workers who are forced to support a growing population of retirees through higher income taxes but who cannot expect similar levels of economic support when they retire.

[2]   Debates surrounding the Bank's model for pension reform concentrate on the arguments around the viability of the PAYG systems. This overlooks the fact that the Bank identifies the collapse of traditional, family based financial transfers to older people as a reason for the implantation of the three pillar model (World Bank 1994).

Thus PAYG systems are seen to create intergenerational inequality (World Bank 1994).

This argument formed the basis of the other part of the Bank's justification for pension reform: maintaining economic competitiveness. It is important to note that the subtitle to *Averting*, which is 'Policies to protect the old and promote growth', makes it clear that pension policies need to be consistent with, if not subordinate to, wider economic policy. PAYG systems were presented as a brake to economic growth and competitiveness by acting as a drain on government resources, crowding out other important goods and services and by distorting the labour market and encouraging black and grey market activities through imposing high payroll taxes. Finally, it was argued that state control over pension funds allowed governments to use the resources for political ends which were not economically optimal and often squandered much of the money that was due to pensioners.

In order to achieve the twin goals of preventing old age poverty and encouraging economic competitiveness the Bank argued that governments should re-organise their pension systems along the three pillar model (World Bank 1994). This comprised of a first pillar, which ought to be universal, state financed and redistributive. This pillar, however, is residual and ought to aim only at providing a basic income for those who have worked a requisite period of time. As Deacon (2007) notes, this fits with the Bank's broader poverty alleviation approach (World Bank 2000, Noël 2006, Hulme and Scott 2010). However, while this seems laudable it is seen to threaten the social solidarity basis of many welfare states. The second pillar should be mandatory, provide income related benefits and ideally be fully funded, privately managed and accumulated in individual pension savings accounts. In theory, this strategy reduces reliance on inefficient state social security administrations and enables systems to take advantage of more efficient private sector management. Finally, a third pillar of voluntary private pension schemes may be created on a variety of different models, potentially with state tax incentives, again invested in individual savings accounts managed by pension funds (World Bank 1994, Fox and Palmer 2001, Blackburn 2002, Orenstein 2003).

Responses to the new economic orthodoxy

Although *Averting* put the Bank's vision at the forefront of the political debate, amid a good deal of debate and controversy, it was not the Bank's official policy (Andrews 2006), nor was it uncontested (Orenstein 2003, Ervik 2005, Deacon 2007). Orenstein (2005) and Ervik (2005) drew attention to the alternative vision promoted by the International Labour Organization (ILO) in *Social Security: A new consensus* (ILO 2001) which saw population ageing as a challenge not a crisis and one that could be resolved through active labour market policies and creating full employment. Hence a number of subsequent documents were published which sought to defend and refine the Bank's initial position. Two years after the report the Bank published a comprehensive technical annex (Palacios 1996) providing a wealth of data in order to support its arguments. This was in turn supported by two much more polemical pieces by James (1996, 1997). In both *Protecting the old and promoting growth* (1996) and *New systems for old age security* (1997) she reasserted the need to reform existing pension systems and continued the attack against PAYG systems:

> existing systems have not always protected the old, they especially will not protect those who grow old in the future, they often have not distributed their benefits in an equitable way, and they have hindered economic growth ... they are simply not sustainable in their present form' (James 1997: 3).

The argument that 'countries concerned about growth should consider pension reform' is strongly emphasised (James 1997: 1). She rejects the ILO and International Social Security Association (ISSA) criticisms of the Bank's proposals on the basis that they do not consider the economic performance of a country (James 1996). However, there is evidence of a growing acknowledgement that there is no one-size-fits-all model for pension reform. She identifies three approaches: a Latin American model, based around the Chilean experience; a 'bold' OECD model, pursued by Switzerland, Australia, Denmark and the UK; and a 'partial' European model, adopted by Sweden, Italy, Latvia and the Czech Republic. Under the 'bold' OECD model, existing occupational pensions have been converted to a second pillar, as with the State Earnings Related Pension Scheme (SERPS) in the UK, while countries like Sweden have partially reorganised their systems by introducing notional direct contribution (DC) accounts (James 1997).

Further steps towards a more open approach were seemingly evident in *New ideas about old age security* (Deacon 2007). In the introduction, Holzmann and Stiglitz (2001), who were then the Head of Social Protection and the Chief Economist of the Bank respectively, acknowledged that greater sensitivity to local conditions was required when recommending multi-pillar reform and that high administration costs of private pension funds and the, then, recent 'dot-com' economic crisis of the early 21st century raised questions about the viability of some aspects of the reform package. This was followed by a highly critical chapter which attacked the 'ten myths of social security systems' and sought to undermine many of the claims made about the superiority of individual privately managed DC accounts over PAYG systems (Orszag and Stiglitz 2001). This was however an isolated contribution and in the remainder of the book authors lined up to refute these claims and to defend the relevance and necessity of multi-pillar reform (Fox and Palmer 2001, Holzmann et al 2001). Arguably, rather than provide evidence for a more balanced approach, this volume acted as a focal point to unite the epistemic community. The epilogue, as Deacon (2007) notes, was that Stiglitz was sacked from the Bank shortly after writing *Ten myths* under pressure from the US government. Despite this it is generally accepted that a more nuanced view was presented in *New ideas* (Ervik 2005, Deacon 2007). This was consolidated in the move away from a dogmatic attachment to the multi-pillar model to the greater consideration of context specific reforms laid out in the Bank's (2001) official document on pension reform *Social Protection Sector Strategy: From Safety Net to Springboard* (World Bank 2001, Andrews 2006).

This proliferation of academic and scholarly activity was a key component of the creation and maintenance of this new pension orthodoxy (Orenstein 2003, Orenstein 2005). In all, the Bank published over 350 articles relating to multi-pillar pension reform between 1984 and 2004. However, a clear theoretical and regional focus is clear. Of these studies

> over 40 percent addressed pension issues in countries that adopted multi-pillar reforms, and a dozen countries account for over four fifths of the studies ... Countries with funded pillars average over four studies apiece, and countries without funded pillars average just over two studies each (Andrews, 2006: 10).

The regional focus was on East Europe, Central Asia and Latin America. This publications strategy was supported a series of promotional tours including more than 100 seminars and presentations on *Averting* and related research. According to an evaluation of the Bank's activities these seminars and workshops, particularly those conducted on a worldwide or regional basis, had a substantial impact on policy makers (Andrews 2006).

The impact of the new economic orthodoxy

Examining the global proliferation of 'generational accounting' ideas and technologies, Ervik (2005) gives an excellent account of how these activities helped to shape the policy debate within Norway. In short, generational accounting measures the burden that current fiscal policies are believed likely to impose on future generations (see Higgs and Gilleard 2015 for an overview). Advocates argued that current accounting practices do not consider the long-term implications of present policies. In contrast, generational accounting estimates the sustainability of a country's public finances by calculating the present value of all future expenditure and comparing it to the present value of all future tax returns. It also identified the set of policy reforms needed to achieve 'generational balance' in which future generations face the same lifetime net tax rates as current generations. Although not exclusively concerned with pension expenditure its relevance for the debate on the sustainability of PAYG systems is clear (Cardarelli et al 1999, Ervik 2005). By drawing on the growing body of Bank literature, importantly the Pension Primer, but mainly through the use of the Bank's Pension Reforms Option Simulation Toolkit (PROST)[3] actuarial analyses software, the Norwegian Pension Commission argued strongly and successfully to reform the pension system along the lines of 'generational accounting' practices (Ervik 2005).[4] The Bank has also been involved in more tangible support for policy reform. Since 1984 the Bank has provided US$5.4 billion in assistance for pension reform in 68 countries. Over half of this was issued between 1998 and 2001. This geographical pattern of funding closely mirrors the Bank's publications on pension reform. The transition economies of Eastern Europe and Central Asia and countries in Latin America and the Caribbean received the majority of the funding. More importantly is the type of reform that qualified for financial assistance. Overall, the Bank has provided greater resources to countries developing multi-pillar systems.

> Although more than four-fifths of all Bank loans supported PAYG reforms, nearly one third of these also supported funded second pillars as part of a multi-pillar reform, and

[3] PROST is employed in more than 80 countries.

[4] Interestingly, the National Institute of Economic and Social Research, a leading independent think tank, is advocating the generational accounting in the UK (Cardarelli et al 1999).

nearly one-third supported voluntary pensions. Overall, more than three-quarters of all projects related to multi-pillar pension reform also included a PAYG component ... Countries implementing multi-pillar systems received half again as many loans for PAYG reforms as countries sticking with their PAYG systems, and over twice as many resources for the PAYG pension component ... Countries legislating and implementing multi-pillar systems also received more loans per country than others. Nearly three quarters of pension loans went to countries in Europe and Central Asia and Latin America and the Caribbean, the only Regions enacting multi-pillar reforms. (Andrews 2006: 13)

There was a very strong suggestion in the report that financial assistance was conditional on pursuing multi-pillar pension reform. Perhaps unsurprisingly this financial assistance yielded notable success. Thirteen of the 23 countries which received four or more pension loans implemented second pillar pensions. Eight of the eleven countries which each received funding of more than US$100 million enacted mandatory funded pension laws. Overall median World Bank lending per country implementing second pillar reforms was US$50 million, compared with US$7 million for those not implementing second pillars (Andrews 2006).

The history of the emergence this new orthodoxy is now fairly well established. However, published data by the World Bank's Independent Evaluation Group (IEG) (Andrews 2006) provide an excellent opportunity to reassess some of the arguments. It is also possible to draw on a range of more recent data from the OECD (2007) and the Social Security Administration (SSA) on the extent and type of reforms carried out in a number of countries. In *Pensions at a glance* (2007, 2013) the authors review the major changes to pension and retirement systems that have taken place within the OECD member states since the 1990s. While this review covers a long time period during which many key documents on pension reform were published, principally *Averting*, the geographical scope is somewhat limited. This is problematic given Deacon's (2007) argument that it was in the developing world, mainly Latin America and the transition economies, where the Bank's reform agenda has had the greatest effect. To attempt to overcome this limitation data have been drawn from 58 of the SSA's monthly series of *International Updates on Developments in Foreign Public and Private Pensions*. These reforms are summarised in Table 7.1. In order to explore pension reform in greater detail they have been classified into six different types. The first deals with changes to the age at which one become eligible for a state pension. The next refers to reforms designed to promote longer working lives. Following this are reforms that relate to changes in the way in which the benefit formula is calculated. After which are reforms that relate directly to the value of the benefits received and whether they have been increased or reduced. Then there are those reforms that change the structure of the pension, such as the introduction of DC schemes. Finally, there are any other reforms. By disaggregating reforms into these, albeit broad, categories a more nuanced analysis is possible as opposed to simply assessing whether reform has taken place or not. It is important to note, however, that the data refer to the number of policies of this type which have been enacted *not* the number of countries enacting such policies. Thus, if a country has passed two policies restricting access to early retirement, for example, then this will count as two reforms of this nature.

These data suggest that this epistemic community has influenced the direction of pension reform, notably in the transition economies and Latin America. These data show that many countries have reduced the value of their pensions and/or shifted responsibility away from publically financed pensions. Of all the policies reviewed 32 of them have reduced the benefits paid out in retirement. In some cases this has been achieved by simply reducing the value of the pension. For example, in the Republic of Korea the replacement rate has been cut from 60% of the final wage to 50% (SSA 2004a). In other countries certain groups of employees have had their pension schemes replaced by less generous schemes. In Jordan military and civil service pensions have been replaced by the general scheme that covers non-governmental employees (SSA 2004b). Likewise, in Taiwan pension benefits for civil servants have been reduced and in Brazil they are subject to a new income tax (SSA 2004c, 2006a).

Other routes to pension reform: indexation and life expectancy

However, the most common ways in which a reduction in the value of the pension have been achieved are through changes in the pension indexation mechanism or by adjusting the pension to either future life expectancy or future dependency ratios within the country. Both of these measures can been seen to meet the World Bank proposed criterion that pension systems need to be economically sustainable (James 1997). The first of these, indexation, refers to the way in which pensions are calculated. In recent years, many OECD countries have moved away from indexation of pension benefits to earnings towards full or partial indexation to prices (OECD, 2007). However, this differs by country. In some member states such as Italy and Portugal, the relative weight of the indexation varies with the value of the pension, tending to be less generous for higher pensions, or, as in Austria, is capped at a certain level of benefit. In the transition economies of Hungary, Poland and the Slovak Republic pensions are now adjusted using a mixed index composed of wage growth and price inflation.

Table 7.1: Reforms to national retirement income systems since 1990

	Pension eligibility age	Adjusted retirement incentives and/or active labour market programmes	Change of years in benefit formula, qualifying conditions and/or coverage	Change in pension value and/or financial sustainability	Change in pension structure	Other
Africa						
Kenya		•	•		•	
Namibia			•		•	
Nigeria	•				•	
Americas						
Brazil	•		•		•	•
Canada		•				•
Chile		•	•			•
Costa Rica			•	•		
Ecuador				•		
El Salvador	•			•	•	
Mexico					•	•
Nicaragua						•
Panama	•		••		•	
Peru						•
USA	•	•				
Asia and Oceania						
Australia	••	••	•	•	•	••
Azerbaijan				•		
China					•	•
Fiji	•					

	Pension eligibility age	Adjusted retirement incentives and/or active labour market programmes	Change of years in benefit formula, qualifying conditions and/or coverage	Change in pension value and/or financial sustainability	Change in pension structure	Other
India			●●		●	●
Israel	●	●				
Japan	●		●	●	●	●
Jordan		●		●		
Kazakhstan					●	
Korea, Rep.	●		●	●	●	
New Zealand	●				●	●
Philippines			●			
Singapore			●			
Taiwan	●			●	●	
Turkey	●		●	●	●	●
Uzbekistan					●	
Vietnam			●		●	
Europe						
Austria	●●	●●	●	●	●	●
Belgium	●	●●●●	●			
Cyprus	●					
Czech Rep.	●	●●			●	
Denmark	●			●		
Estonia		●			●	
Finland	●	●●●	●	●●	●	
Germany	●	●		●●	●	●
France		●●●●	●●●	●●		●
Greece	●	●				
Hungary	●	●	●	●●●	●	●
Ireland		●		●	●	●
Italy	●●	●	●	●		
Lithuania					●	
Macedonia	●				●	
Malta	●●	●●	●	●		
Netherlands					●●	●

	Pension eligibility age	Adjusted retirement incentives and/or active labour market programmes	Change of years in benefit formula, qualifying conditions and/or coverage	Change in pension value and/or financial sustainability	Change in pension structure	Other
Norway		•	••	•	•	•
Poland		•	•	•	••	
Portugal	•	•••	•	••	•	
Romania	•	•			•	•
Russia			•		•	
Serbia	•					
Slovak Rep.	•		•	•	•	
Spain.		•				
Sweden			•	•	•	•
Switzerland	•	•				•
UK	••	•••		••	•	•
Ukraine		•			•	

Sources: (OECD 2007, OECD 2013, OECD 2015); SSA selected years

In Finland and Switzerland this model has been in place for some time. However, there have been adjustments in the relative index to favour prices. In Turkey the periodic pension benefit index mechanism has been changed from the monthly consumer price index (CPI) to an annual adjustment based on a combination of the CPI and gross domestic product. Although it is argued that indexing pensions to prices preserves the purchasing power of pensions it means that pensioners do not share in the general growth in living standards. Thus the relative value of the pension, to wages, decreases over time raising the risk of the increased economic marginalisation of older people.

The second method for reducing the value of the pension has been to introduce a 'financial sustainability' factor in to the calculation of benefits. Effectively this either explicitly or implicitly adjusts benefits to increasing life expectancy and/or the future dependency ratio. Such schemes have been proposed or implemented in around half of OECD countries (OECD 2007, Whitehouse 2007). The most common way in which this has been achieved has been through the introduction of DC schemes, funded or notional, which automatically adjust benefits to life expectancy. In these schemes pension capital is accumulated in an individual account which is transformed into a regular pension payment at retirement. Annuity benefits will be reduced the higher life expectancy is at the time of retirement because of the longer expected duration of the pension payment. Since the late 1990s, Hungary, the Slovak Republic and the Netherlands have replaced part or all of their public defined benefit (DB) pension schemes with funded DC plans. In other countries, such as Italy, Poland, the Czech Republic and Sweden, notional DC schemes have been implemented (SSA 2004c, OECD 2007). Many countries in Latin America and Asia have also set up mandatory DC schemes or individual funded accounts. Uruguay and El Salvador have closely followed the Chilean model and introduced mandatory individual accounts and, in the case of the latter, wound up their PAYG public pension system for new entrants (SSA 2004b, 2004d). In Asia the most celebrated case is Kazakhstan which replaced its entire PAYG system with mandatory individual accounts in 1996 (SSA 2005a). Other countries in the region have also more or less followed suit. China, Taiwan, Uzbekistan and India have all set up similar accounts although not totally at the expense of their public schemes and, in the case of the latter, only for civil servants (SSA 2003b, 2004b, 2005b). In Africa the Nigerian government set up new compulsory retirement savings accounts in 2004 (SSA 2004e). Namibia launched an Agricultural Retirement Fund, which aims to extend coverage to agricultural labourers, as a funded DC scheme (SSA 2005b).

Other countries have used other methods to recalculate pension value. Germany has adjusted the value of the pension in line with life expectancy through changes in the points system used to calculate benefits effectively linking pension payments to the dependency ratio. Japan has also adjusted the value of its basic pension based on expected future dependency ratios. Against this only eight policies were introduced, over this time period, which increased the value of the pension. These policies have been almost exclusively enacted in Latin American and transition countries. In Costa Rica the value of the minimum contributory public pension and all means-tested components have been increased (SSA 2005c). In Ecuador a sliding scale of increases to the value of the average pension have been approved, to the advantage of poorer pensioners (SSA 2004f). While in El Salvador, although not strictly an increase in the value of the pension, the government has made pension subsidies available to retirees whose benefits are lower under the new individual account system than they would have been under the previous PAYG system (SSA 2003b). In Russia a blanket increase of 300 roubles on the average pension came into effect from the end of 2007 and in Azerbaijan the minimum pension level has been increased to be at least equal to the poverty level (SSA 2006b, 2007b).

Other reforms have changed the formula used to calculate benefits in retirement. This can be achieved by any or all of the following three means: i) by increasing the number of contribution years used to calculate pension benefits; ii) by changing the valorisation of past earnings; or iii) by changing the definition of what counts as a contribution. Within the OECD, seven states have extended the period over which earnings are measured in the past two decades. France has moved from the best 10 years to the best 25 years in the public scheme. Both Australia and Austria have extended the averaging period from the 15 highest paid years to the 40 best years or a percentage thereof. In Finland, Poland, Portugal and Sweden, governments have passed laws to move to a lifetime average earnings measure. The most dramatic change occurred in the Slovak Republic where the calculation changed from the best five years from the final ten years of work to lifetime average earnings. The majority of OECD countries now use a lifetime earnings measure, or a close proxy for it, to calculate pension benefits (OECD 2007). These changes are also found outside the OECD. In Costa Rica the changes are arguably as dramatic as those seen in the Slovak Republic. Instead of being based on the highest 48 monthly contributions in the final five years of coverage benefits will now be calculated based on average earnings over the last 20 years adjusted for inflation (SSA 2005c).

In addition to this some countries have changed the way in which past earnings are revalued, or valorised, to take account of changes in living standards between the time pension rights accrued and the time they are claimed. Several OECD countries have moved away from valorising past earnings in line with economy-wide wage growth and have substituted prices for all or part of the calculation. France, for example, moved to price valorisation in the public scheme as early as 1985 and in the occupational schemes in 1996. In Finland and Poland, where a mix of wage and price growth is already used to valorise past earnings, reforms have accorded greater weight to prices (OECD 2007).

However, although there is clear evidence that the Bank has actively devoted resources to supporting pension reform in a number of countries it does not automatically follow that the three pillar system has become the global model for pension reform. As Ervik (2005) notes, the presence of the Bank's ideas, personnel or even money does not necessarily mean that the Bank is forcing its reform agenda onto unwilling national governments. The process of policy transfer is far more complex and complicated. As writers from a historical 'institutionalist' perspective argue, the character of national policy making institutions plays a crucial part in mediating these forms of exchange (Pierson 1998, 2001b). So too do national political actors, economic circumstances and wider political culture. Thus rather than global actors imposing their agenda it might very well be the case that reform minded national political elites use these arguments and technologies to strengthen their case. This seems to be what happened in Norway where the Ministry of Finance was able to employ generational accounting techniques and arguments to force a national reform agenda (Ervik 2005). Moreover, despite the conclusion by the IEG that the Bank's activities have been largely successful in influencing the pension reform debate, there are examples where this was not the case. For example, despite being strong candidates for reform governments neither in Slovenia nor the Czech Republic were interested in pursuing this policy or seeking assistance. Nor were the Bank's relations with government agencies always successful. Illustrating the importance of national actors the report notes that 'in Uruguay and Hungary, the Bank had a good relationship with the Ministry of Economy/ Budget and Planning Office and Ministry of Finance, respectively, but was unable to influence the country's Social Security agency' (Andrews 2006:52).

The active ageing epistemic community: An alternative politics of later life?

However, notwithstanding the evidence for success of the 'new pensions orthodoxy', there are other competing organisations and ideas which constitute alternative models for meeting the challenge of population ageing. The IEG report notes that the Bank is not the sole global actor engaged with these issues but has to work in a 'multi-donor environment' alongside other INGO's like the EU and USAID. Alongside this supranational activity several nation states also act as global models for pension reform. The report observes that 'Notional Defined Contribution reforms in Sweden and Italy became the model for a number of countries in Europe and Central Asia, and the Chilean reform influenced policy makers in both that region and in Latin America and the Caribbean' (Andrews 2006: 15). The Norwegian Pension Commission, for example, referred to the Swedish experience to frame its arguments for pension reform (Ervik 2005, Ervik et al 2006).

Figure 7.6: The main components of the Active Ageing epistemic community

From among these competing ideas it is possible to identify an emergent, alternative epistemic community forming around the concept and practice of 'active ageing'. Active ageing, along with productive ageing, successful ageing and healthy ageing, has increasingly become part of the nomenclature to describe new, more positive aspects of contemporary later life. However, it has also acquired currency among several INGOs, including the ILO, EU, WHO and UN, as part of their approach to population ageing. Figure 7.6 illustrates the components of this active ageing epistemic community.

The WHO provides perhaps the most comprehensive definition of the different aspects that 'active ageing' might encompass.

> Active ageing is the process of optimizing opportunities for health, participation and security in order to enhance quality of life as people age. It applies to both individuals and population groups. Active ageing allows people to realize their potential for physical, social, and mental well-being throughout the life course and to participate in

society, while providing them with adequate protection, security and care when they need. The word "active" refers to continuing participation in social, economic, cultural, spiritual and civic affairs, not just the ability to be physically active or to participate in the labour force. Older people who retire from work, ill or live with disabilities can remain active contributors to their families, peers, communities and nations. Active ageing aims to extend healthy life expectancy and quality of life for all people as they age. (World Health Organization 2010)

However, despite the advantage that such a broad definition has for attracting a wide range of possible supporters, active ageing has tended to be more narrowly defined in terms of the labour market participation rates of older people. This is reflected in the position taken by the ILO. As already mentioned the ILO has been the main source of opposition to the new pension orthodoxy (James 1996). Despite a number of previous challenges to the Bank's description of and prescription for the demographic 'crisis' (Gillion et al 2000) the ILO set out its alternative arguments and analyses for meeting the challenge of population ageing in its 2001 publication *Social Security: A new consensus*. They argued that the forecast financial crisis of an ageing population was neither inevitable nor was it the product of any inherent unsustainability in PAYG pension systems. Instead the blame was clearly laid at the feet of policies that promoted early LME and failed to create employment in the formal sector. They concluded that '[a]n ageing society need not face any crisis, as long as it is able to provide jobs for its ageing workforce' (ILO 2001: 83). This was illustrated by showing that if a country with a de facto retirement age of 60 and a female labour force participation rate similar to that of the Netherlands was to raise the de facto retirement age to 67 and increase female labour force participation to the present highest levels in Europe (those of Sweden) then the combined unemployment and old age pensioner dependency ratio would only rise from 62 dependents per 100 employed persons, in 2001, to about 68 per 100 by 2030. In contrast if retirement age and female labour force participation rates stayed the same that ratio would be 80 to 100, or about 18 per cent higher. In the developing world, however, they argue that the main challenge to the sustainability of old age security was the low levels of employment found in the formal sector which leads in turn to a low tax base as well as low pension coverage (ILO 2001).

Perhaps the clearest example of the spread and support for these ideas can be seen in the 'active ageing' policies implemented by the EU in 1999 (Kasneci 2007). This was given further impetus at the 2001 Stockholm European Council where, in response to concerns raised about population ageing, the Council 'agreed to set an EU target for increasing the average EU employment rate among older women and men (55–64) to 50% by 2010' (Stockholm European Council 2001). This was upheld the following year in Barcelona and an additional commitment to reducing early LME was agreed upon.

> [E]arly retirement incentives for individuals and the introduction of early retirement schemes by companies should be reduced. Efforts should be stepped up to increase opportunities for older workers to remain in the labour market, for instance, through flexible and gradual retirement formulas and guaranteeing real access to lifelong learning. A progressive increase of about 5 years in the effective average age at which people stop working in the European Union should be sought by 2010. (Barcelona European Council 2002: 12)

These aims represented a clear departure from many of the policies enacted during the 1980s and 1990s which, by design or accident, facilitated early LME (Kohli and Rein 1991, Guillemard 2003).

Active ageing as a global agenda

However, these ideas are not restricted to the EU. The UN is a key, if not *the* key, global actor within this epistemic community. In the 2007 *World Economic and Social Survey* the UN clearly comes out in support of the ILO recommendations. In their analyses of the effects of the liberalisation of labour markets in many low and middle income economies the report's authors conclude that the expected growth in formal sector employment has failed to happen. Instead growth has come from the informal sector reducing the potential tax base from which to finance public pensions and, in some cases, pension coverage rates in the population at large have fallen. Turning to the more advanced economies the authors reported:

> The analysis of the Survey suggests that the greatest potential for counteracting the projected changes in labour force growth lies in raising the participation rates

of women and older workers. Indeed, many countries still possess considerable scope for enacting measures aiming at increasing the participation rate of older workers—typically those aged 55–64—by bringing the effective retirement age more closely in line with the statutory retirement age. (UN 2007: xi–xii)

In order to achieve this they recommended removing incentives for early retirement, providing better workplace design to meet the needs of an ageing workforce, an end to age discrimination, the promotion of positive images of older workers, and the provision of opportunities for continuing professional development and lifelong learning (UN 2007). In fact, these recommendations are perhaps best seen as a development of ideas set out five years earlier in the UN's *Madrid International Plan of Action on Aging* and a reflection of policies already enacted by many member states in response to the plan. The *Madrid Plan* is arguably as important a document as *Averting* in the global discourse on population ageing. According to the UN's Head of the Social Integration Branch of the Division for Social Policy and Development, 'The Madrid International Plan of Action on Ageing reflects a global consensus on the social dimensions of ageing that has evolved during preceding decades through multilateral activity and work conducted at the United Nations' (Zelenev 2006). In all, 159 countries attended the conference and contributed to ideas and support for a 'society for all ages'. This concept built on the United Nations Principles for Older Persons (UN 2001) and the success of the International Year of Older Persons in 1999. The *Madrid Plan* outlined 18 issues of priority concern with 35 specific objectives that were to be implemented in 239 specific recommendations for action. It is possible to identify three broad priority areas: i) Older persons and development; ii) advancing health and wellbeing into old age, and; iii) ensuring enabling and supportive environments (Zelenev 2006). In order to ensure that these recommendations were implemented, the UN set up a number of regional commissions, in Europe, Asia and the Pacific, and Latin America. The outcome of these commissions was the ten regional implementation strategies (RIS).

These ten strategies cover a wide range of issues from housing and healthcare to the political participation and perceptions of older people. On the fifth anniversary of the Madrid Declaration, at the United Nations Economic Commission for Europe (UNECE) Ministerial Conference on Ageing in Leon, governments were asked to submit reports on what progress, if any, had been made in implementing these strategies. In all, 34 countries ranging from Azerbaijan to America returned reports covering a host of issues. However, the three RIS that most directly relate to the debate on financing later life and active ageing are:

- RIS 3: Promotion of equitable and sustainable economic growth in response to population ageing.
- RIS 4: Adjustment of social protection systems in response to demographic changes and their social and economic consequences.
- RIS 5: Enabling labour markets to respond to the economic and social consequences of population ageing.

As noted above there are a number of different ways in which governments aimed to meet these challenges. A number of governments, such as Armenia, Latvia and the UK, have introduced policies aimed at deferring the age at which older workers retire. For example, the Spanish government agreed to a package of financial incentives to encourage workers to work beyond the state retirement age. In Portugal, as part of the *National Strategy for Active Ageing*, a flexible retirement age coupled with a bonus mechanism for each effective month of additional work month done beyond state retirement age have been introduced. Similar initiatives have been reported by the SSA. The Australian government introduced a lump sum bonus for those who choose to defer their public pension and in Finland and France the value of the pension will be increased for anyone choosing to work beyond 68 years and 60 years of age respectively (OECD 2007). Chile, Austria, the Czech Republic and Belgium have all reduced access to early retirement by raising the minimum requirements for early retirement pension. Belgium has also restricted access to its unemployment pension (SSA 2004a). Other countries have made early retirement less attractive by reducing the value of the early pension or similar benefits. For example, Israel has made early pension payments subject to the full tax rate (SSA 2003a) while Germany and Malta have both reduced the value of their early retirement benefits (SSA 2006c, OECD 2007).

Extending working life

Another common set of reforms are those which change the age at which one becomes eligible to claim a state pension. Between them 30 countries have enacted 32 policies which have raised the state pension age. In some countries, such as Hungary, Greece, the UK and Portugal, these policies aim to unify the hitherto different retirement ages for men and women, raising the latter in line with the former (OECD 2007, SSA 2008a). In others the retirement age for specific groups of workers, such as civil servants in the UK and Cyprus, have been raised in line with the general retirement age for the population (SSA 2005a, 2005d). However, in the main such policies have simply resulted in a general increase in the retirement age for the whole population. Japan, New Zealand, the Republic of Korea, Turkey and Malta have all raised their overall retirement age to 65 years (SSA 2005a, 2008b, OECD 2007). The USA and Germany have increased it to 67 years and, under a flexible retirement policy, in Finland people can remain in work until 68 years of age (OECD 2007, SSA 2007b). In Austria the government has introduced a 'retirement corridor' which allows people to retire between 62 and 67 years of age with differing financial incentives (SSA 2005a). However, in a number of countries, such as Panama, although increases in the age of retirement have been enacted for the whole population, gender-specific retirement ages have not been removed (SSA 2004c, 2005e). This can be seen in Brazil, where although the age of eligibility for a pension has been raised by seven years for both men and women, differential retirement ages, of 60 years and 55 years respectively, still remain (SSA 2004c). Finally, it is worth noting that two policies have been put into place which run counter to this general trend and have reduced the age of eligibility for the state pension. In Fiji the age of retirement for civil servants has been reduced from 60 to 55 years (SSA 2007d) while in Denmark the official retirement age was briefly reduced from 67 to 65 years (SSA 2004g). However, the Danish parliament soon reversed this and linked retirement age to life expectancy estimates (SSA 2005d).

However, the main focus of many governments has been to improve the LMP rates of pre-retirement age older workers, typically 55 to 65 years of age. The representatives of EU member states who reported back to the conference reasserted their commitment to the Stockholm and Barcelona European Council Declarations. The USA also echoed these objectives. A high number of countries, such as Belgium, Estonia and Malta, reported that they had implemented labour market activation programmes aimed at older workers. In Finland the government has implemented two programmes, the *Finnish Workplace Development Programme* (TYKES) and *Promoting the Attractiveness of Working Life* (VETO), to improve the LMP rates of older workers. Both Germany and the UK have introduced similar programmes targeted at the over 50s. In Germany the *Act to Improve the Employment Opportunities of Older*

Persons came into force on 1 May 2007 as part of the *50plus Initiative* of the Federal Government.

A number of governments have also looked towards what might be called demand side approaches to increasing LMP by introducing incentives for employers to hire older workers. For example, in Austria the government has initiated a number of projects, such as the *Productive Ageing* project with Magna Steyr Vehicle Technology, to increase dialogue with employers about how best to utilise the skills of older workers. However, the most common policy has been to offer financial incentives, such tax breaks or wage subsidies, to employers who employer older workers. Sweden, Germany, Hungary and Romania have all exempted employers from making unemployment contributions, healthcare contributions or both for new employees aged over 50 years, or 55 years in Sweden. Wage subsidies have also been introduced in Germany and Denmark. Again similar programmes are reported in the SSA reports. The Portuguese government is reported to have developed a 'national strategy for the promotion of active ageing' that is designed to encourage older workers to remain in the labour force (Paul 2007, SSA 2007a).

Another approach has been to focus on reskilling older workers to increase their employability in the new economy. The Canadian government has invested $70 million Canadian dollars in the *Targeted Initiative for Older Workers* to improve the skills and work experience of older workers. Similarly, the Portuguese government introduced the *Senior Intervention Programme* in 2005 to provide professional guidance, retraining and work experience opportunities in the voluntary and community sector. In Hungary the government has removed the age ceiling on all professional, language and general training courses.

This is coupled, in many countries, with additional support for older workers seeking employment. Countries like France and Austria have introduced 'age awareness' campaigns throughout their job centres. In other countries more active measures have been taken. In Lithuania an informal vocational guidance and counselling programme, *Social integration of elderly people*, was developed to help those aged over 60 to seek employment and training. This was followed up in 2006 with the launch of *Seigniors' Bank* website by the Lithuanian Labour Exchange. Similarly, in Romania the National Agency for Employment has created 'job bourses' to support personalised action plans, vocational training and e-learning for older workers, especially those from rural areas, seeking employment. In the UK, as part of the New Deal programme mentioned earlier, a Skills Coaching trial was introduced to offer an enhanced guidance service for low-skilled unemployed people.

A few countries have taken a more direct, legalistic, approach. Austria, Denmark, Estonia, Finland and the UK have all either introduced new laws to ban age discrimination or removed articles for existing legislation which were seen as disadvantageous to older workers' employment (Taylor and Walker 1997, Taylor 2002, 2003). In several Canadian provinces employers are no longer able to force workers to retire at 65 years of age (SSA 2006d). This has been supported in Austria, Denmark and the UK with efforts to improve the workplace and job design to meet the needs of an ageing workforce. In Austria the *Alternsgerechtes Arbeiten* (Ageing and Work) project is designed to provide specialised training for labour inspectors about health and safety risks for the ageing workforce, to consult employers and employees about concerning health and safety risks for older workers, and to discuss how age related risk assessments could be effectively implemented.

Finally, a number of governments have sought to promote positive images of older workers. In France the *Plan National d'Action Concerté pour l'Emploi des Seniors* included a public information campaign to showcase the potential of older workers. The Danish government followed a similar route setting up a major campaign to point out to both enterprises and older workers the advantages and possibilities of staying in the labour market longer.

Conclusion

In this chapter we have identified three key epistemic communities that are operating within the field of ageing and later life. Their existence once again questions the dominance of methodological nationalism in the formulation of both the policies and the cultures of old age. They also challenge, once again, the too simplistic equation of globalisation with the imagery of an unstoppable juggernaut which operates with its own deterministic logic. We have also deliberately included the idea that anti-ageing can be seen as an epistemic community because it also recognises that the processes that we have been looking at are not just confined to the 'normal' arenas associated with ageing such as pension reform and labour market participation. Our examples show that we have to move away from the either/or of national or global actors being determinant for the production of the conditions for ageing and later life and rather that we need to examine the assemblages of actors across different spatialities. In doing this it also becomes apparent that the debates globalisation and discourses about the changing nature of later life have emerged over roughly the same period of time. However, there has been little cross-fertilisation between them. Moreover, many of these debates have wrong-footed gerontologists who have played key roles in establishing and maintaining older paradigms of later life. We constantly need to be aware that academics and researchers are caught up in these epistemic communities as, in Zygmunt Bauman's terms, both interpreters and legislators (Bauman 2013)

This awareness of the limitations of globalisation does not mean that global actors are absent or unimportant. These new biotemporalities are creating novel spatial assemblages around ageing and health(iness). The regulatory and policy spaces of the national 'welfare' state that were traditionally seen to have responsibility for the health and wellbeing of the older population have shifted in part to multiple overlapping spatial logics. The shifting temporality of later life from one of biological and cognitive decline to one of renewability and reversibility can be seen to be mirrored in multiple overlapping spatialities. A range of new social actors are competing to fill the cultural space opened up by these new biotemporalities. This is evident in composition and activities of each of the epistemic communities. The structure of the anti-ageing enterprise clearly illustrates the complex, heterarchical nature of spatial logics in the current period as it unites actors across a range of levels, from the local (such as individual spas), the national (national governments), the regional (EU directives) and the global (MNCs). Moreover, we can see how national, regional and global regulatory spaces overlap and criss-cross each other. Hence the extension of national certification to foreign hospitals shows that juridical and geographical borders may no longer neatly coincide but increasingly have to interact with one another.

We witness the same complex interplay of different spatial actors operating in the pensions and retirement ideoscapes. So that while global economic flows may have had a marginal impact on the economic activities and financial wellbeing of older people (as shown in Chapter Five), these new actors, in the form of epistemic communities, are actively working to shape the nature and direction of ageing and later life. In those countries which have followed the new pension orthodoxy, pensions have moved away from the relative security of the nation state as the guarantor of benefits and are increasingly reliant on the much more turbulent, short-term focused, global market (Blackburn 2002, 2012). As such the timing and nature of retirement has become much more contingent than it was in the classical modernist period. However, it is also clear that no one spatial logic is dominant but that in order to be successful these communities must align groups across a wide range of spatialities. Nor is the case that these alignments run from the global down. Actors at any level can seek to recruit others into their community to advance their goals.

Part 3
Concluding remarks

EIGHT

Conclusion

The aim of this book has been to map out the present day time-spaces of ageing and later life. In drawing together the wide range of different contexts in which old age occurs a number of inferences can be made. The main conclusion is that there does not seem to be one single global time-space of later life. Instead the economic, political and cultural coordinates of later life are located in a series of overlapping, sometimes conflicting, and sometimes co-ordinated spatial logics and temporal frames. This can be illustrated through a number of subsidiary conclusions that relate to the individual chapters. These show that: i) there is evidence that the third age has become what could be described as a free floating global signifier; ii) that material aspects of globalisation have a very weak effect on the conditions of later life; and iii) that there are a number of emerging epistemic communities that are actively involved in trying to shape later life. These findings are, however, conditional and impel us to develop new theoretical models within gerontology which would allow us to handle the complex interrelations between these spatial logics as they develop.

New spaces for old? Multiple spatialities of ageing and later life

The analyses presented throughout the book lend overwhelming support to the argument that there has been a more or less radical transformation of the temporal coordinates of later life during the past few decades. However, the spatial (re)configuration of these new temporalities does not easily map on to a single logic of globalisation. Thus, to answer to the primary research question investigated in the book, there is little evidence for a global time-space of ageing and later life. Yet neither is it the case that we see the continuing presence of a set of mutually exclusive time-spaces of ageing and later life contained within separate nation states. Instead of a simple model we see a number of variegated landscapes which change depending on the lens that is being used. Consequently, when we look at topics such as engagement with consumer culture or patterns of tourism we can see a relatively global landscape. However, when we look at health or the financial circumstances of older people we see a much more uneven terrain with different regions or individual nation states standing apart from each other. The multiplicity of spatial logics and the lack of a global time-space lead to the conclusion that it is not possible to definitively describe the state of the world's older population, rather the picture that emerges from the data is one of spatial variation. In the earlier chapters of the book we have artificially separated the various aspects of ageing and later life to allow for clearer analyses of the conditions and experiences of older people. Here they are reconfigured to permit the exploration of the intersectionalities as well as the inter-spatialities that exist between them.

It is important to note that while we might not have moved into a completely global time-space of ageing and later life, there is strong evidence for the existence of global processes and actors in later life that cut across a number of the different 'scapes' we have identified. The clearest examples of this are the emergence of the third age as a free floating global signifier as well as some aspects of the spread of medical tourism and the activities of the epistemic communities connected to ageing and later life. The increased fluidity around the age and timing of LME does seem to coincide with a desire by many older people to push back the onset of old age. This has opened up new spaces in the life course as the end of working life and the start of old age become more and more disconnected. This provides powerful evidence that the third age has transcended its sociocultural moorings in the UK and USA and increasingly suggests that a more globalised dimension to the time-space of later life is currently emerging. The spread of these ideas also comes at the same time as the diffusion of the material conditions for the realisation of a third age, such as improved health and income, now extends beyond Western Europe and North America. This is most clearly evident in the spread of consumer culture among older people in East Asia. Here is a clear example of a 'global' rather than a 'regional' diffusion of third age identities and practices. In a regional diffusion we would expect these practices to spread out from a regional core, for example the USA, to adjoining countries in neighbouring regions or, alternatively, to countries that belong to a similar welfare regime type if we were to take Esping-Andersen's (1990) approach. However, our analyses show that these practices have migrated across regions however they may be defined. They show that global consumer capitalism seeks to open up new markets wherever it can take hold and that it has found a market within East Asia. These results suggest that consumerism seemingly has the ability to overcome the assumed cultural differences between the East and West and is capable of creating a shared experience of later life constructed around cultural consumption.

If the spread of the third age represented a possible global 'ethnoscape' of ageing and later life, then the activities of the various epistemic communities that we have identified in the book constitute a number of competing global 'ideoscapes'. Each of the three epistemic communities which we identified (the new pension orthodoxy, the active ageing approach and the global ageing enterprise) contained actors operating within different spatial logics. In concert with this, global actors such as the World Bank and the UN form key constituents of these communities. They occupy crucial positions for the dissemination of information, funding of programmes and as *fora* for discussions and institutions in the coordination of action. However, they do not operate alone. Regional, national and local actors are present in each of these communities. Neither do they operate in a regulatory void. Instead the multiplicity of spatialities has created a super-regulatory field with many overlapping regimes. This was clearly evident in the analyses of the 'global' cosmetics and cosmeceutical industry. These analyses, and those for pensions and retirement, show that the regulatory spaces of health and financial wellbeing have not simply shifted 'up' to a global level but have also moved 'down' and include actors at each spatial level. Our analyses support our central argument that there appears to be no single time-space of ageing and later life. Instead we see a mosaic of different spatial logics through which the conditions and meaning of later life are constructed and contested.

This conclusion is evidenced when we look at the issue of medical tourism. Although it is important to be cautious about the data on this phenomenon we would argue that it exemplifies this complexity and operates in a multiplicity of spaces. It is possible to see how it touches on and incorporates all the spatial layers, from the global to the local. A global dynamic clearly exists with older people from many countries travelling to medical tourist hubs in Asia, Europe and Latin America. However this is overlaid with regional patterns. The majority of medical tourists tend to travel to neighbouring countries. At the same time regional bodies, such as the EU, are trying to create a common market for these services within their borders. Contrary to the globalisation literature, nation states also play a huge role in both the receiving and sending countries. These hubs or hospitals which operate at the local level are highly connected to, as well as being supported by, their national governments as well as by their economic and health policies. On the other side of the equation, governments in the sending countries have extended their juridical boundaries to include these hubs by giving them forms of accreditation. In this way the nation states and regions remain key actors in the production and reproduction of the conditions of later life. Instead of disappearing it could be argued that they have adapted to the multi-scalar environment.

Indeed, throughout the chapters in this book there has been ample evidence of the importance of regional patterns and actors for the various dimensions of ageing and later life. The fact that population ageing remains relatively confined to the advanced industrial nations is perhaps the most potent argument against the emergence of a global time-space for later life. What we see, instead, is an intersection between economic geography and demography. So, while it is true that life expectancy is increasing and fertility rates are declining in almost all countries, at present and in the near future, older people only make up a small proportion of the population in many developing countries. The fact that these countries tend to be concentrated in the global South adds a broader regional dimension to these analyses. Thus international or intraregional variation sit alongside inter-regional patterns which partition the world in the relatively more aged and less aged populations. This is reflected in many of the policy discourses pertaining to these regions. As noted earlier the Millennium Development Goals neglect any mention of older people as a key group and are instead overwhelmingly focused on children and those of working age. Conversely the issues of pensions and 'old age' care feature largely in Europe and North American politics. These twin discourses reflect and reinforce the different time-spaces of ageing and later life in the economically more- and less-prosperous world(s). These analyses are also important as they caution us from wrongly extrapolating from one indicator, life expectancy, to another, population ageing. They also point to problem of treating demographic trends as static and politically neutral. Rises in life expectancy might stall or even reverse, as they did in Russia after the fall of Communism, due to economic shocks and/or poor health behaviours, notably alcoholism.

This uneven 'bioscape' of population ageing is an important corrective to a rather simplistic view which treats population ageing as a uniform global phenomenon and draws our attention to the impact that different spatial formations have on the experience and expectations of later life around the world. This is important given that it sets up a number of the key demographic parameters that drive and to some extent are driven by the impact of population ageing. Hence, from the World Report on Health and Ageing and the most recent Global Burden of Disease statistics we also see highly regionalised patterns of morbidity and mortality. This again shows us that, far from a global time-space of health in later life, we see a largely divided world in which older people in the more advanced industrial economies are much more likely to die from non-communicable diseases while those in the developing world are subject to a double burden of disease with both communicable and non-communicable diseases presenting threats to life.

Similar regional patterns are identifiable across the 'financescapes' of later life when we look at the data on labour market participation. Our analyses extended those done elsewhere (see Kohli and Rein 1991, Hofäcker 2010) by looking outside of the advanced industrial economies of the OECD or EU region in order to explore these trends more clearly. The results show a clear distinction between the global North and the global South. This bifurcation, with people working much later in life in the developing world, is reflected in a dual discourse in which the aim in the North is to encourage older workers to work longer, while in the South there is real concern that older workers do not have the opportunity to retire. However, even within the more advanced industrialised economies the pattern is neither completely homogenous nor completely fragmented. Here there is tacit support for Esping-Andersen's (1990) typology of welfare regimes. Countries in the social democratic category tend to have higher rates of labour market participation in later life as one would expect from their more state interventionist approach and greater commitment to labour market activation programmes. In opposition to this, the corporatist countries could be classified as being part of an 'early exit' regime. There is also evidence that the East Asian countries have a similarly high rate of LMP in later life. Although these countries fall outside Esping-Andersen's original formulation these data, along with the relatively low levels of spending on healthcare in these countries, do fit with a classification of the productivist-welfare regime (Hort and Kuhnle 2000, Gough 2001). Again, data add additional support to the argument that different political and welfare structures produce different responses to the issue of population ageing. Furthermore, they demonstrate that there are a number of regional time-spaces which sit alongside those of the nation and set specific constraints on policy direction and change.

The overlap between these regional bioscapes and financescapes is most clearly seen in the data for the former communist economies of East and Central Europe. In these countries poverty and poor health are still the dominant experience for older people. In many respects ageing and later life in these countries continue to be constructed along modernist spatial and temporal lines. The data from these countries offers some of the most convincing evidence for the existence of regional dynamics of later life. While the patterns for self-rated health, disability and poverty are generally marked by a wide degree of international variation with very little global or regional homogeneity, this part of the world stands out as the exception. Moreover, despite having rates of life expectancy and LME that are comparable to their Western European neighbours, older people from the former Soviet Union and Eastern Bloc countries are grouped at the most disadvantaged end of the distribution on health and wellbeing. This finding is interesting as, unlike the EU or ASEAN, there are no longer any formal regional political or economic institutions that unite these countries. In fact, an increasing number are to be found within the EU. Nonetheless, it is clear that older people in these countries share a common set of experiences which lends support to the new regionalist argument that present day regions are greater than their associated political institutions (Hettne 2005).

Finally, these global and regional patterns are overlaid with high levels of international variation. This is particularly noticeable when we consider older people's subjective accounts of their situation along a number of different dimensions. Despite the clear evidence for distinct regional patterns of mortality and morbidity, we need to be cautious not to read off other aspects of the bioscapes of ageing from these demographic patterns. The evidence shows that these do not neatly intersect with older people's attitudes to health. Here these regional patterns are largely crosscut by national differences, strongly suggesting that subjective assessments of health in later life are highly culture-bound and that older people draw on a range of social comparisons from within their own country to make sense of their health. Following on from this and despite having relatively low life expectancy and higher rates of morbidity, older people in India have the highest rate of very good self-rated health. This may be due to some form of survivor effect: compared to those who did not survive into later life, those who did survive rate their health as good. This reinforces the need to contextualise the meaning of health in later life within a national cultural framework in most cases. We see similar apparently contradictory spatial patterns operating across the financescapes too. Notwithstanding our earlier observation regarding the uniformly negative assessment of financial wellbeing among older people living in the former Soviet bloc countries, subjective assessments of income satisfaction in later life appear to be highly dependent on one's national cultural context. This leads to the seemingly anomalous situation that in countries where older people appear to be objectively worse off they report that they are highly satisfied with their income. Again this leads us to conclude that they are taking the national, rather than the global, context as their normative horizon when making social comparisons. Hence older people in Ecuador are probably not comparing their income situation with their peers in the USA when they say that they are largely satisfied with their income but are perhaps comparing it to previous generations who did not have access to a social pension.

The spatial limits to globalisation and the continued salience of national time-spaces are clearest when looking at the impact of the material dimensions of globalisation on the conditions of ageing and later life. It is clear that global actors have not created a 'race to the bottom' in the services and institutions that aim to ensure the wellbeing of older people. Rather there are still wide international variations in spending on healthcare, rates of labour market participation and pension provision. The evidence clearly shows that exposure to economic openness has little or no impact on these aspects. These findings are in line with the historical institutionalist argument that welfare institutions create a set of path dependencies that achieve a certain degree of inertia over time. When one considers that the pension and healthcare systems in some of the advanced industrialised economies have been in existence, in some form or another, for over 100 years such a conclusion makes sense. It seems that national governments still have a good deal of discretion in determining how and where to spend their money. Moreover, there is some evidence that high social spending and economic openness are quite compatible. This international variation is also partially overlaid with 'regional' patterns. The data on healthcare spending show that at the extreme ends of the distribution on expenditure and privatisation there are identifiable clusters of countries among the Scandinavian, North American and Asian regions. Thus when we look at spending on pensions and the make-up of pension income, such regional or welfare clusters are much less evident than they are for rates of labour market participation in later life. Here the picture is clearly one of international variation. There is very little regional homogeneity between countries who share similar welfare structures, such as Sweden and Denmark. However, these international, or intraregional, differences do not appear to be the product of direct global economic flows. Exposure to economic globalisation appears to be unrelated to social expenditure on pensions or to their composition. Yet this does not mean that they are unaffected by global actors, or more precisely by 'global' discourses on ageing. As noted above there is evidence that it is the activities of a number of epistemic communities that have had a greater impact on population ageing, through the setting agendas and/or policy goals, than the more material aspects of globalisation that are usually mentioned. As a result, the evidence from across all these different arenas allows us to argue that we have yet to enter a global time-space. This is not to deny that globalisation is a real phenomenon, but rather to posit that it is not the dominant spatial logic. Neither is it inevitable or irreversible. A closer examination of economic, cultural and political life reveals a far more complex pattern that cannot be simply examined through the binary distinction of national versus global planes. The world and the action that takes place within it is a mosaic of different, sometimes competing, sometimes cooperating, spatial logics. The global and the national operate alongside the local and the regional. Each spatiality has its own set of logics as well as its own actors. The relations between them may continually shift, but none can be said to be reducible to the others.

Here be monsters: theorising later life in a global era

These conclusions raise a number of empirical and theoretical challenges for gerontology. We would argue that these can be rather crudely summarised in the answers to three broad questions: 1) Where are we measuring? 2) What are we measuring? 3) What are we analysing? Turning to the first of these it is clear that at present any attempt to analyse the state of the global ageing population is constrained by the spatial limits in data coverage. While there have been some real strides forward in this area, such as the Survey of Global Ageing (SAGE) and the work done by HelpAge International in the creation of their Global Age Watch Index, there are still many countries where we do not have much or any data on the experiences of ageing and later life. This is not to overlook the many good studies done with older people in Africa and other less developed regions. Yet the great majority of these are small-scale, qualitative studies. While these are immensely valuable, for example in demonstrating the complexity of family relations in these countries (see Aboderin 2004b), their limited scope and the lack of a standardised set of questions make it very difficult to draw comparisons with older people in other countries. For our analyses we have been fortunate to be able to use data from a number of more 'global' surveys, the ISSP and WVS, which include some middle and lower income countries. However, these are general population surveys, rather than surveys of older people. As a result, in countries with low rates of population ageing, it is often difficult to get sufficiently large numbers of older people into surveys to have any confidence in statistical analyses. Hence, although throughout the book we have made every effort to ensure that data were presented from as wide a range of countries as possible, it is simply the case that very few cross-national studies include countries from Africa or Central Asia. This is a potentially serious drawback when trying to conduct comparative research in order to draw conclusions about the nature of ageing and later life around the world. An additional consideration relates to the balance of breadth and depth of analyses. This is reflected in our decision throughout the book to look at older people in as many countries as possible. But this has been at the expense of looking at social-demographic variations, such as gender and social class, among the older population and how these might intersect with different spatialities. It also has to be acknowledged that because our aim was to explore these 'global' dynamics a certain degree of depth has had to be sacrificed to achieve maximum breadth. This it is potentially problematic given that it possibly ascribes a false homogeneity to older people living in different countries. We are unable to see, for example, if older women in different countries have more in common with each other than they have with men in their own countries, or whether or not there are gendered forms of globalisation. We fully recognise that these are important issues that hopefully can be explored in the future. Thus our first challenge as gerontologists must be to extend the breadth and depth of data collection about ageing and later life to encompass all countries around the world.

Our second challenge is to be clear about what it is we are measuring. A common argument of much of the more recent gerontological literature is that contemporary patterns of ageing call for a reassessment of the frames we use to study later life (Phillipson 1998, Gilleard and Higgs 2000, 2005, Metz and Underwood 2005, Jones et al 2008). This does not merely entail extending the field of enquiry to include areas such as leisure, consumption and lifestyle, but requires us to critically reflect on the utility of the definitions used to identify older people themselves. As Harper and Laws (1995: 200) noted 'the age variable itself, its social and spatial construction' is a key concern within geographical gerontology. A central issue that appears throughout the book is the problematic nature of the measurement of later life. In line with both critical and cultural gerontology, we have shown that the temporalities of later life in late or reflexive modernity have become more unstable, more complex and more varied. Although it might be premature to declare the complete collapse of the modernist life course it is fairly apparent that the sociodemographic indicators that have previously been used to demarcate the boundary between mid and late life have become decoupled from one another, and from chronological age. Older, modernist temporalities of decline and finitude have been replaced by more open, positive, but also contingent, temporalities of renewal. The transformation of the sociodemographic markers of later life, such as health, retirement and poverty, has been reflexively incorporated in to the world views of older people themselves. This is seen in the data on the subjective assessment of the onset and characteristics of old age. The markers by which older people seek to fix or locate these boundaries are themselves mobile and subject to change. Yet the shifting and contested discourses around the age of retirement and the rapid growth of anti-ageing technologies provide a very unstable basis on which to fashion a new life course. Almost as soon as new parameters are established, they dissolve to be replaced by new goals and ever more fantastic potentialities. Hence regardless of which of the dimensions of ageing that are considered, it is clear that chronological age is a poor indictor for later life. The shift to a more pluralistic set of identities and lifestyles, as well as the increasing malleability of later life indicate that these methodological challenges are also theoretical challenges too. Hence there is an evident tension in the book between an awareness of these issues and our reliance on chronological age for many of our analyses. This is a product of the continued absence of alternative measures of age in many large-scale surveys and official statistics, despite evidence that older people often actively employ alternative temporal schema, such as subjective age, cognitive age and desired age to locate themselves. This issue is not confined to our analyses but takes on an added saliency when undertaking international comparisons as it raises additional questions about whether the meaning of being aged 60 differs for someone who lives in a country with a life expectancy of 65 compared with someone who lives in a country where they can expect to live to 80 or 90 years of age. Consequently, we need to adopt a much more critical perspective when we are forced to rely on chronological age as well as lobbying for survey organisers to include alternative measures of age when conducting cross-national studies.

The third challenge relates how we treat space in our analyses. As we hope to have shown we are not advocating an abandonment of the nation state as a meaningful spatial frame through which to understand ageing and later life. Rather, we are arguing that we need to develop better theoretical and empirical models that can deal with the complexity of multiple spatialities as well as the interrelationships between them. From a social gerontology perspective this means that we should not rush to discard the nation state as a key focus of study. It does mean, however, that we do need a new vocabulary or set of analogies to describe its present incarnations. Urry (2002), drawing on Bauman's dichotomous representations of the state as either 'gamekeeper' or 'gardener', argues that we have returned to the state as gamekeeper due to the complex mobilities which render the ability of the nation state to control flows, objects and information relatively ineffectual. However, the image of the gamekeeper is imperfect so long as it relies on the notion that the state still presides over a distinct geographical area (the grounds). The analyses presented throughout the book illustrate the argument that this is no longer the case. Today the state has to manage not only the flows within its borders, but has itself become fluid; managing relations and people through a range of bilateral, multilateral and international policies. If, therefore, we are looking for a new agricultural analogy, maybe the 'cowboy state' would be a better choice. Here the state has a 'loose' control over its mobile mass, while itself being increasingly mobile. Under such circumstances, it retains loose control over the general direction of travel (mainly through reactive policies at the national and supranational levels) but it cannot control the herd in all circumstances. In this analogy the state loses some cattle, gains others and has some stolen, while all the time it is constantly at risk of a stampede. For all its insights, it could be argued that this analogy also has its drawbacks as it suggests a largely free floating state untethered to others. This is also not the case in the real world. Instead, the data, most notably those on medical tourism, suggest that the 'plastic state' might be a better term to denote a state that shifts its juridical borders in expectation and response to global flows. While the search for analogies is certain to go on, it is equally true that we need to be constantly more critical about what the 'national' spaces (for example, political, juridical, geographical, and so on) are when we look at how state agencies extend their reach beyond the confines of the nation.

The need for more nuanced models is perhaps most clearly illustrated when looking at the activities of the various epistemic communities. These have been critical for our understanding of the shifting landscapes of ageing and later life in this book. If we were to limit our analyses to one spatial frame, for example the global, we would miss the complex interplay between different actors operating at different scales. The analyses show that these are incredibly important networks which connect actors across a range of organisations and spatial levels. In so doing they operate as multi-layered spatial assemblages of power seeking to project their vision for ageing and later life. The way in which these networks come together, their membership and their means of operation are crucial issues for gerontology. In particular, we should aim to understand the relationships between members of these communities and how they seek to capture the roles of key actors operating across different spatialities. While certain actors may be more central to particular communities they must also mobilise actors at other levels to ensure their own success. It is clear from the three examples of epistemic communities used in this book that each of them has been able to achieve a high degree of alignment and include actors from every scale who share similar goals. It is also clear that when they fail to recruit actors within a certain scale, as was noted in the IEG report on the activities of the new pension orthodoxy (Andrews 2006), they are also largely unable to realise their goals. Therefore, rather than seeing the relationships between these actors in reductionist terms, they are best seen as 'elective affinities', to borrow a term from Albrow (1996).

Ultimately, our conclusions are relatively simple. It is a paradox that as population structures become more homogenous, the experience of ageing and later life becomes more heterogeneous. There has definitely been a collapse of chronological age as a meaningful marker for the identification of old age within social gerontology. There is no longer a single spatial or temporal fix for its understanding. It has become much more contingent and fluid. Alongside this, the economic, political and cultural coordinates of later life have also become increasingly located in a series of overlapping spatial logics and temporal frames. It is therefore a problem that present approaches to globalisation within social gerontology have been often too narrowly focused on either the global or the (inter)national to be able to explore the complex ways in which these different spatialities, along with those of the regional and the local, interconnect to produce specific spatial (and temporal) constellations. If this book has had one implicit overriding aim, it has been to re-orientate the gerontological understanding of globalisation so that it can better address these complex and interlocking levels that provide much of the context of contemporary later life.

References

Aboderin, I. (2004a). 'Decline in material family support for older people in Urban Ghana, Africa: Understanding processes and causes of change.' *Journals of Gerontology Series B-Psychological Sciences and Social Sciences* **59**(3): S128–S137.

Aboderin, I. (2004b). 'Modernisation and ageing theory revisited: Current explanations of recent developing world and historical Western shifts in material family support for older people.' *Ageing and Society* **24**: 29–50.

Adema, W., P. Fron and M. Ladaique (2011). 'Is the European Welfare State Really More Expensive? Indicators on Social Spending, 1980–2012.' *OECD Social, Employment and Migration Working Papers No. 124.*

Agheyisi R. (2013). *Cosmeceuticals: Products and global markets.* BCC Research, Wellesley.

Albert, S. M. and M. G. Cattell (1994). Family relationships of the elderly: Living arrangements. *Old Age in a Global Perspective: Cross-cultural and cross-national views.* S. M. Albert and M. G. Cattell. New York, G.K Hall & Co.

Albrow, M. (1996). *The Global Age.* Stanford, CA: Standford University Press.

Alderson, A. S. (2004). 'Explaining the upswing in direct investment: A test of mainstream and heterodox theories of globalization.' *Social Forces* **83**(1): 81–122.

Aldous, J. (1962). 'Urbanization, the extended family and kinship ties in West Africa.' *Social Forces* **41**: 6–12.

Allan, J. P., and Scruggs, L. (2004). Political partisanship and welfare state reform in advanced industrial societies. *American Journal of Political Science*, **48**(3), 496-512.

Allen, S., S. Beales, D. Busolo, F. Clark, C. Eldridge, O. Gonzalez, M. Gorman, C. Hall, A. Heslop, P. Hinchliff, A. Humphreys, J. James, C. López-Clavero, L. McGowan, J. Pannirselvam and K. Peachey (2002). *The state of the world's older people 2002.* London: Help Age International.

Alley, D. E., N. M. Putney, M. Rice and V. L. Bengtson (2010). 'The Increasing Use of Theory in Social Gerontology: 1990–2004.' *The Journals of Gerontology Series B: Psychological Sciences and Social Sciences* **65B**(5): 583–590.

Althusser, L. (1969). *For Marx.* London: Verso.

American Society for Aesthetic Plastic Surgery (ASAPS) (2006). *Cosmetic surgery national data bank statistics.* New York: ASAPS Communications Office.

ASAPS (2009). *Cosmetic surgery national data bank statistics.* New York: ASAPS Communications Office.

An, J. Y., K. An, L. O'Connor and S. Wexler (2008). 'Life satisfaction, self-esteem, and perceived health status among elder Korean women: Focus on living arrangements.' *Journal of Transcultural Nursing* **19**(2): 151–160.

Ana Aslan International Foundation. (2010). Our Philiosophy. www.brainageing.ro

Anderson, B. (2004). *Imagined Communities: Reflections on the Origin and Spread of Nationalism.* London: Verso.

Anderson, M. (1971). *Family structure in 19th century Lancashire.* Cambridge: Cambridge University Press.

Andrade, F. C. D., P. E. Guevara, M. L. Lebrao, Y. A. D. Duarte and J. L. F. Santos (2010). 'Gender Differences in Life Expectancy and Disability-Free Life Expectancy Among Older Adults in Sao Paulo, Brazil.' *Womens Health Issues* **21**(1): 64–70.

Andrews, E. S. (2006). *Pension reform and the development of pension systems. An evaluation of World Bank assistance.* Washington DC: World Bank.

Angus, J. and P. Reeve (2006). 'Ageism: A threat to 'Aging well' in the 21st century.' *Journal of Applied Gerontology* **25**(2): 137–152.

Annual Survey of Hours and Earnings (2010). 'Annual Survey of Hours and Earnings 2010.' www.statistics.gov.uk

Antonovsky, A. (1968). 'Social class and the major cardiovascular diseases.' *Journal of Chronic Diseases* **21**: 65–106.

Appadurai, A. (1996). *Modernity at large: Cultural dimensions of globalization.* Minneapolis: University of Minnesota Press.

Arita, T. and P. McCann (2002). 'The spatial and hierarchical organization of Japanese and US multinational semiconductor firms.' *Journal of International Management* **8**: 121–39.

ASEAN Cosmetics (2007). 'ASEAN Cosmetics Association.' www.aseancosmetics.org

Askham, J., D. Ferring and G. Lamnra (2007). Personal relationships in later life. *Ageing in society: 3rd edition.* J. Bond, S. Peace, F. Dittmann-Kohli and G. J. Westerhof. London: Sage, pp. 186–208.

Asquith, N. (2009). 'Positive ageing, neoliberalism and Australian sociology.' *Journal of Sociology* **45**(3): 255–69.

Australian Bureau of Statistics. (2011). '6530.0 Household Expenditure Survey, Australia: Detailed Expenditure Items, 2009–10.' www.abs.gov.au/AUSSTATS/abs@.nsf/DetailsPage/6530.02009–10?OpenDocument

Baars, J. (2015). 'Time in late modern ageing.' *Routledge Handbook of Cultural Gerontology*. J. Twigg and W. Martin. London: Routledge, pp. 397–403.

Bain, R. (1945). 'The ages of man.' *American Sociological Review* **10**: 97–103.

Balaban, V. and C. Marano (2010). 'Medical tourism research: A systematic review.' *International Journal of Infectious Diseases* **14**: e135.

Balestat, G. and G. Lafortune (2007). 'Trends in severe disability among elderly people: assessing the evidence in 12 OECD countries and the future implications.' *OECD Health Working Papers*, 26. OECD. Paris: OECD.

Bambra, C., G. Netuveli and T. A. Eikemo (2010). 'Welfare State Regime Life Courses: The Development of Western European Welfare State Regimes and Age-Related Patterns of Educational Inequalities in Self-Reported Health.' *International Journal of Health Services* **40**(3): 399–420.

Banerjee, S., S. Nath, N. Dey and H. Eto (2015). 'Global Medical Tourism: A Review' in H. Eto (ed), *New Business Opportunities in the Growing E-Tourism Industry*. Hershey, PA: IGI Global: 114–31.

Barak, B. (1987). 'Cognitive Age - A New Multidimensional Approach to Measuring Age Identity.' *International Journal of Aging & Human Development* **25**(2): 109–28.

Barak, B. (2009). 'Age identity: A cross-cultural global approach.' *International Journal of Behavioral Development* **33**(1): 2–11.

Barak, B. and S. Gould (1985). 'Alternative Age Measures - A Research Agenda.' *Advances in Consumer Research* **12**: 53–8.

Baran, P. and P. Sweezy (1966). *Monopoly Capital: An Essay on the American Economic and Social Order*. New York: Monthly Review Press.

Barcelona European Council (2002). *Presidency conclusions*. Brussels: EU.

Bardage, C., S. M. F. Pluijm, N. L. Pedersen, D. J. H. Deeg, M. Jylhä, M. Noale, T. Blumstein and Á. Otero (2005). 'Self-rated health among older adults: a cross-national comparison.' *European Journal of Ageing* **2**(2): 149–58.

Bardasi, E., S. P. Jenkins and J. A. Rigg (2002). 'Retirement and the income of older people: a British perspective.' *Ageing and Society* **22**: 131–59.

Barker, G. and R. Hancock (2000). 'The income dimension' in D. Hirsch (ed), *Life after 50: Issues for policy and research*. York: Joseph Rowntree Foundation, pp. 44–91.

Bass, S. and J. Caro (2001). 'Productive aging: A conceptual framework.' in (eds), *Productive aging. Concepts and challenges*. Baltimore, MD: John Hopkins University Press, pp. 37–78.

Baudrillard, J. (1989). *From Marxism to Postmodernism and beyond*. Cambridge: Polity Press.

Bauman, Z. (1998). *Globalization. The human consequences*. Cambridge: Polity Press.

Bauman, Z. (2000). *Liquid Modernity*. Cambridge: Polity Press.

Bauman, Z. (2001). *The Individualized Society*. Cambridge: Polity Press.

Bauman, Z. (2007). *Liquid Times. Living in an age of uncertainty*. Cambridge: Polity Press.

Bauman, Z. (2013). *Legislators and interpreters: On modernity, post-modernity and intellectuals*. New Jersey: John Wiley & Sons.

BBC (2006). 'Baby boom sets Japan '2007 problem'.' news.bbc.co.uk/1/hi/world/asia-pacific/5263514.stm

Beard, J. and C. Petitot (2010). 'Ageing and Urbanization: Can Cities be Designed to Foster Active Ageing?' *Public Health Reviews* **32**: 427–50.

Beck, U. (1999). *What is globalization?* Cambridge: Polity Press.

Beck, U. (2002). 'The Cosmopolitan Society and its Enemies.' *Theory, Culture & Society* **19**: 17–44.

Beck, U. and C. Lau (2005). 'Second modernity as a research agenda: theoretical and empirical explorations in the 'meta-change' of modern society.' *British Journal of Sociology* **56**(4): 525–57.

Beeson, M. (2005). 'Rethinking regionalism: Europe and East Asia in comparative historical perspective.' *Journal of European Public Policy* **12**(6): 969–85.

Belfield, C., J. Cribb, A. Hood and R. Joyce (2014). *Living standards, poverty and inequality in the UK: 2014*. London: Institute for Fiscal Studies.

Belsky, D. W., A. Caspi, R. Houts, H. J. Cohen, D. L. Corcoran, A. Danese, H. Harrington, S. Israel, M. E. Levine, J. D. Schaefer, K. Sugden, B. Williams, A. I. Yashin, R. Poulton and T. E. Moffitt (2015). 'Quantification of biological aging in young adults.' *Proceedings of the National Academy of Sciences* **112**(30): E4104–E4110.

Ben-Shlomo, Y. and D. Kuh (2002). 'A life course approach to chronic disease epidemiology: conceptual models, empirical challenges and interdisciplinary perspectives.' *International Journal of Epidemiology* **31**(2): 285–93.

Bengtson, V. L., E. O. Burgess and T. M. Parrott (1997). 'Theory, Explanation, and a Third Generation of Theoretical Development in Social Gerontology.' *The Journals of Gerontology Series B: Psychological Sciences and Social Sciences* **52B**(2): S72–S88.

Benner, M. (2003). 'The Scandinavian challenge – The future of advanced welfare states in the knowledge economy.' *Acta Sociologica* **46**(2): 132–49.

Berger, P. L. (2002). 'The Cultural Dynamics of Globalization' in (eds), *Many Globalizations. Cultural Diversity in the Contemporary World*. New York: Oxford University Press, pp. 1–16.

Bernard, M. and J. Phillips (2000). 'The challenge of ageing in tomorrow's Britain.' *Ageing and Society* **20**: 33–54.

Bernard, M., C. Phillipson, J. Phillips and J. Ogg (2001). 'Continuity and change in the family and community life of older people.' *Journal of Applied Gerontology* **20**(3): 259–78.

Berney, L. R. and D. B. Blane (1997). 'Collecting retrospective data: Accuracy of recall after 50 years judged against historical records.' *Social Science & Medicine* **45**(10): 1519–25.

Beyeler, M. (2003). 'Globalization, Europeanization and domestic state reforms. New institutionalist concepts.' *Global Social Policy* 3: 153–72.

Bhabha, H. K. (1994). *The Location of Culture*. London: Routledge.

Biggiero, L. (2006). 'Industrial and knowledge relocation strategies under the challenges of globalization and digitalization: the move of small and medium enterprises among territorial systems.' *Entrepreneurship and Regional Development* **18**(6): 443–71.

Biggs, S. (2001). 'Toward critical narrativity - Stories of aging in contemporary social policy.' *Journal of Aging Studies*, **15**(4): 303–316.

Biggs, S. (2004). 'Age, gender, narratives, and masquerades.' *Journal of Aging Studies* **18**(1): 45–58.

Biggs, S., C. Phillipson, A. M. Money and R. Leach (2006). 'The age-shift: Observations on social policy, ageism and the dynamics of the adult lifecourse.' *Journal of Social Work Practice* 20(3): 239–50.

Binstock, R. H. (2003). 'The war on 'anti-aging medicine'.' *Gerontologist* **43**(1): 4–14.

Binstock, R. H., J. R. Fishman and T. E. Johnson (2006). 'Anti-Aging Medicine and Science. Social Implications' in (eds), *Handbook of Aging and the Social Sciences*, 6th edition. London: Academic Press, pp. 437–57.

Blackburn, R. (2002). *Banking on death*. London: Verso.

Blackburn, R. (2012). *Age Shock: How Finance is Failing Us*. London: Verso Books.

Blair, C. (2014). *Securing Pension Provision: The Challenge of Reforming the Age of Entitlement*. Houndmills: Palgrave Macmillan.

Blane, D., L. Berney, G. D. Smith, D. J. Gunnell and P. Holland (1999). 'Reconstructing the life course: health during early old age in a follow-up study based on the Boyd Orr cohort.' *Public Health* **113**(3): 117–24.

Blane, D., C. Gilleard, P. Higgs, M. Hyde and D. Wiggins (2004). 'Third age consumerism: The relative influence of class of origin versus class at labor market exit.' *Gerontologist* **44**: 512.

Blane, D., P. Higgs, M. Hyde and R. D. Wiggins (2004). 'Life course influences on quality of life in early old age.' *Social Science & Medicine* **58**(11): 2171–9.

Blomström, M., S. Globerman and A. Kokko (2000). 'Regional integration and foreign direct investment. Some general issues' in J. H. Dunning (ed), *Regions, globalization and the knowledge-based economy*. Oxford: Oxford University Press, pp. 109–30.

Blossfeld, H. P., S. Buchholz and D. Hofäcker (2006). *Globalization, uncertainty and late careers in society*. Oxford: Routledge.

Blundell, R. and I. Preston (1998). 'Consumption inequality and income uncertainty.' *Quarterly Journal of Economics* **113**(2): 603–40.

Bone, M. (1995). *Trends in dependency among older people living in England*. London: OPCS.

Bongaarts, J. and Z. Zimmer (2001). *Living arrangements of older adults in the developing world: An analysis of the DHS household surveys*. Washington DC: World Bank Policy Research Division.

Bongaarts, J. and Z. Zimmer (2002). 'Living arrangements of older adults in the developing world: An analysis of demographic and health survey household surveys.' *Journals of Gerontology Series B-Psychological Sciences and Social Sciences* **57**(3): S145-S157.

Borghans, L. and B. ter Weel (2002). 'Do older workers have more trouble using a computer than younger workers?' *The Economics of Skills Obsolescence* **21**: 139–73.

Borsch, X. (2002). 'Two billion people older than 60 years by 2050, warns UN Secretary General.' *The Lancet* **359**: 1321.

Bowling, A. (2006). 'Lay perceptions of successful ageing: findings from a national survey of middle aged and older adults in Britain.' *European Journal of Ageing* **3**: 123–36.

Bowling, A. and P. Dieppe (2005). 'What is successful ageing and who should define it?' *British Medical Journal* **331**(7531): 1548–51.

Boyle, P. (1994). 'Metropolitan Out-Migration in England And Wales, 1980–81.' *Urban Studies* **31**(10): 1707–22.

Bradley, D. E. (2011). 'Litwak and Longino's Developmental Model of Later-Life Migration: Evidence From the American Community Survey, 2005–2007.' *Journal of Applied Gerontology* **30**(2): 141–58.

Bradley, D. E., C. F. Longino, E. P. Stoller and W. H. Haas (2008). 'Actuation of mobility intentions among the young-old: An event-history analysis.' *Gerontologist* **48**(2): 190–202.

Brandt, F., A. Cazzaniga and M. Hann (2011). 'Cosmeceuticals: Current Trends and Market Analysis.' *Seminars in Cutaneous Medical Surgery* **30**: 141–3.

Braudel, F. (1993). *A History of Civilizations*. London: Penguin.

Braudel, F. (2002). *The wheels of commerce. Civilization and capitalism 15th-18th century. Volume 2*. London: Orion House.

Braverman, H. (1976). *Labor and Monopoly Capital: The Degradation of Work in the Twentieth Century*. New York: Monthly Review Press.

Breeze, E., D. Jones, P. Wilkinson, C. Bulpitt, C. Grundy, A. Latif and A. Fletcher (2005). 'Area deprivation, social class, and quality of life among people aged 75 years and over in Britain.' *International Journal of Epidemiology* **34**(2): 276–83.

Brenner, N. (2004). *New State Spaces: Urban Governance and the Rescaling of Statehood*. Oxford: Oxford University Press.

Brittain, K., L. Corner, L. Robinson and J. Bond (2010). 'Ageing in place and technologies of place: the lived experience of people with dementia in changing social, physical and technological environments.' *Sociology of Health & Illness* **32**(2): 272–87.

Bromley, D. (1981). *The Psychology of Human Ageing*. London: Pelican.

Brown, N. (2003). 'Under one roof: The evolving story of three generation housing in Japan' in (eds), *Demographic change and the family in Japan's aging society*. New York: SUNY, p. 53–72.

Buffel, T., C. Phillipson and T. Scharf (2012). 'Ageing in urban environments: Developing 'age-friendly' cities.' *Critical Social Policy* **32**(4): 597–617.

Burgoon, B. (2001). Globalization and welfare compensation: disentangling the ties that bind. *International Organization*, **55**(3), 509-551.

Burt, S. and M. Gabbott (1995). 'The elderly consumer and non-food purchase behaviour.' *European Journal of Marketing* **29**(2): 43–57.

Busch, K. (2010). World Economic Crisis and the Welfare State. International Policy Analysis. Friedrich Ebert Stiftung. Berlin. http://library.fes.de/pdf-files/id/ipa/07000.pdf

Buzan, B. and O. Wæver (2003). *Regions and powers: the structure of international security*. Cambridge: Cambridge University Press.

Cagney, K. A., C. R. Browning and M. Wen (2005). 'Racial Disparities in Self-Rated Health at Older Ages: What Difference Does the Neighborhood Make?' *The Journals of Gerontology Series B: Psychological Sciences and Social Sciences* **60**(4): S181–S190.

Calasanti, T. (2003). 'Work and retirement in the 21st century: Integrating issues of diversity and globalization.' *Ageing International* **28**: 3–20.

Cardarelli, R., J. Sefton and L. J. Kotlikoff (1999). *Generational accounting in the UK*. London: NIESR.

Carmel, E., K. Hamblin and T. Papadopoulos (2007). 'Governing the activation of older workers in the European Union: The construction of the 'activated retiree'.' *International Journal of Sociology and Social Policy* **27**(9/10): 387–400.

Carrera, P. and N. Lunt (2010). 'A European perspective on medical tourism: The need for a knowledge base.' *International Journal of Health Services* **40**: 469–84.

Carrigan, M. and I. Szmigin (2000). 'Advertising in an ageing society.' *Ageing and Society* **20**: 217–33.

Casey, B. and A. Yamada (2002). *Getting older, getting poorer? A study of the earnings, pensions, assets and living arrangements of older people in nine countries*. Paris: OECD.

Castells, M. (2000). 'Materials for an exploratory theory of the network society.' *British Journal of Sociology* **51**(1): 5–24.

Chan, A. (1997). 'An overview of the living arrangements and social support exchanges of older Singaporeans.' *Asia Pac Popul J* **12**(4): 35–50.

Cheung, C. K. and K. K. Leung (2007). 'Relating social welfare to life satisfaction in the postmodern era of Hong Kong.' *Social Indicators Research* **84**(1): 53–70.

Choi, C. M. and D. S. Berson (2006). 'Cosmeceuticals.' *Seminars in Cutaneous Medicine and Survery* **25**: 163–8.

Chou, K. L. (2007). 'Cross-border retirement migration plan in Hong Kong middle-aged adults.' *Habitat International* **31**(3–4): 366–74.

Chou, K. L., N. W. S. Chow and I. Chi (2006). 'Economic status of the elderly in Hong Kong – Homogeneous or heterogeneous?' *International Social Work* **49**(2): 218–32.

Chung, S. and S. J. Park (2008). 'Successful ageing among low-income older people in South Korea.' *Ageing & Society* **28**: 1061–74.

Cini, M. (2007). 'Introduction' in M. Cini (ed), *European Union politics*. Oxford: Oxford University Press, pp. 1–10.

Clapson, M. (2003). *Suburban century: social change and urban growth in England and the United States*. Oxford: Berg.

Clark, W. A. V. and K. White (1990). 'Modeling elderly mobility.' *Environment and Planning A* **22**(7): 909–24.

Clarke, J. (2001). 'Globalization and welfare states. Some unsettling thoughts' in (eds), *Globalization and European welfare states. Challenges and change.* Houndmills: Palgrave, pp. 19–37.

Clarke, L. H. and M. Griffin (2008). 'Visible and invisible ageing: beauty work as a response to ageism.' *Ageing & Society* **28**: 653–74.

Clarke, L. H., M. Griffin and K. Maliha (2009). 'Bat wings, bunions, and turkey wattles: body transgressions and older women's strategic clothing choices.' *Ageing & Society* **29**: 709–26.

Cloke, P. (1985). 'Counterurbanisation: a rural perspective.' *Geoforum* **70**: 13–23.

Cloutier-Fisher, D. and J. Harvey (2009). 'Home beyond the house: Experiences of place in an evolving retirement community.' *Journal of Environmental Psychology* **29**(2): 246–55.

Cohen, L. (1994). 'Old-Age – Cultural and Critical Perspectives.' *Annual Review of Anthropology* **23**: 137–58.

Cohen, R. and P. Kennedy (2007). *Global sociology.* 2nd edition. Houndmills: Palgrave.

Committee on Ageing Issues. (2006). *Report on the Ageing Population.* Singapore. http://app.msf.gov.sg/Portals/0/Summary/research/CAI_report.pdf

Cooper, M. (2006). 'Resuscitations: Stem Cells and the Crisis of Old Age.' *Body & Society* **12**(1): 1–23.

Cosmetics Design (2010). 'Cosmetics Design.' www.cosmeticsdesign.com

Cosmetic, Toiletry & Perfumery Association (CTPA). (2016). GB Market Statistics Overview. http://www.ctpa.org.uk/content.aspx?pageid=310. Accessed 21/03/2016

Cosmetics Europe (2014). CE Statistics 2014. https://www.cosmeticseurope.eu/publications-cosmetics-europe-association/statistics.html. Accessed 21/03/2016

Coupland, J. (2009). 'Time, the body and the reversibility of ageing: commodifying the decade.' *Ageing & Society* **29**: 953–76.

Cowgill, D. and L. Holmes (1972). *Aging and modernization.* New York: Appleton-Century-Crofts.

Cowgill, D. O. (1974). 'Aging of populations and societies.' *Annals of the American Academy of Political and Social Science* **415**(SEP): 1–18.

Cox, E. and J. Hunter (2015). *Full steam ahead: Business attitudes towards the northern powerhouse.* Manchester: IPPR North.

Cox, K. R. (2004). 'Globalization and the politics of local and regional development: the question of convergence.' *Transactions of the Institute of British Geographers* **29**(2): 179–94.

Crimmins, E. M. (2004). 'Trends in the health of the elderly.' *Annual Review of Public Health* **25**: 79–98.

Crimmins, E. M. and H. Beltran-Sanchez (2011). 'Mortality and Morbidity Trends: Is There Compression of Morbidity?' *Journals of Gerontology Series B-Psychological Sciences and Social Sciences* **66**(1): 75–86.

Crimmins, E. M., M. D. Hayward and Y. Saito (1994). 'Changing Mortality and Morbidity Rates and the Health-Status and Life Expectancy of the Older Population.' *Demography* **31**(1): 159–75.

Crimmins, E. M., Y. Saito and S. L. Reynolds (1997). 'Further evidence on recent trends in the prevalence and incidence of disability among older Americans from two sources: The LSOA and the NHIS.' *Journals of Gerontology Series B-Psychological Sciences and Social Sciences* **52**(2): S59–S71.

Crouch, D. (2015). 'Denmark wants to rebrand part of Sweden as 'Greater Copenhagen'', *The Guardian*, 5 March.Cumming, E. and W. Henry (1961). *Growing Old. The Process of Disengagement*. New York: Basic Books.

Curran, C.-S., S. Bröring and J. Leker (2010). 'Anticipating converging industries using publicly available data.' *Technological Forecasting and Social Change* **77**(3): 385–95.

Cutler, D. M. (2001a). 'Declining disability among the elderly.' *Health Affairs* **20**(6): 11–27.

Cutler, D. M. (2001b). 'The reduction in disability among the elderly.' *Proceedings of the National Academy of Sciences of the United States of America* **98**(12): 6546–7.

Dahlgren, G. (2008). 'Neoliberal reforms in Swedish primary health care: for whom and for what purpose?' *International Journal Of Health Services: Planning, Administration, Evaluation* **38**(4): 697–715.

Daly, M. (2001). *Globalization and the Bismarckian welfare states. Globalization and European welfare states: Challenges and change.* Houndmills, Basingstoke, Hampshire: Palgrave.

Dannefer, D. (2003). 'Cumulative advantage/disadvantage and the life course: Cross-fertilizing age and social science theory.' *Journals of Gerontology Series B-Psychological Sciences and Social Sciences* **58**(6): S327–S337.

Dannefer, D. and R. Settersten (2010). 'The study of the life course: Implications for social gerontology' in D. Dannefer and C. Philipson (eds), *The SAGE handbook of social gerontology*. London: Sage, pp. 3–20.

Danson, M. W. (2007). 'Fuzzy concepts, scanty evidence, policy distance: the case for rigour and policy relevance in critical regional studies.' *Regional Studies* **41**: S175–S190.

Davis, M. (2006). *Planet of Slums*. London: Verso.

de Grey, A. (2010). 'Reaping the Longevity Dividend in Time: Biogerontology Heavyweights Advocate Seeking Late-Onset Interventions Against Aging.' *Rejuvenation Research* **13**(4): 383–5.

De Vos, S. and G. Sandefur (2002). 'Elderly living arrangements in Bulgaria, the Czech Republic, Estonia, Finland, and Romania.' *European Journal of Population-Revue Europeenne De Demographie* **18**(1): 21–38.

De Vroom, B. (2004). 'The shift from early to late exit: Changing institutional conditions and individual preferences. The case of the Netherlands' in (eds), *Ageing and the transition to retirement. A comparative analysis of European welfare states*. Aldershot: Ashgate, pp. 120–54.

Deacon, B. (2007). *Global social policy and governance*. London: Sage.

Demakakos, P., E. Hacker and E. Gjonça (2004). 'Perceptions of ageing' in (eds), *Retirement, health and relationships of the older population in England. The 2004 English Longitudinal Study of Ageing (wave 2)*. London: IFS, pp. 339–68.

Dent, C. M. (2008). 'The Asian Development Bank and developmental regionalism in East Asia.' *Third World Quarterly* **29**(4): 767–86.

Department for Communities and Local Government (2008). *Lifetime Homes, Lifetime Neighbourhoods: A National Strategy for Housing in an Ageing Society*. London: TSO.

Department of Statistics Singapore. (2013). 'Report on the Household Expenditure Survey, 2012/13.' www.singstat.gov.sg/publications/household-expenditure-surveyDepartment of Work and Pensions (2006). *Pensioner's Income Series 2005/6*. London, HMSO.

Department of Work and Pensions (2007). *Pensioner Income Series 2006/7*. London, HMSO.

Desforges, L. (2000). 'Traveling the world – Identity and travel biography.' *Annals of Tourism Research* **27**(4): 926–45.

Desmond, H. J. (2000). 'Older and greyer – third age workers and the labour market.' *The International Journal of Comparative Labour Law and Industrial Relations* **16**: 235–50.

Devine, F. (1992). *Affluent workers revisited: privatism and the working class*. Edinburgh: Edinburgh University Press.

Dex, S. and C. Phillipson (1986). 'Social policy and the older worker' in (eds), *Ageing and social policy. A critical assessment*. Aldershot: Gower, pp. 45–66.

Dicken, P. (2007). *Global Shift: Mapping the Changing Contours of the World Economy*. London: Sage.

Dicken, P., P. F. Kelly, K. Olds and H. Wai-Chung Yeung (2001). 'Chains and networks, territories and scales: towards a relational framework for analysing the global economy.' *Global Networks-a Journal of Transnational Affairs* **1**: 89–112.

Dixon, M. and J. Margo (2006). *Population politics*. London: Institute for Public Policy Research.

Donegan, B. (2006). 'Governmental regionalism: Power/knowledge and neoliberal regional integration in Asia and Latin America.' *Millennium-Journal of International Studies* **35**(1): 23–51.

Dorling, D., J. Rigby, B. Wheeler, D. Ballas, B. Thomas, E. Fahmy, D. Gordon and R. Lupton (2007). *Poverty and wealth across Britain 1968 to 2005*. York: Joseph Rowntree Foundation.

Draelos, Z. D. (2009). 'Cosmeceuticals: undefined, unclassified, and unregulated.' *Clinics in Dermatology* **27**(5): 431–4.

Dreher, A. (2006). 'Does globalization affect growth? Evidence from a new index of globalization.' *Applied Economics* **38**(10): 1091–110.

Dubos, R. (1965). *Man Adapting*. New Haven and London: Yale University Press.

Dunning, J. H. (2000). 'Regions, globalization and the knowledge economy: the issues stated' in J. H. Dunning (ed), *Regions, globalization and the knowledge-based economy*. Oxford: Oxford University Press, pp. 7–41.

Dunning, J. H. (2009). 'Location and the multinational enterprise: A neglected factor?' *Journal of International Business Studies* **40**(1): 5–19.

Dunning, J. H., Y. S. Pak and S. Beldona (2007). 'Foreign ownership strategies of UK and US international franchisors: An exploratory application of Dunning's envelope paradigm.' *International Business Review* **16**(5): 531–48.

Easthope, H. (2009). 'Fixed Identities in a Mobile World? The Relationship Between Mobility, Place, and Identity.' *Identities-Global Studies in Culture and Power* **16**(1): 61–82.

Ebbinghaus, B. (2006). *Reforming early retirement in Europe, Japan and the USA*. Oxford: Oxford University Press.

Economic and Social Commission for Western Asia (2007). *Annual review of developments in globalization and regional integration in the Arab countries 2006*. New York: UN.

Egger, P. and M. Pfaffermayr (2004). 'Foreign direct investment and European integration in the 1990s.' *World Economy* **27**(1): 99–110.

Eisenstadt, S. N. (1999). 'Multiple modernities in an age of globalization.' *Canadian Journal of Sociology-Cahiers Canadiens De Sociologie* **24**(2): 283–95.

Eisenstadt, S. N. (2000). 'Multiple modernities.' *Daedalus* **129**(1): 1–29.

Eisenstadt, S. N. (2002). Some observations on multiple modernities: in Sachsenmaier D, S.N Eisenstadt and J Riedel (eds) *Reflections on Multiple Modernities: European, Chinese and Other Interpretations.* Brill Publishers. Leiden: 27–41

Ekerdt, D. J. and E. Clark (2001). 'Selling retirement in financial planning advertisements.' *Journal of Aging Studies* **15**(1): 55–68.

Elder, G. H. (1975). 'Age differentiation and life course.' *Annual Review of Sociology* **1**: 165–90.

Elder, G. H. (1994). 'Time, Human Agency, and Social-Change – Perspectives on the Life-Course.' *Social Psychology Quarterly* **57**(1): 4–15.

Elder, G. H. (1998). 'The life course as developmental theory.' *Child Development* **69**(1): 1–12.

Elliott, A., M. Katagiri and A. Sawai (2014). *Routledge Companion to Contemporary Japanese Social Theory: From Individualization to Globalization in Japan Today.* Oxford: Routledge.

Eraydin, A. and B. Armatli-Koroglu (2005). 'Innovation, networking and the new industrial clusters: the characteristics of networks and local innovation capabilities in the Turkish industrial clusters.' *Entrepreneurship and Regional Development* **17**: 237–66.

Ervik, R. (2005). 'The battle for future pensions. Global accounting tools, international organizations and pension reforms.' *Global Social Policy* **5**: 29–54.

Ervik, R., I. Helgoy and D. A. Christensen (2006). 'Ideas and policies on active ageing in Norway and the UK.' *International Social Science Journal* **58**(190): 571–84.

Esping-Andersen, G. (1990). *The three worlds of welfare capitalism.* Cambridge: Polity Press.

Estes, C. L. (1980). *The Aging Enterprise.* San Francisco: Jossey-Bass Publishers.

Estes, C. L. (1986). 'The Aging Enterprise – In Whose Interests.' *International Journal of Health Services* **16**(2): 243–51.

Estes, C. L. and C. Phillipson (2002). 'The globalization of capital, the welfare state, and old age policy.' *International Journal of Health Services* **32**(2): 279–97.

Eto, H. and P. Mahujchariyawong (2015). 'Feasibility and Acceptability of Long-Staying Healthcare Service Facilities in Developing Areas.' *Open Journal of Social Sciences* **3**(11): 215–24.

Eurydice (2011). 'Countries'. https://webgate.ec.europa.eu/fpfis/mwikis/eurydice/index.php/Countries

Facchini, C. and M. Rampazi (2009). 'No longer young, not yet old Biographical uncertainty in late-adult temporality.' *Time & Society* **18**(2–3): 351–72.

Falkingham, J. and C. Victor (1991). 'The myth of the Woopie? Incomes, the elderly and targeting welfare.' *Ageing & Society* **11**: 471–93.

Fan, R. (2007). 'Which care? Whose responsibility? And why family? A Confucian account of long-term care for the elderly.' *Journal of Medicine and Philosophy* **32**: 495–517.

Feo, O. and C. E. Siqueira (2004). 'An alternative to the neoliberal model in health: the case of Venezuela.' *International Journal of Health Services: Planning, Administration, Evaluation* **34**(2): 365–75.

Ferraro, K. F. and T. P. Shippee (2009). 'Aging and Cumulative Inequality: How Does Inequality Get Under the Skin?' *Gerontologist* **49**(3): 333–43.

Ferreira, F. R., C. C. Cesar, V. P. Camargos, M. F. Lima-Costa and F. A. Proietti (2010). 'Aging and Urbanization: The Neighborhood Perception and Functional Performance of Elderly Persons in Belo Horizonte Metropolitan Area-Brazil.' *Journal of Urban Health-Bulletin of the New York Academy of Medicine* **87**(1): 54–66.

Fishman, J. R., R. H. Binstock and M. A. Lambrix (2008). 'Anti-aging science: The emergence, maintenance, and enhancement of a discipline.' *Journal of Aging Studies* **22**(4): 295–303.

Fishman, J. R., R. A. Settersten Jr and M. A. Flatt (2010). 'In the vanguard of biomedicine? The curious and contradictory case of anti-ageing medicine.' *Sociology of Health & Illness* **32**(2): 197–210.

Fogel, R. W. (1994). 'Economic growth, population theory, and physiology: The bearing of long-term processes on the making of economic policy.' *American Economic Review* **84**: 369–95.

Folts, W. E. and K. B. Muir (2002). 'Housing for Older Adults: New Lessons from the Past.' *Research on Aging* **24**(1): 10–28.

Fon Sim, O., J. P. Kitchen and T. J. Ata (2008). 'Consumption patterns and silver marketing: an analysis of older consumers in Malaysia.' *Marketing Intelligence & Planning* **26**(7): 682–98.

Fon Sim, O. and D. R. Phillips (2007). 'Older Consumers in Malaysia.' *International Journal of Ageing and Later Life* **2**: 85–117.

Foner, N. (1984). 'Age and social change' in (eds), *Age and anthropological theory*. New York: Cornell University Press, pp. 64–87.

Forrest, R. and P. Leather (1998). 'The ageing of the property owning democracy.' *Ageing and Society* **18**: 35–63.

Förster, M. and M. D'Ercole (2005). *Income distribution and poverty in OECD countires in the second half of the 1990s.* Paris: OECD.

Foster, L. and A. Walker (2015). 'Active and Successful Aging: A European Policy Perspective.' *The Gerontologist* **55**(1): 83–90.

Fox, L. (1994). *Old age security in transitional economies.* Washington DC: World Bank.

Fox, L. and E. Palmer (2001). 'New approaches to multi-pillar pension systems: What in the world is going on?' in (eds), *New ideas about old age security. Towards sustainable pension systems in the 21st century.* Washington DC: World Bank, pp. 90–132.

Fox, N. J. (2005). 'Cultures of ageing in Thailand and Australia. (What can an ageing body do?)' *Sociology – the Journal of the British Sociological Association* **39**(3): 481–98.

Francis, D. (1992). 'The great transition' in (ed), *Classic Disputes in Sociology.* Oxford: Routledge, pp. 1–35.

Frank, A. G. (1967). *Capitalism and underdevelopment in Latin America.* New York: Monthly Review Press.

Frank, E. (2001). 'Aging and the market in the United States.' *International Journal Of Health Services: Planning, Administration, Evaluation* **31**(1): 133–46.

Freedman, V. A., E. Crimmins, R. F. Schoeni, B. C. Spillman, H. Aykan, E. Kramarow, K. Land, J. Lubitz, K. Manton, L. G. Martin, D. Shinberg and T. Waidmann (2004). 'Resolving inconsistencies in trends in old-age disability: Report from a technical working group.' *Demography* **41**(3): 417–41.

Freedman, V. A. and L. G. Martin (1998). 'Understanding trends in functional limitations among older Americans.' *Am J Public Health* **88**(10): 1457–62.

Freedman, V. A., L. G. Martin and R. F. Schoeni (2002). 'Recent trends in disability and functioning among in the United States – A systematic review.' *Jama-Journal of the American Medical Association* **288**(24): 3137–46.

Freedman, V. A., R. F. Schoeni, L. G. Martin and J. C. Cornman (2007). 'Chronic conditions and the decline in late-life disability.' *Demography* **44**(3): 459–477.

Friedrichs, J. (2001). 'The meaning of new medievalism.' *European Journal of International Relations* **7**(4): 475–501.

Fries, J. F. (1984). 'Aging, Natural Death, and he Compression of Morbidity.' *New England Journal of Medicine* **310**(10): 659–60.

Fries, J. F. (2000). 'Compression of morbidity in the elderly.' *Vaccine* **18**(16): 1584–9.

Fries, J. F. (2002). 'Aging, natural death, and the compression of morbidity.' *Bulletin of the World Health Organization* **80**(3): 245–50.

Fries, J. F. (2005a). 'The compression of morbidity.' *Milbank Quarterly* **83**(4): 801–23.

Fries, J. F. (2005b). 'Frailty, heart disease, and stroke – The compression of morbidity paradigm.' *American Journal of Preventive Medicine* **29**(5): 164–8.

Fries, J. F., L. W. Green and S. Levine (1989). 'Health Promotion and the Compression of Morbidity.' *Lancet* **1**(8636): 481–3.

Fröbel, J., J. Heinrichs and O. Kreye (1981). *The New International Division of Labour*. Cambridge: Cambridge University Press.

Fukuyama, F. (2004). *State-building: governance and world order in the 21st century*. New York: Cornell University Press.

Garrett, G., and Mitchell, D. (2001). Globalization, government spending and taxation in the OECD. *European Journal of Political Research*, **39**(2), 145-177.

George, S. and I. Bache (2001). *Politics in the European Union*. Oxford: Oxford University Press.

Geyman, J. P. (2004). 'Privatization of Medicare: toward disentitlement and betrayal of a social contract.' *International Journal of Health Services: Planning, Administration, Evaluation* **34**(4): 573–94.

Giddens, A. (1991a). *Modernity and self identity: Self and society in the late modern age*. Cambridge: Polity Press.

Giddens, A. (1991b). *The Consequences of Modernity*. California: Stanford University Press.

Giddens, A. (1994). 'Living in a Post-Traditional Society' in (eds) *Reflexive modernization. Politics, tradition and aesthetics in the modern social order*. Cambridge: Polity Press, 56–109.

Giddens, A. (2002). *Runaway World*. London: Profile Books.

Gilleard, C. (1996). 'Consumption and identity in later life: Toward a cultural gerontology.' *Ageing and Society* **16**: 489–98.

Gilleard, C. and P. Higgs (2000). *Cultures of ageing. Self, citizen and the body*. London: Prentice Hall.

Gilleard, C., & Higgs P. (2002). The third age: class, cohort or generation? *Ageing & Society*, **22**(03), 369-382.

Gilleard, C. and P. Higgs (2005). *Contexts of ageing. Class, cohort and community*. Cambridge: Polity Press.

Gilleard, C. and P. Higgs (2007). 'The Third Age and the Baby Boomers. Two Approaches to the Social Structuring of Later Life.' *International Journal of Ageing and Later Life* **2**: 13–30.

Gilleard, C. and P. Higgs (2009). 'The Power of Silver: Age and Identity Politics in the 21st Century.' *Journal of Aging & Social Policy* **21**(3): 277–95.

Gilleard, C. and P. Higgs (2011). 'The Third Age as a cultural field' in (eds), *Gerontology in the era of the Third Age: Implications and next steps*. New York: Springer, pp. 33–51.

Gilleard, C. and P. Higgs (2013). *Ageing, Corporeality and Embodiment*. London: Anthem Press.

Gilleard, C. and P. Higgs (2015). 'The cultural turn in gerontology' in (eds), *Routledge Handbook of Cultural Gerontology*. London: Routledge, pp. 29–36.

Gilleard, C., P. Higgs, M. Hyde, R. Wiggins and D. Blane (2005). 'Class, cohort, and consumption: The British experience of the third age.' *Journals of Gerontology Series B-Psychological Sciences and Social Sciences* 60(6): S305–S310.

Gillion, C., J. Turner, C. Bailey and D. Latulippe (2000). *Social Security Pensions: Development and Reform*. Geneva: ILO.

Ginn, J. (2004). 'European Pension Privatisation: Taking Account of Gender.' *Social Policy & Society* 3: 123–34.

Ginn, J. and S. Arber (2001). 'Pension prospects of minority ethnic groups: inequalities by gender and ethnicity.' *British Journal of Sociology* 52(3): 519–39.

Golant, S. M. (1975). 'Residential Concentrations of the Future Elderly.' *The Gerontologist* 15(1 Part 2): 16–23.

Goldblatt, D., J. Perraton, D. Held and A. McGrew (1999). *Global transformations: Politics, economics, culture*. Cambridge: Polity Press.

Gordon, I. R. and P. McCann (2000). 'Industrial clusters: complexes, agglomerations and/or social networks.' *Urban Studies* **37**: 513–32.

Gough, I. (2001). 'Globalization and Regional Welfare Regimes.' *Global Social Policy* **1**(2): 163–89.

Graham, J. E., A. B. Mitnitski, A. J. Mogilner and K. Rockwood (1999). 'Dynamics of cognitive aging: Distinguishing functional age and disease from chronologic age in a population.' *American Journal of Epidemiology* **150**(10): 1045–54.

Graham, P., T. Blakely, P. Davis, A. Sporle and N. Pearce (2004). 'Compression, expansion, or dynamic equilibrium? The evolution of health expectancy in New Zealand.' *Journal of Epidemiology and Community Health* **58**(8): 659–66.

Grech, A. G. (2015). 'Convergence or divergence? How the financial crisis affected European pensioners.' *International Social Security Review* **68**(2): 43–62.

Greco, A.J. (1986), "The fashion-conscious elderly: a viable, but neglected market segment", *Journal of Consumer Marketing*, **3**(4), pp. 71-75.

Greco, A. J. (1993). 'The Fashion-Conscious Elderly: A Viable, but Neglected Market Segment.' *Journal of Consumer Marketing* **3**(4): 71–5.

Greider, W. (1998). *One world, ready or not. The manic logic of global capitalism.* London: Penguin.

Grenier, A. (2012). *Transitions and the lifecourse: Challenging the construction of 'growing old'.* Bristol: Policy Press.

Grimes, W. (2012). 'Financial Regionalism after the Global Financial Crisis: Regionalist Impulses and National Strategies' in (eds), *The Consequences of the Global Financial Crisis: The Rhetoric of Reform and Regulation.* Oxford: Oxford University Press, pp. 88–109.

Gu, D., M. E. Dupre, D. F. Warner and Y. Zeng (2009). 'Changing health status and health expectancies among older adults in China: Gender differences from 1992 to 2002.' *Social Science & Medicine* **68**(12): 2170–9.

Guillemard, A. M. (2003). 'France: Struggling to find a way out of the early exit culture.' *Geneva Papers on Risk and Insurance-Issues and Practice* **28**(4): 558–74.

Gunter, B. (1998). *Understanding the Older Consumer: The Grey Market.* London: Routledge.

Gupta, V. and R. Subramanian (2008). 'Seven perspectives on regional clusters and the case of Grand Rapids office furniture city.' *International Business Review* **17**(4): 371–84.

Gustafson, P. (2001). 'Retirement migration and transnational lifestyles.' *Ageing and Society* **21**: 371–94.

Gustafson, P. (2002). 'Tourism and seasonal retirement migration.' *Annals of Tourism Research* **29**(4): 899–918.

Gustafson, P. (2008). 'Transnationalism in retirement migration: the case of North European retirees in Spain.' *Ethnic and Racial Studies* **31**(3): 451–75.

Ha, Y. C. (2007). 'Late industrialization, the state, and social changes – The emergence of neofamilism in South Korea.' *Comparative Political Studies* **40**(4): 363–82.

Haas, P. M. (1989). 'Do regimes matter? Epistemic communities and Mediterranean pollution control.' *International Organization* **43**(03): 377–403.

Haas, P. M. (1992). 'Epistemic Communities and International-Policy Coordination – Introduction.' *International Organization* **46**(1): 1–35.

Haas, W. H. and W. J. Serow (2002). 'The baby boom, amenity retirement migration, and retirement communities: Will the Golden Age of Retirement continue?' *Research on Aging* **24**(1): 150–64.

Hallerberg, M. (2013). 'Challenges for the German Welfare State before and after the Global Financial Crisis.' *Cato Journal* **33**(2): 263–7.

Halliday, J. (2005). 'REACH clarifies use of chemicals in cosmetics.' CosmeticsDesign.com, www.cosmeticsdesign.com/Formulation-Science/REACH-clarifies-use-of-chemicals-in-cosmetics

Hansson, R. O., P. D. Dekoekkoek, W. M. Neece and D. W. Patterson (1997). 'Successful Aging at Work: Annual Review, 1992–1996: The Older Worker and Transitions to Retirement.' *Journal of Vocational Behavior* **51**(2): 202–33.

Hareven, T. K. (1994). 'Aging and Generational Relations – A Historical and Life-Course Perspective.' *Annual Review of Sociology* **20**: 437–61.

Harper, S. (2000). 'Ageing 2000-questions for the 21st century.' *Ageing and Society* **20**: 111–22.

Harper, S. and G. Laws (1995). 'Rethinking the Geography of Aging.' *Progress in Human Geography* **19**(2): 199–221.

Harvey, D. (1989). *The Condition of Postmodernity*. Oxford: Wiley-Blackwell.

Harvey, D. (2006). *Spaces of Global Capitalism: Towards a Theory of Uneven Geographical Development*. London: Verso Books.

Hay, C. (2001). 'Globalization, economic change and the welfare state. The 'vexatious inquisition of taxation'' in R. Sykes, B. Palier and P. M. Prior (eds), *Globalization and European welfare states. Challenges and change.* Houndmills: Palgrave, pp. 38–58.

Hazan, H. (1994). *Old age constructions and deconstructions*. Cambridge, Cambridge University Press.

Held, D. and A. McGrew (2003). *The global transformations reader: An introduction to the globalization debate*. Cambridge: Polity Press.

Held, D. and A. McGrew (2007). *Globalization/Anti-Globalization: Beyond the great divide*. Cambridge: Polity Press.

Hendricks, J., R. Applebaum and S. Kunkel (2010). 'A World Apart? Bridging the Gap Between Theory and Applied Social Gerontology.' *The Gerontologist* **50**(3): 284–93.

Henkens, K. and J. Schippers (2012). 'Active ageing in Europe: the role of organisations.' *International Journal of Manpower* **33**(6): 604–11.

Henkens, K. and F. Tazelaar (1994). 'Early Retirement of Civil-Servants in the Netherlands.' *Journal of Applied Social Psychology* **24**(21): 1927–43.

Henkens, K. and F. Tazelaar (1997). 'Explaining retirement decisions of civil servants in the Netherlands – Intentions, behavior, and the discrepancy between the two.' *Research on Aging* **19**(2): 139–73.

Hershey, D. A., K. Henkens and H. P. van Dalen (2010). 'What drives retirement income worries in Europe? A multilevel analysis.' *European Journal of Ageing* **7**(4): 301–11.

Hettne, B. (2001). 'Europe. Paradigm and paradox' in (eds), *Regionalization in a globalizing world. A comparative perspective on forms, actors and processes.* New York: Zed Books, pp. 22–41.

Hettne, B. (2005). 'Beyond the 'new' regionalism.' *New Political Economy* **10**(4): 543–71.

Heymann, L. A. (1997). 'The cosmetic/drug dilemma: FDA regulation of alpha-hydroxy acids.' *Food and Drug Law Journal* **52**(4): 357–75.

Higgs, P. (1995). 'Citizenship and old age: The end of the road?' *Ageing & Society* **15**: 535–50.

Higgs, P. and C. Gilleard (2010). 'Generational conflict, consumption and the ageing welfare state in the United Kingdom.' *Ageing & Society* **30**: 1439–51.

Higgs, P. and C. Gilleard (2015). 'Generational Justice, generational habitus and the problem of the baby boomers' in C. Torp (ed). *Challenges of Aging: Pensions, Retirement and Generational Justice.* Houndmills: Palgrave Macmillan, pp. 251–64.

Higgs, P., M. Hyde, C. Gilleard, C. Victor, R. Wiggins and I. R. Jones (2009). 'From passive to active consumers? Later life consumption in the UK from 1968–2005.' *The Sociological Review* **57**: 102–24.

Higgs, P. and I. R. Jones (2009). *Medical Sociology and Old Age.* Oxford: Routledge.

Hills, J. (2004). *Inequality and the state.* Oxford: Oxford University Press.

Hills, J. and K. Stewart (2005). *A more equal society? New labour, poverty, inequality and exclusion.* Bristol: Policy Press.

Hirst, P. and E. P. Thompson (2000). *Globalization in Question: The International Economy and the Possibilities of Governance.* Cambridge: Polity Press.

Hirst, P. and G. Thompson (2000). 'Globalization and the history of the international economy' in (eds), *The global transformations reader.* Cambridge: Polity Press, pp. 274–87.

Hofäcker, D. (2010). *Older workers in a globalizing world: an international comparison of retirement and late-career patterns in Western industrialized countries.* Cheltenham: Edward Elgar.

Holden, C. (2005). 'Privatization and trade in health services: a review of the evidence.' *International Journal of Health Services: Planning, Administration, Evaluation* **35**(4): 675–89.

Holland, P., L. Berney, D. Blane, G. D. Smith, D. J. Gunnell and S. M. Montgomery (2000). 'Life course accumulation of disadvantage: childhood health and hazard exposure during adulthood.' *Social Science & Medicine* **50**(9): 1285–95.

Holzmann, R., E. James, A. Börsch-Supan, P. Diamond and S. Valdés-Prieto (2001). 'Comments on re-thinking pension reform: Ten myths about social security systems' in (eds), *New ideas about old age security. Towards sustainable pension systems in the 21st century*. Washington DC: World Bank, pp. 57–89.

Holzmann, R. and J. E. Stiglitz (2001). 'Introduction' in R. Holzmann and J. E. Stiglitz (eds), *New ideas about old age security. Towards sustainable pension systems in the 21st century*. Washington DC: World Bank, pp. 1–16.

Holzner, B. (1968). *Reality construction in Society*. Cambridge: Schenkman.

Holzner, B. and J. Marx (1979). *Knowledge affiliation: the Knowledge system in society*. Boston: Allyn and Bacon.

Hoogvelt, A. (2001). *Globalization and the postcolonial world: The new political economy of development*. Baltimore, MD: Johns Hopkins University Press.

Hort, S. O. and S. Kuhnle (2000). 'The coming of East and South-East Asian welfare states.' *Journal of European Social Policy* **10**(2): 162–84.

Howard, R. W. (2008). 'Western retirees in Thailand: motives, experiences, wellbeing, assimilation and future needs.' *Ageing & Society* **28**: 145–63.

Huber, E. and J. D. Stephens (2001). 'Welfare state and production regimes in the era of retrenchment' in P. Pierson (ed), *The new politics of the welfare state*. Oxford: Oxford University Press, pp. 107–45.

Hulme, D. and J. Scott (2010). 'The Political Economy of the MDGs: Retrospect and Prospect for the World's Biggest Promise.' *New Political Economy* **15**(2): 293–306.

Hung, W. W., J. S. Ross, K. S. Boockvar and A. L. Siu (2011). 'Recent trends in chronic disease, impairment and disability among older adults in the United States.' *BMC Geriatrics* **11**(1): 1–12.

Hungerford, T. L. (2003). 'Is there an American way of aging? Income dynamics of the elderly in the United States and Germany.' *Research on Aging* **25**(5): 435–55.

Hurd Clarke, L. and E. Bennett (2015). 'Gender, ageing and appearance' in (eds), *Routledge Handbook of Cultural Gerontology*. Oxford: Routledge, pp. 133–40.

Hurd, M. D. (1989). 'The Economic-Status of the Elderly.' *Science* **244**(4905): 659–64.

Hussain, D. (2009). 'Fencing off Bangladesh', *The Guardian*, 5 September.Hyde, M. (2015). 'Travel and tourism in later life' in (eds), *Routledge Handbook of Cultural Gerontology*. London: Routledge, pp. 337–44.

Hyde, M., P. Higgs, C. Gilleard, C. Victor, R. Wiggins and I. R. Jones (2009). 'Ageing, cohorts, and consumption: The British experience 1968–2005' in (eds), *Consumption and generational change. The rise of consumer lifestyles*. New Brunswick, NJ: Transactions Publishers, pp. 93–128.

Hyde, M., P. Higgs and S. Newman (2008). 'The health profile of ageing populations' in (eds), *Chronic Physical Illness: Self Management and Behavioural Interventions*. Milton Keynes: Open University Press, pp. 3–27.

Idler, E. L. and Y. Benyamini (1997). 'Self-rated health and mortality: A review of twenty-seven community studies.' *Journal of Health and Social Behavior* **38**: 21–37.

ILO (2001). *Social security: A new consensus*. Geneva: International Labour Organization.

Inkeles, A. (1969). 'Making men modern: On the causes and consequences on individual change in six developing countries.' *The American Journal of Sociology* **75**: 208–25.

Inkeles, A. (1998). *One World Emerging? Convergence and Divergence in Industrial Societies*. New York: Westview Press.

INSERM (2013). 'The latest trends in healthy life expectancy in the European Union.' Press release, 17 April. http://presse.inserm.fr/en/the-latest-trends-in-healthy-life-expectancy-in-the-european-union/7858

International Labour Organization (ILO) (2015). 'Main statistics (annual) – Economically active population.' http://laborsta.ilo.org/applv8/data/c1e.html

ISSP Research Group (2015a). *International Social Survey Programme: Citizenship – ISSP 2004*. ISSP. Cologne, GESIS Data Archive.

ISSP Research Group (2015b). *International Social Survey Programme: Family and Changing Gender Roles IV – ISSP 2012*. ISSP. Cologne, GESIS Data Archive.JAAM (2010). 'Japanese Society of Anti-Aging Medicine.' www.anti-aging.gr.jp/english/anti.phtmlJackson, P. (2004). 'Local consumption cultures in a globalizing world.' *Transactions of the Institute of British Geographers* **29**(2): 165–78.

Jackson, R. and N. Howe (2003). *The 2003 Aging Vulnerability Index. An assessment of the capacity of twelve developed countries to meet the aging challenge*. Washington DC: CSIS & Watson Wyatt.

Jackson, S. H. D., M. R. Weale and R. A. Weale (2003). 'Biological age – what is it and can it be measured?' *Archives of Gerontology and Geriatrics* **36**(2): 103–15.

Jagger, C., C. Gillies, F. Moscone, E. Cambois, H. Van Oyen, W. Nusselder and J.-M. Robine (2008). 'Inequalities in healthy life years in the 25 countries of the European Union in 2005: a cross-national meta-regression analysis.' *The Lancet* **372**(9656): 2124–31.

James, E. (1996). *Protecting the old and promoting growth. A defense of Averting the Old Age Crisis.* Washington DC: World Bank.

James, E. (1997). *New systems for old age security. Theory, practice and empirical evidence.* Washington DC: World Bank.

Janevic, M., E. Gjonça and M. Hyde (2004). 'Physical and social environment' in (eds), *Health, wealth and lifestyles of the older population in England: THE 2002 ENGLISH LONGITUDINAL STUDY OF AGEING.* London: IFS, pp. 301–16.

Japanese Statistics Bureau (2014). 'Family Income and Expenditure Survey, 2014.' www.e-stat.go.jp/SG1/estat/ListE.do?lid=000001135066

Jayasuriya, K. (2001). 'Globalization and the changing architecture of the state: the regulatory state and the politics of negative co-ordination.' *Journal of European Public Policy* **8**(1): 101–23.

Jayasuriya, K. (2004). 'The new regulatory state and relational capacity.' *Policy and Politics* **32**(4): 487–501.

Jeevan, R. and A. Armstrong (2008). *Cosmetic tourism and the burden on the NHS.* London: BAPRAS.

Jenkins, S. (2015). *The income distribution in the UK: A picture of advantage and disadvantage.* Discussion paper 8835. Bonn: Institute for the Study of Labor (IZA).

Jessop, B. (1994). 'Post-Fordism and the State' in A. Amin (ed), *Post-Fordism: A reader.* Oxford: Wiley-Blackwell, pp. 251–80.

Jessop, B. (2003). 'State theory, regulation and autopoieses: debates and controversies.' *Capital and Class* **75**: 83–92.

Jeune, B. and H. Brønnum-Hansen (2008). 'Trends in health expectancy at age 65 for various health indicators, 1987–2005, Denmark.' *European Journal of Ageing* **5**(4): 279–85.

Jones, G. (2000). *Merchants to multinationals. British trading companies in the nineteenth and twentieth centuries.* Oxford: Oxford University Press.

Jones, I. R. and P. F. Higgs (2010). 'The natural, the normal and the normative: contested terrains in ageing and old age.' *Soc Sci Med* **71**(8): 1513–19.

Jones, I. R., M. Hyde, C. Victor, R. Wiggins, C. Gilleard and P. Higgs (2008). *Ageing in a consumer society. From passive to active consumption in Britain.* Bristol: Policy Press.

Kaplan, G. A. and J. E. Keil (1993). 'Socioeconomic factors and cardiovascular disease: a review of the literature.' *Circulation* **88**: 1973–98.

Karl, U and Torres, S. (2016) *Ageing in Contexts of Migration.* Routledge: Oxford.

Kasneci, D. (2007). 'Active Ageing: the EU Policy Response to the Challenge of Population Ageing.' *European Papers on the New Welfare* **8**: 1–9.

Katz, S. and T. Calasanti (2015). 'Critical Perspectives on Successful Aging: Does It 'Appeal More Than It Illuminates'?' *The Gerontologist* **55**(1): 26–33.

Katz, S. and B. Marshall (2003). 'New sex for old: lifestyle, consumerism, and the ethics of aging well.' *Journal of Aging Studies* **17**(1): 3–16.

Keese, M. (2006). *Live longer, work longer.* Paris: Organisation for Economic Co-operation and Development.

Keohane, R. O. and J. S. Nye (2000). *International relations theory: Power and interdependence.* Harlow: Prentice Hall.

Kertzer, D. I. (1983). 'Generation as a sociological problem.' *Annual Review of Sociology* **9**: 125–49.

Kettler, D., & Loader, C. (2004). Temporizing with Time Wars: Karl Mannheim and Problems of Historical Time. *Time & Society*, **13**(2-3), 155-172.

Kim, J. Y. and L. Y. Zhang (2008). 'Formation of foreign direct investment clustering – a new path to local economic development? The case of Qingdao.' *Regional Studies* **42**(2): 265–80.

Kim, S. (2011). 'Intra-regional residential movement of the elderly: testing a suburban-to-urban migration hypothesis.' *Annals of Regional Science* **46**(1): 1–17.

Kimuna, S. R. (2005). 'Living arrangements of older people in Zimbabwe.' *African Population Studies* **20**: 143–63.

King, R., T. Warnes and A. M. Williams (2000). *Sunset Lives: British Retirement Migration to the Mediterranean.* London: Berg.

Klein, N. (2001). *No Logo.* London: HarperCollins.

Knight, J. and J. W. Traphagan (2003). 'The study of the family in Japan: Integrating anthropological and demographic approaches' in (eds), *Demographic change and the family in Japan's aging society.* New York: SUNY: 3–22.

Knodel, J. and N. Debavalya (1997). 'Living arrangements and support among the elderly in South East Asia. An introduction.' *Asia Pac Popul J* **12**: 5–16.

Kohli, M. and M. Rein (1991). 'The changing balance of work and retirement' in Gunsteren (eds), *Comparative studies of early exit from the labor force*. Cambridge: Cambridge University Press, pp. 1–35.

Korpi, W. (2001). 'Contentious institutions – An augmented rational-action analysis of the origins and path dependency of welfare state institutions in Western countries.' *Rationality and Society* **13**(2): 235–83.

Korpi, W., and Palme, J. (2003). New politics and class politics in the context of austerity and globalization: Welfare state regress in 18 countries, 1975-95. *American Political Science Review*, **97**(3), 425-446.

Kovrig, B. (1986). 'Hungarian Socialism: the Deceptive Hybrid.' *East European Politics & Societies* **1**(1): 113–34.

Krugman, P. (1998). *The accidental theorist: And other dispatches from the dismal science*. New York: W. W. Norton.

Kuh, D., Y. Ben-Shlomo, J. Lynch, J. Hallqvist and C. Power (2003). 'Life course epidemiology.' *Journal of Epidemiology and Community Health* **57**(10): 778–83.

Kumar, S. (2005). 'Exploratory analysis of global cosmetic industry: major players, technology and market trends.' *Technovation* **25**(11): 1263–72.

Kupari, M., M. Lindroos, A. M. Iivanainen, J. Heikkilä and R. Tilvis (1997). 'Congestive heart failure in old age: prevalence, mechanisms, and 4-year prognosis in the Helsinki Ageing Study.' *Journal of Internal Medicine* **241**: 387–94.

Laczko, F. and C. Phillipson (1991). *Changing work and retirement*. Milton Keynes: Open University Press.

Lafontaine, C. (2009). 'Regenerative Medicine's Immortal Body: From the Fight against Ageing to the Extension of Longevity.' *Body & Society* **15**(4): 53–71.

Lamb, V. L. and G. C. Myers (1999). 'A comparative study of successful aging in three Asian countries.' *Population Research and Policy Review* **18**(5): 433–49.

Lanska, D. J. and X. Mi (1993). 'Decline in US stroke mortality in the era before antihypertensive therapy.' *Stroke* **24**: 1382–8.

Lash, S. and J. Urry (1993). *Economies of signs and space*. London: Sage.

Laslett, P. (1977). 'Characteristics of Western family life considered over time.' *Journal of Family History* **2**: 89–115.

Laslett, P. (1987). 'The emergence of the Third Age.' *Ageing & Society* **7**: 133–60.

Laslett, P. (1996). *A fresh map of life*. 2nd edition. London: MacMillan Press.

Laslett, P. (1997). 'Interpreting the demographic changes.' *Philosophical Transactions of the Royal Society of London Series B-Biological Sciences* **352**(1363): 1805–09.

Laslett, P. and R. Wall (1972). *Household and family in past time.* Cambridge: Cambridge University Press.

Lee, C. G. (2010). 'Health care and tourism. Evidence from Singapore.' *Tourism Management* **31**: 486–8.

Lenin, V. I. (1975 [1916]). *Imperialism, the highest stage of capitalism.* Peking: Foreign Languages Press.

Lerner, D. (1964). *The passing of traditional society: modernizing the Middle East.* Virginia: Free Press of Glencoe.

Lewis, D. C. (2009). 'Aging Out of Place: Cambodian Refugee Elders in the United States.' *Family and Consumer Sciences Research Journal* **37**: 376–87.

Lewis, R. and S. Gillam (2003). 'Back to the market: yet more reform of the National Health Service.' *International Journal Of Health Services: Planning, Administration, Evaluation* **33**(1): 77–84.

Lindenschmidt, R. C., F. B. Anastasia, M. Dorta and L. Bansil (2001). 'Global cosmetic regulatory harmonization.' *Toxicology* **160**(1–3): 237–41.

Litwak, E. (1959). 'The use of extended family groups in the achievement of social goals: some policy implications.' *Social Problems* **7**: 177–87.

Litwak, E. and C. F. Longino (1987). 'Migration Patterns among the Elderly – A Developmental Perspective.' *Gerontologist* **27**(3): 266–72.

Lloyd-Sherlock, P. (1997). *Old age and urban poverty in the developing world: the shanty towns of Buenos Aires.* London: St Martin's Press.

Lloyd-Sherlock, P. (2002a). *Living arrangements of older persons and poverty.* New York: United Nations, Population Division, Dept. of Economic and Social Affairs.

Lloyd-Sherlock, P. (2002b). 'Social policy and population ageing: challenges for north and south.' *International Journal of Epidemiology* **31**(4): 754–57.

Lloyd-Sherlock, P. (2010). *Population ageing and international development: from generalisation to evidence.* Bristol: Policy Press.

Loader, B. and R. Burrows (1994). 'Towards a post-Fordist welfare state? The restructuring of Britain, social policy and the future of welfare' in (eds), *Towards a post-Fordist welfare state?* London: Routledge, pp. 1–13.

Long, N. (1998). 'Broken down by age and sex – Exploring the ways we approach the elderly consumer.' *Journal of the Market Research Society* **40**(2): 73–91.

Longino, C. F. and D. E. Bradley (2003). 'A first look at retirement migration trends in 2000.' *Gerontologist* **43**(6): 904–07.

Łopaciuk, A. and Łoboda, M. (2013). Global beauty industry trends in the 21st century. Management, Knowledge and Learning International Conference 2013 - Active Citizenship by Knowledge Management & Innovation.

Lorenz, P. and H. Zinke (2005). 'White biotechnology: differences in US and EU approaches?' *Trends in Biotechnology* **23**(12): 570–4.

Lumpkin, J. R. (1984). 'The Effect of Retirement Versus Age on the Shopping Orientations of the Older Consumer.' *The Gerontologist* **24**(6): 622–7.

Mak, J., L. Carlile and S. Dai (2005). 'Impact of Population Aging on Japanese International Travel to 2025.' *Journal of Travel Research* **44**(2): 151–62.

Mannheim, K. (1952). 'The Problem of Generations' in K. Mannheim (ed), *Essays on the Sociology of Knowledge*. London: RKP.

Manton, K. G. (1982). 'Changing concepts of morbidity and mortality in the elderly population.' *Milbank Quartlery* **60**: 183–244.

Manton, K. G., E. Stallard and L. Corder (1995). 'Changes in Morbidity and Chronic Disability in the Us Elderly Population – Evidence from the 1982, 1984, and 1989 National Long-Term-Care Surveys.' *Journals of Gerontology Series B-Psychological Sciences and Social Sciences* **50**(4): S194–S204.

Manton, K. G., E. Stallard and L. Corder (1997). 'Education specific estimates of life expectancy and age specific disability in the U.S. elderly population: 1982 to 1991.' *Journal of Aging and Health* **9**: 419–50.

Marchand, M. H. (2001). 'North American regionalisms and regionalization in the 1990s' in (eds), *Regionalization in a globalizing world. A comparative perspective on forms, actors and processes*. New York: Zed Books, pp. 198–211.

Markusen, A. (1996). 'Sticky places in slippery space: A typology of industrial districts.' *Economic Geography* **72**(3): 293–313.

Markusen, A. (2007). 'Fuzzy concepts, scanty evidence, policy distance: The case for rigour and policy relevance in critical regional studies.' *Regional Studies* **41**: S175–S190.

Martin, D., Metzger, J. and Pierre, P. (2006). The Sociology of Globalization: Theoretical and Methodological Reflections. *International Sociology*, **21**(2), pp.499-521

Martínez, A. D. (2012). 'Ideoscapes' in *The Wiley-Blackwell Encyclopedia of Globalization*. John Wiley & Sons.

Massey, D. (2008). *for space*. London: Sage.

Mathers, C. (1996). 'Trends in health expectancies in Australia 1981–1993.' *Journal of the Australian Population Association* **13**: 1–15.

Maule, A. J. (1995). 'Early Retirement Schemes – Factors Governing their Success and how these Differ Across Job Categories.' *Personnel Review* **24**(8): 6–16.

Mayer, K. U. and U. Schoepflin (1989). 'The State and the Life Course.' *Annual Review of Sociology* **15**: 187–209.

Mba, C. J. (2007). 'Gender disparities in living arrangements of older people in Ghana. Evidence from the 2003 Ghana demographics and health survey.' *Journal of International Women's Studies* **9**: 493–522.

McCann, P., T. Arita and I. R. Gordon (2002). 'Industrial clusters, transaction costs and the institutional determinants of MNE location behaviour.' *International Business Review* **11**: 647–63.

McCanne, D. R. (2009). 'The Organization for Economic Cooperation and Development and Health Care Reform in the United States.' *International Journal of Health Services: Planning, Administration, Evaluation* **39**(4): 699–704.

McDonald, L. and P. Donahue (2000). 'Poor health and retirement income: the Canadian case.' *Ageing and Society* **20**: 493–522.

McGreal, C. (2011). 'The battle of the US-Mexico frontier', *The Guardian*, 20 February.

McHugh, K. E. (2000a). 'The 'ageless self'? Emplacement of identities in sun belt retirement communities.' *Journal of Aging Studies* **14**(1): 103–15.

McHugh, K. E. (2000b). 'Inside, outside, upside down, backward, forward, round and round: a case for ethnographic studies in migration.' *Progress in Human Geography* **24**(1): 71–89.

McHugh, K. E. (2003). 'Three faces of ageism: society, image and place.' *Ageing and Society* **23**: 165–85.

McHugh, K. E. and E. M. Larson-Keagy (2005). 'These white walls: The dialectic of retirement communities.' *Journal of Aging Studies* **19**(2): 241–56.

McHugh, K. E. and R. C. Mings (1996). 'The circle of migration: Attachment to place in aging.' *Annals of the Association of American Geographers* **86**(3): 530–50.

McKelvey, J. B. (2009). 'Globalization and ageing workers: constructing a global life course.' *International Journal of Sociology and Social Policy* **29**: 49–59.

Mertz, B. and N. Stephens (1986). 'Marketing to older American consumers.' *International Journal of Aging & Human Development* **23**: 47–58.

Metz, D. and M. Underwood (2005). *Older, richer, fitter. Identifying the consumer needs of Britain's ageing population.* London: Age Concern Books.

Meyer, M. and S. Molyneux-Hodgson (2010). 'Introduction: The Dynamics of Epistemic Communities.' *Sociological Research Online* **15**(2): 14.

Middleton, S., R. Hancock, K. Kellard, J. Beckhelling, V. H. Phung and K. Perren (2007). *Measuring resources in later life. A review of the data.* York: Joseph Rowntree Foundation.

Migration Policy Team (2013). *Migration Profile: Jordan.* Paris: MPC.

Miilunpalo, S., I. Vuori, P. Oja, M. Pasanen and H. Urponen (1997). 'Self-rated health status as a health measure: The predictive value of self-reported health status on the use of physician services and on mortality in the working-age population.' *Journal of Clinical Epidemiology* **50**: 517–28.

Millikan, L. E. (2001). 'Cosmetology, cosmetics, cosmeceuticals: definitions and regulations.' *Clinics in Dermatology* **19**(4): 371–4.

Minicuci, N. and M. Noale (2005). 'Influence of level of education on disability free life expectancy by sex: the ILSA study.' *Experimental Gerontology* **40**: 997–1003.

Minkler, M. and P. Fadem (2002). '"Successful Aging": A Disability Perspective.' *Journal of Disability Policy Studies* **12**: 229–42.

Minkler, M., E. Fuller-Thomson and J. M. Guralnik (2006). 'Gradient of disability across the socio-economic spectrum in the United States.' *New England Journal of Medicine* **355**: 695–703.

Mishra, R. (1999). *Globalization and the welfare state.* Cheltenham: Edward Elgar.

Moller, L., T. S. Kristensen and H. Hollnagel (1996). 'Self rated health as a predictor of coronary heart disease in Copenhagen, Denmark.' *Journal of Epidemiology and Community Health* **50**: 423–8.

Montanari, I. (2001). 'Modernization, globalization and the welfare state: a comparative analysis of old and new convergence of social insurance since 1930.' *British Journal of Sociology* **52**(3): 469–94.

Moody, H. R. (2000). *Aging: Concepts and Controversies.* New Jersey: Pine Forge Press.

Morgan, N. J., A. Pritchard and S. Abbott (2001). 'Consumers, travel and technology: A bright future for the Web or television shopping?' *Journal of Vacation Marketing* **7**(2): 110–24.

Morganti, P. and S. Paglialunga (2008). 'EU borderline cosmetic products review of current regulatory status.' *Clinics in Dermatology* **26**(4): 392–7.

Moschis, G. (1994). 'Consumer behavior in later life: Multidisciplinary contributions and implications for research.' *Journal of the Academy of Marketing Science* **22**(3): 195–204.

Moschis, G. P. (2009). 'Generational Marketing' in (eds), *Consumption and Generational Change*. New Brunswick and London: Transactions Publishers, pp. 149–70.

Muise, A. and S. Desmarais (2010). 'Women's Perceptions and Use of 'Anti-Aging' Products.' *Sex Roles* **63**(1–2): 126–37.

Müller, K. (2003). 'The making of pension privatization in Latin America and Eastern Europe' in (eds), *Pension reform in Europe: Process and progress*. Washington DC: World Bank, pp. 47–78.

Mykytyn, C. E. (2006). 'Contentious terminology and complicated cartography of anti-aging medicine.' *Biogerontology* **7**(4): 279–85.

Mykytyn, C. E. (2010). 'A history of the future: the emergence of contemporary anti-ageing medicine.' *Sociology of Health & Illness* **32**(2): 181–96.

Myles, J. and P. Pierson (2001). 'The comparative political economy of pension reform' in (ed), *The new politics of the welfare state*. Oxford: Oxford University Press, pp. 305–34.

Naghavi, M., H. Wang, R. Lozano, A. Davis, X. Liang and M. Zhou (2015). 'Global, regional and national age-sex specific all-cause and cause-specific mortality for 240 causes of death, 1990–2013: a systematic analysis for the global burden of disease study, 2013.' *Lancet* **385**(9963): 117–71.

Nam, J., R. Hamlin, H. J. Gam, J. H. Kang, J. Kim, P. Kumphai, C. Starr and L. Richards (2007). 'The fashion-conscious behaviours of mature female consumers.' *International Journal of Consumer Studies* **31**(1): 102–08.

Nassab, R. and P. Harris (2013). 'Cosmetic surgery growth and correlations with financial indices: a comparative study of the United Kingdom and United States from 2002–2011.' *Aesthet Surg J* **33**(4): 604–08.

Nasto, B. (2007). 'Biotech at the beauty counter.' *Nature Biotechnology* **25**(6): 617–19.

National Statistics Taiwan. (2014). 'Survey of Family Income and Expenditure in Taiwan, 2014.' http://eng.stat.gov.tw/ct.asp?xItem =3458&CtNode=1597&mp=5

Navarro, V., J. Schmitt and J. Astudillo (2004). 'Is globalization undermining the welfare state? The evolution of the welfare state in developed capitalist countries during the 1990s.' *International Journal Of Health Services: Planning, Administration, Evaluation* **34**(2): 185–227.

Neilson, B. (2003). 'Globalization and the biopolitics of aging.' *Cr-the New Centennial Review* **3**(2): 161–86.

Neumayer, E. (2006). 'Unequal access to foreign spaces: how states use visa restrictions to regulate mobility in a globalized world.' *Transactions of the Institute of British Geographers* **31**(1): 72–84.

Noël, A. (2006). 'The new global politics of poverty.' *Global Social Policy* **6**: 304–33.

Norton, M. and S. West (2014). *Age UK Evidence Review: Poverty in Later Life*. London: Age UK.Nyangweso, M. A. (1998). 'Transformations of care of the aged among Africans - a study of the Kenyan situation.' *Aging & Mental Health* **2**(3): 181–5.

O'Brien, E. (2015). 'Planning for population ageing: implications of local demographic, spatial and fiscal differences.' *International Planning Studies*: 1–12.

Oakley, A. (1974). *The Sociology of Housework*. London: Robertson.

Odén, B. (2001). 'Regionalization in Southern Africa. The role of the dominant' in (eds), *Regionalization in a globalizing world. A comparative perspective on forms, actors and processes*. New York: Zed Books, pp. 82–99.

OECD (2001). *Ageing and income. Financial resources and retirement in 9 OECD countries*. Paris: OECD.

OECD (2007). *Pensions at a glance*. Paris: OECD.

OECD (2013). *Pensions at a Glance 2013*. Paris: OECD Publishing.

OECD (2015a). *Pensions at a Glance 2015*. Paris: OECD Publishing.

OECD (2015b). Social expenditure – aggregated data. https://stats.oecd.org/Index.aspx?DataSetCode=SOCX_AGG. Accessed 10/08/2015

Office for National Statistics (2014). *Statistical Bulletin: Health Expectancies at Birth and Age 65 in the United Kingdom, 2009–11*. London: ONS.

Office for National Statistics (2015a). *Family Spending 2014. Table A.11: Detailed household expenditure by age of household reference person*. London: ONS.

Office for National Statistics (2015b). *Travel Trends, 2014*. London: ONS.

Official Statistics of Finland (2014). *Households' consumption*. Helsinki: Statistics Finland. http://tilastokeskus.fi/til/ktutk/index_en.html

Ofstedal, M. B., J. Knodel and N. Chayoran (1999). 'Intergenerational support and gender. A comparison of four Asian countries.' *Southeast Asian Journal of Social Science* **27**: 21–42.

Ohmae, K. (1990). *The Borderless World*. London: HarperCollins.

Öjendal, J. (2001). 'Southeast Asia at a constant crossroads. An ambiguous 'new region" in (eds), *Regionalization in a globalizing world. A comparative perspective on forms, actors and processes*. New York: Zed Books, pp. 147–72.

Olds, K. (1995). 'Globalization and the production of new urban spaces: Pacific Rim megaprojects in the late 20th century.' *Environment and Planning A* **27**(11): 1713–43.

Olshansky, S. J. and A. B. Ault (1986). 'The 4th Stage of the Epidemiologic Transition – The Age of Delayed Degenerative Diseases.' *Milbank Quarterly* **64**(3): 355–91.

Olshansky, S. J., B. Carnes, R. G. Rogers and L. Smith (1997). 'Infectious diseases – New and ancient threats to world health.' *Population Bulletin* **52**(2): 1–52.

Omran, A. (1971). 'The Epidemiologic Transition: A theory of the epidemiology of population change.' *Milbank Memorial Quarterly* **XLIX**: 509–38.

Orenstein, M. (2003). 'Mapping the diffusion of pension innovation' in (eds), *Pension reform in Europe. Process and progress*. Washington DC: World Bank, pp. 171–94.

Orenstein, M. (2005). 'The new pension reform as global social policy.' *Global Social Policy* **5**: 175–202.

Orszag, P. R. and J. E. Stiglitz (2001). 'Rethinking pension reform: Ten myths about social security systems' in (eds), *New ideas about old age security. Towards sustainable systems in the 21st century*. Washington DC: World Bank, pp. 17–56.

Oxfam International (2015). *Wealth: Having it all and wanting more*. Oxford: Oxfam GB.

Padiak, J. (2005). 'The role of morbidity in the mortality decline of the nineteenth century: Evidence from the military population at Gibraltar 1818–1899.' *Journal of the History of Medicine and Allied Sciences* **60**(1): 73–95.

Pain, K. (2008a). 'Examining 'core–periphery' relationships in a global city-region: The case of London and South East England.' *Regional Studies* **42**(8): 1161–72.

Pain, K. (2008b). 'Gateways and Corridors in Globalization: Changing European Global City Roles and Functions.' *GaWC Research Bulletin* 287.

Palacios, R. (2002). 'The future of global ageing.' *International Journal of Epidemiology* **31**(4): 786–91.

Palacios, R. J. (1996). *Averting the old-age crisis. Technical Annex*. Washington DC: World Bank.

Palmore, E. (1971). 'Trends in Relative Status of Aged.' *Social Forces* **50**(1): 84–91.

Pampel, F. C. and M. Hardy (1994). 'Status Maintenance and Change During Old-Age.' *Social Forces* **73**(1): 289–314.

Parra, D. C., L. F. Gomez, O. L. Sarmiento, D. Buchner, R. Brownson, T. Schimd, V. Gomez and F. Lobelo (2010). 'Perceived and objective neighborhood environment attributes and health related quality of life among the elderly in Bogota, Colombia.' *Social Science & Medicine* **70**(7): 1070–6.

Parry, J. H. (2000). *Trade and dominion. The European overseas empires in the eighteenth century.* London: Phoenix Press.

Parsons, T. (1955). *The social system.* New York: Free Press.

Parsons, T. (1971). *The system of modern societies.* New Jersey: Prentice-Hall.

Paul, C. (2007). *Employment and labour market policies for an ageing workforce and initiatives in the workplace. National overview report: Portugal.* Dublin: European Foundation for the Improvement of Living and Working Conditions.

Paul, T. V. and N. M. Ripsman (2004). 'Under pressure? Globalisation and the national security state.' *Millennium-Journal of International Studies* **33**(2): 355–80.

Peace, S., H. W. Wahl, H. Mollenkopt and F. Oswald (2007). 'Environment and ageing' in (eds), *Ageing in Society.* 3rd edition. London: Sage, pp. 209–34.

Pearson, A., B. Sleap and A. Walker (2008). *An untapped resource. How supporting older people with social protection will help achieve the Millennium Development Goals (MDGs).* London: HelpAge International.

Peng, X., S. Song, S. Sullivan, J. Qiu and W. Wang (2010). 'Ageing, the Urban-Rural Gap and Disability Trends: 19 Years of Experience in China – 1987 to 2006.' *PLoS ONE* **5**(8): e12129.

Percival, J. (2002). 'Domestic spaces: uses and meanings in the daily lives of older people.' *Ageing & Society* **22**: 729–49.

Peterson, R. T. (1992). 'The Depiction of Senior-Citizens in Magazine Advertisements - A Content-Analysis.' *Journal of Business Ethics* **11**(9): 701–06.

Phillipson, C. (1982). *Capitalism and the Construction of Old Age.* London: Palgrave Macmillan.

Phillipson, C. (1990). 'The sociology of retirement' in (eds), *Ageing in society. An introduction to social gerontology.* London: Sage, pp. 144–60.

Phillipson, C. (1998). *Reconstructing Old Age: New Agendas in Social Theory and Practice.* London: Sage.

Phillipson, C. (2002). 'Ageism and globalization. Citizenship and social rights in transnational settings.' *3rd International Symposium on Cultural Gerontology*. Tampere: Swedish Gerontological Society.

Phillipson, C. (2003). 'Globalisation and the Future of Ageing: Developing a Critical Gerontology.' *Sociological Research Online* **8**.

Phillipson, C. (2007). 'The 'elected' and the 'excluded': sociological perspectives on the experience of place and community in old age.' *Ageing & Society* **27**: 321–42.

Phillipson, C. (2013a). *Ageing*. Cambridge: Polity Press.

Phillipson, C. (2013b). 'Commentary: The future of work and retirement.' *Human Relations* 66(1): 143–53.

Phillipson, C. (2015). 'The Political Economy of Longevity: Developing New Forms of Solidarity for Later Life.' *The Sociological Quarterly* **56**(1): 80–100.

Phillipson, C. and J. Baars (2007). 'Social theory and social ageing' in (eds), *Ageing in society*. London: Sage, pp. 68–84.

Phillipson, C., M. Bernard, J. Phillips and J. Ogg (1999). 'Older people's experiences of community life: patterns of neighbouring in three urban areas.' *Sociological review* **47**(4): 715–43.

Phillipson, C. and T. Scharf (2005). 'Rural and urban perspectives on growing old: developing a new research agenda.' *European Journal of Ageing* **2**(2): 67–75.

Pierson, C. (1994). 'Continuity and discontinuity in the emergance of the 'post-Fordist' welfare state' in (eds), *Towards a Post-Fordist Welfare State*. London: Routledge, pp. 95–113.

Pierson, C. (1998). 'Contemporary challenges to welfare state development.' *Political Studies* **46**(4): 777–94.

Pierson, C. (2006). *Beyond the Welfare State?* Cambridge: Polity Press.

Pierson, P. (2001a). 'Post industrial pressures on the mature welfare states' in P. Pierson (ed), *The new politics of the welfare state*. Oxford: Oxford University Press, pp. 80–104.

Pierson, P. (2001b). 'Coping with permanent austerity: welfare state restructuring in different democracies' in P. Pierson (ed), *The new politics of the welfare state*. Oxford: Oxford University Press, pp. 410–56.

Pierson, P. (2001c). 'Investigating the welfare state at the century's end' in P. Pierson (ed), *The new politics of the welfare state*. Oxford: Oxford University Press, pp. 1–16.

Pilcher, J. (1994). 'Mannheim's Sociology of Generations: An Undervalued Legacy.' *The British Journal of Sociology* **45**: 481–95.

Pinder, J. and S. Usherwood (2007). *The European Union: A Very Short Introduction*. Oxford: Oxford University Press.

Piven, F. F. and R. A. Cloward (2000). 'Power repertoires and globalization.' *Politics & Society* **28**(3): 413–30.

Polivka, L. (2001). 'Globalization, population ageing and ethics.' *Journal of Aging and Identity* **6**: 147–63.

Polivka, L. and E. A. Borrayo (2002). 'Globalization, population aging and ethics, part II. Towards a just global society.' *Journal of Aging and Identity* **7**: 195–211.

Powell, J. L. and C. F. Longino (2002). 'Post-modernism versus modernism: Rethinking theoretical tensions in social gerontology.' *Journal of Aging and Identity* **7**: 219–226.

Powell, M. and A. Barrientos (2004). 'Welfare regimes and the welfare mix.' *European Journal of Political Research* **43**(1): 83–105.

Raab, M., M. Ruland, B. Schonberger, H. P. Blossfeld, D. Hofacker, S. Buchholz and P. Schmelzer (2008). 'GlobalIndex: A sociological approach to globalization measurement.' *International Sociology* **23**(4): 596–631.

Rae, M. J., R. N. Butler, J. Campisi, A. D. N. J. de Grey, C. E. Finch, M. Gough, G. M. Martin, J. Vijg, K. M. Perrott and B. J. Logan (2010). 'The Demographic and Biomedical Case for Late-Life Interventions in Aging.' *Science Translational Medicine* **2**(40).

Rama, M. (2003). 'Globalization and the Labor Market.' *The World Bank Research Observer* **18**(2): 159–86.

Ramarez de Arellano, A. (2007). 'Patients without borders: the emergence of medical tourism.' *International Journal of Health Services: Planning, Administration, Evaluation* **37**(1): 193–8.

Raymer, J., G. Abel and P. W. F. Smith (2007). 'Combining census and registration data to estimate detailed elderly migration flows in England and Wales.' *Journal of the Royal Statistical Society Series a-Statistics in Society* **170**: 891–908.

Raymo, J. M. and T. Kaneda (2003). 'Changes in the living arrangements of Japanese elderly. The role of demographic factors' in (eds), *Demographic change and the family in Japan's aging society.* New York: SUNY, pp. 27–52.

Regidor, E., P. Guallar-Castillon, J. L. Gutierrez-Fisac, J. R. Banegas and F. Rodriguez-Artalejo (2010). 'Socioeconomic Variation in the Magnitude of the Association between Self-Rated Health and Mortality.' *Annals of Epidemiology* **20**(5): 395–400.

Restrepo, H. E. and M. Rozental (1994). 'The Social Impact of Aging Populations – Some Major Issues.' *Social Science & Medicine* **39**(9): 1323–38.

Reyes-Ortiz, C. A., G. V. Ostir, M. Pelaez and K. J. Ottenbacher (2006). 'Cross-national comparison of disability in Latin American and Caribbean persons aged 75 and older.' *Archives of Gerontology and Geriatrics* **42**(1): 21–33.

Rhodes, M. (1996). 'Globalization and West European Welfare States: a Critical Review of Recent Debates.' *Journal of European Social Policy* **6**(4): 305–27.

Riach, K. and W. Loretto (2009). 'Identity work and the 'unemployed' worker: age, disability and the lived experience of the older unemployed.' *Work Employment and Society* **23**(1): 102–19.

Riain, S. O. (2000). 'States and markets in an era of globalization.' *Annual Review of Sociology* **26**: 187–213.

Rieger, E. and S. Leibfried (1998). 'Welfare state limits to globalization.' *Politics & Society* **26**(3): 363–90.

Riley, M. W. (1971). 'Social Gerontology and the Age Stratification of Society.' *The Gerontologist* **11**: 79–87.

Riley, M. W. (1973). 'Aging and Cohort Succession: Interpretations and Misinterpretations.' *Public Opinion Quarterly* **37**(1): 35–49.

Riley, M. W. (1974). 'The Perspective of Age Stratification.' *The School Review* **83**: 85–91.

Robertson, R. (1995). 'Glocalization: Time-Space and Homogeneity-Heterogenity' in (eds), *Global Modernities*. London: Sage pp. 25–44.

Robine, J. M., P. Mormiche and C. Sermet (1998). 'Examination of the causes and mechanisms of the increase in disability-free life expectancy.' *J Aging Health* **10**(2): 171–91.

Robinson, M. (2008). 'Hybrid states: Globalisation and the politics of state capacity.' *Political Studies* **56**(3): 566–83.

Robinson, T. and D. Umphery (2006). 'First- and third-person perceptions of images of older people in advertising: An inter-generational evaluation.' *International Journal of Aging & Human Development* **62**(2): 159–73.

Robles, F. (2001). 'Latin American corporate strategy under the new regionalism' in (eds), *Responding to globalization*. London: Routledge, pp. 171–204.

Roche, M. (2003). 'Mega-Events, Time and Modernity: On time structures in global society.' *Time & Society* **12**(1): 99–126.

Roubini, N. (2014). 'Economic insecurity and the rise of nationalism', *The Guardian*, 2 June.

Roux, A. V. D., L. N. Borrell, M. Haan, S. A. Jackson and R. Schultz (2004). 'Neighbourhood environments and mortality in an elderly cohort: results from the cardiovascular health study.' *Journal of Epidemiology and Community Health* **58**(11): 917–23.

Rubinstein, R. L. and K. de Medeiros (2015). "Successful Aging,' Gerontological Theory and Neoliberalism: A Qualitative Critique.' *The Gerontologist* **55**(1): 34–42.

Rugman, A. M. (2000). *The end of globalization*. London: Random House.

Rugman, A. M. (2005). *The regional multinationals. MNEs and 'global' strategic management*. Cambridge: Cambridge University Press.

Russell, C. (2007). 'What do older women and men want? Gender differences in the 'Lived experience' of ageing.' *Current Sociology* **55**(2): 173–92.

Russell, R. V. (2003). 'Tourists and refugees – Coinciding sociocultural impacts.' *Annals of Tourism Research* **30**(4): 833–46.

Ryder, N. B. (1985). 'The cohort as a concept in the study of social change' in (eds), *Cohort analysis in social research. Beyond the identification problem*. New York: Springer-Verlag, pp. 9–44.

Sassen, S. (1998). *Globalization and its discontents*. New York: The New Press.

Sassen, S. (2000). 'Regulating immigration in a global age: A new policy landscape.' *Annals of the American Academy of Political and Social Science* **570**: 65–77.

Sassen, S. (2001). *The Global City: New York, London, Tokyo*. 2nd edition. New Jersey: Princeton University Press.

Sassen, S. (2004). 'Local Actors in Global Politics.' *Current Sociology* **52**(4): 649–70.

Sassen, S. (2006). *Territory, Authority, Rights. From medieval to global assemblages*. Princeton: Princeton University Press.

Savage, M., G. Bagnall and B. Longhurst (2005). *Globalization and belonging*. London: Sage.

Sawchuck, K. A. (1995). 'From Gloom to Boom: Age, Identity and Target Marketing' in (eds), *Images of Aging. Cultural representations*. London: Routledge, pp. 17–187.

Scharf, T. and B. Bartlam (2008). 'Ageing and social exclusion in rural communities' in (ed), *Rural ageing: A good place to grow old?* Bristol: The Policy Press, pp. 97–108.

Scharf, T. and J. D. Gierveld (2008). 'Loneliness in urban neighbourhoods: an Anglo-Dutch comparison.' *European Journal of Ageing* **5**(2): 103–15.

Scheve, K. and M. J. Slaughter (2004). 'Economic Insecurity and the Globalization of Production.' *American Journal of Political Science* **48**(4): 662–74.

Schoeni, R. F., V. A. Freedman and L. G. Martin (2008). 'Why is late-life disability declining?' *Milbank Quarterly* **86**(1): 47–89.

Schoeni, R. F., V. A. Freedman and R. B. Wallace (2001). 'Persistent, consistent, widespread, and robust? Another look at recent trends in old-age disability.' *Journals of Gerontology Series B-Psychological Sciences and Social Sciences* **56**(4): S206–S218.

Schoeni, R. F., L. G. Martin, P. M. Andreski and V. A. Freedman (2005). 'Persistent and Growing Socioeconomic Disparities in Disability Among the Elderly: 1982–2002.' *Am J Public Health* **95**(11): 2065–70.

Scholte, J. A. (1998). 'Beyond the buzzword. Towards a critical theory of globalization' in (eds), *Globalization. Theory and practice*. London: Pinter, pp. 43–57.

Scholte, J. A. (2005). *Globalization. A critical introduction*. 2nd edition. Houndmills: Palgrave.

Schulz, M., F. Söderbaum and J. Öjendal (2001). 'A framework for understanding regionalization' in (eds), *Regionalization in a globalizing world. A comparative perspective on forms, actors and processes*. New York: Zed Books, pp. 1–21.

Schwartz, H. (2000). *States versus markets. The emergence of a global economy*. 2nd edition. Houndmills: Macmillan Press.

Schwartz, H. (2001). 'Round up the usual suspects! Globalization, domestic politics and welfare state change' in P. Pierson (ed), *The new politics of the welfare state*. Oxford: Oxford University Press, pp. 17–45.

Sedgley, D., A. Pritchard and N. Morgan (2011). 'Tourism and ageing: A transformative research agenda.' *Annals of Tourism Research* **38**(2): 422–36.

Settersten, R. A. and K. U. Mayer (1997). 'The measurement of age, age structuring, and the life course.' *Annual Review of Sociology* **23**: 233–61.

Shaffer, E. R. and J. E. Brenner (2004). 'International trade agreement: Hazards to health?' *International Journal of Health Services* **34**: 467–81.

Shahar, S. (2005). 'The Middle Ages and Renaissance' in P. Thane (ed), *The Long History of Old Age*. London: Thames and Hudson, pp. 71–112.

Sharkey, B. J. (1987). 'Functional vs Chronological Age.' *Medicine and Science in Sports and Exercise* **19**(2): 174–8.

Sheller, M. and J. Urry (2006). 'The new mobilities paradigm.' *Environment and Planning A* **38**(2): 207–26.

Shetty, P. (2010). 'Medical tourism booms in India, but at what cost?' *The Lancet* **376**(9742): 671–2.

Shipiro, A. (2008) 'Sun, sea and surgery – the advent of medical tourism.' *JuniorDr*.

Short, J. (2001). *Global Dimensions: Space, Place and the Contemporary World*. London: Reaktion Books.

Simcock, P. and L. Sudbury (2006). 'The invisible majority? Older models in UK television advertising.' *International Journal of Advertising* **25**(1): 87–106.

Skala, N. (2009). 'The potential impact of the World Trade Organization's general agreement on trade in services on health system reform and regulation in the United States.' *International Journal of Health Services: Planning, Administration, Evaluation* **39**(2): 363–87.

Slaughter, A. M. (1997). 'The real new world order.' *Foreign Affairs* **76**(5): 183–197.

Smallman-Raynor, M. and D. Phillips (1999). 'Late stages of epidemiological transition: health status in the developed world.' *Health & Place* **5**(3): 209–22.

Smart, B. (1992). *Modern conditions, postmodern controversies*. London: Routledge.

Smith, A. D. (2003). 'Towards a Global Culture?' in (eds), *The Global Transformations Reader*. Cambridge: Polity Press, pp. 278–87.

Social Exclusion Unit (2005). *Excluded older people: Social Exclusion Unit report*. London: Office of the Deputy Prime Minister.

Soong, G. (2011). 'Taiwan's future is 'super-aged", *The China Post*, 12 July.SSA (2003a). *International Update: Recent Developments in Foreign Public and Private Pensions*. October. Washington: Social Security Administration's Office of Policy.

SSA (2003b). *International Update: Recent Developments in Foreign Public and Private Pensions*. December. Washington: Social Security Administration's Office of Policy.

SSA (2004a). *International Update: Recent Developments in Foreign Public and Private Pensions*. June. Washington: Social Security Administration's Office of Policy.

SSA (2004b). *International Update: Recent Developments in Foreign Public and Private Pensions*. July. Washington: Social Security Administration's Office of Policy.

SSA (2004c). *International Update: Recent Developments in Foreign Public and Private Pensions*. January. Washington: Social Security Administration's Office of Policy.

SSA (2004d). *International Update: Recent Developments in Foreign Public and Private Pensions*. March. Washington: Social Security Administration's Office of Policy.

SSA (2004e). *International Update: Recent Developments in Foreign Public and Private Pensions*. September. Washington: Social Security Administration's Office of Policy.

SSA (2004f). *International Update: Recent Developments in Foreign Public and Private Pensions.* August. Washington: Social Security Administration's Office of Policy.

SSA (2004g). *International Update: Recent Developments in Foreign Public and Private Pensions.* February. Washington: Social Security Administration's Office of Policy.

SSA (2005a). *International Update: Recent Developments in Foreign Public and Private Pensions.* January. Washington: Social Security Administration's Office of Policy.

SSA (2005b). *International Update: Recent Developments in Foreign Public and Private Pensions.* February. Washington: Social Security Administration's Office of Policy.

SSA (2005c). *International Update: Recent Developments in Foreign Public and Private Pensions.* May. Washington: Social Security Administration's Office of Policy.

SSA (2005d). *International Update: Recent Developments in Foreign Public and Private Pensions.* July. Washington: Social Security Administration's Office of Policy.

SSA (2005e). *International Update: Recent Developments in Foreign Public and Private Pensions.* June. Washington: Social Security Administration's Office of Policy.

SSA (2006a). *International Update: Recent Developments in Foreign Public and Private Pensions.* March. Washington: Social Security Administration's Office of Policy.

SSA (2006b). *International Update: Recent Developments in Foreign Public and Private Pensions.* April. Washington: Social Security Administration's Office of Policy.

SSA (2006c). *International Update: Recent Developments in Foreign Public and Private Pensions.* May. Washington: Social Security Administration's Office of Policy.

SSA (2006d). *International Update: Recent Developments in Foreign Public and Private Pensions.* November. Washington: Social Security Administration's Office of Policy.

SSA (2007a). *International Update: Recent Developments in Foreign Public and Private Pensions.* February. Washington: Social Security Administration's Office of Policy.

SSA (2007b). *International Update: Recent Developments in Foreign Public and Private Pensions.* December. Washington: Social Security Administration's Office of Policy.

SSA (2008a). *International Update: Recent Developments in Foreign Public and Private Pensions.* April. Washington: Social Security Administration's Office of Policy.

SSA (2008b). *International Update: Recent Developments in Foreign Public and Private Pensions*. June. Washington: Social Security Administration's Office of Policy.

Stallings, B. and W. Streeck (1995). 'Capitalisms in conflict? The United States, Europe and Japan in a post-Cold War world' in B. Stallings (ed), *Global change, regional response. The new international context of development*. Cambridge: Cambridge University Press, pp. 67–100.

Standing, G. (1997). 'Globalization, Labour Flexibility and Insecurity: The Era of Market Regulation.' *European Journal of Industrial Relations* **3**(1): 7–37.

Statistics Lithuania. (2013). 'Household Budget Survey.' http://osp.stat.gov.lt/en/viesos-duomenu-rinkmenos/-

Statistics Norway. (2013). 'Norway Survey of Consumption Expenditure, 2012.' www.ssb.no/en/inntekt-og-forbruk/statistikker/fbu/aar/2013–12–17Stockholm European Council (2001). *Presidency conclusions*. Brussels: EU.

Storper, M. (1997a). *The regional world*. New York: The Guilford Press.

Storper, M. (1997b).' Territories, flows and hierarchies in the global economy' in R. Cox (ed), *Spaces of globalization. Reasserting the power of the local*. New York: The Guilford Press, pp. 19–44.

Strange, S. (1996). *The Retreat of the State: The Diffusion of Power in the World Economy*. Cambridge: Cambridge University Press.

Strehler, B. (1962). *Time, Cells and Aging*. New York: Academic Press.

Streib, G. F. (2002). 'An Introduction to Retirement Communities.' *Research on Aging* **24**(1): 3–9.

Subramanian, S. V., L. Kubzansky, L. Berkman, M. Fay and I. Kawachi (2006). 'Neighborhood Effects on the Self-Rated Health of Elders: Uncovering the Relative Importance of Structural and Service-Related Neighborhood Environments.' *The Journals of Gerontology Series B: Psychological Sciences and Social Sciences* **61**(3): S153–S160.

Sunil, T. S., V. Rojas and D. E. Bradley (2007). 'United States' international retirement migration: the reasons for retiring to the environs of Lake Chapala, Mexico.' *Ageing & Society* **27**: 489–510.

Swank, D. (1998). 'Funding the welfare state: Globalization and the taxation of business in advanced market economies.' *Political Studies* **46**(4): 671–92.

Swank, D. (2001). 'Political institutions and welfare state restructuring. The impact of institutions on soical policy change in developed democracies' in P. Pierson (ed), *The new politics of the welfare state*. Oxford: Oxford University Press, pp. 197–237.

Swank, D. (2006). Tax policy in an era of internationalization: Explaining the spread of neoliberalism. *International Organization*, **60**(04), 847-882.

Szmigin, I. and M. Carrigan (2001a). 'Introduction to special issue on cognitive age and consumption.' *Psychology & Marketing* **18**(10): 999–1002.

Szmigin, I. and M. Carrigan (2001b). 'Time, consumption, and the older consumer: An interpretive study of the cognitively young.' *Psychology & Marketing* **18**(10): 1091–116.

Taylor, P. (2002). *New policies for older workers*. Bristol: Policy Press.

Taylor, P. (2003). 'Older workers, employer behaviour and public policy.' *Geneva Papers on Risk and Insurance-Issues and Practice* **28**(4): 553–7.

Taylor, P. and A. Walker (1997). 'Age discrimination and public policy.' *Personnel Review* **26**(4): 307–18.

Terry, N. P. (2007). 'Under-Regulated Health Care Phenomena in a Flat World: Medical Tourism and Outsourcing.' *Western New England Law Review* **29**: 421–472.

Thane, P. (2005). 'The age of old age' in P. Thane (ed), *The long history of old age*. London: Thames and Hudson, pp. 9–30.

The Gallup Organisation (2007). *Cross-border health services in the EU*. Brussels: EU.

Therborn, G. (2000). 'Globalizations.' *International Sociology* **15**(2): 151–79.

Thompson, E. P. (1967). 'Time, Work-Discipline, and Industrial Capitalism.' *Past and Present* 38(1): 56–97.

Thornton, A. and T. E. Fricke (1987). 'Social-Change and the Family – Comparative Perspectives from the West, China, and South-Asia.' *Population Index* **53**(3): 419–20.

Thorpe, N. (2015). 'Migrant crisis: Hungary surge as fence slowly rises.' *BBC News*, 24 August. www.bbc.co.uk/news/world-europe-34043344Thrift, N. (1999). 'A hyperactive world' in (eds), *Geographies of global change. Remapping the world in the late twentieth century*. Oxford: Blackwell, pp. 24–49.

Tomassini, C., K. Glaser, D. A. Wolf, V. G. M.I.B and E. Grundy (2004). 'Living arrangements among older people. An overview of trends in Europe and the USA.' *Population Trends* **114**: 24–34.

Topmiller, M., F. J. Conway and J. Gerber (2010). 'US Migration to Mexico: Numbers, Issues, and Scenarios.' *Mexican Studies-Estudios Mexicanos* **27**(1): 45–71.

Torres, S. (2001). 'Understandings of successful ageing in the context of migration: the case of Iranian immigrants in Sweden.' *Ageing & Society* **21**: 333–55.

Townsend, P. (1963). *The family life of older people.* London: Pelican Books.

Townsend, P. (1981). 'The Structured Dependency of the Elderly: A Creation of Social Policy in the Twentieth Century.' *Ageing & Society* **1**(01): 5–28.

Tshuma, L. (2000). 'Hierarchies and government versus networks and governance: Competing regulatory paradigms in global economic regulation.' *Social & Legal Studies* **9**(1): 115–42.

Turner, A., J. Drake and J. Hills (2004). *A new pension settlement for the twenty-first century. The second report of the Pensions Commission.* London: HMSO.

Twigg, J. (2007). 'Clothing, age and the body: a critical review.' *Ageing & Society* **27**: 285–305.

Twigg, J. and W. Martin (2015). 'The Field of Cultural Gerontology: An Introduction' in (eds), *Routledge Handbook of Cultural Gerontology.* London: Routledge, p. 1–16.

Uhlenberg, P. (1992). 'Population Aging and Social Policy.' *Annual Review of Sociology* **18**: 449–74.

UN (2001). *United Nations Principles for Older Persons.* Geneva: UN.

UN (2004). *Living arrangements of older people around the world.* Geneva: United Nations Population Division.

UN (2007). *World economic and social survey.* Geneva: UN.

United Nations Human Settlements Programme (2003). *The challenge of slums: global report on human settlements.* London: Earthscan Publications.

Unwin, D. W. (2007). 'The European Community: From 1945 to 1985' in M. Cini (ed), *European Union Politics.* 2nd edition. Oxford: Oxford University Press, pp. 13–29.

UNWTO (2010). *Tourism Highlights 2010 Edition.* Geneva: UNWTO.

Uotinen, V. (1998). 'Age identification: A comparison between Finnish and North-American cultures.' *International Journal of Aging & Human Development* **46**(2): 109–24.

Urry, J. (2000). *Sociology Beyond Societies. Mobilities for the Twenty-First Century.* London: Routledge.

Urry, J. (2002). *Global complexity.* Cambridge: Polity Press.

van Dalen, H. P. and K. Henkens (2002). 'Early-retirement reform: can it and will it work?' *Ageing and Society* **22**: 209–31.

Van Der Bly, M. C. E. (2005). 'Globalization. A triumph of ambiguity.' *Current Sociology* **53**: 875–93.

Verbrugge, L. (1984). 'Longer life but worsening health? Trends in health and mortality of middle-aged and older persons.' *Milbank Memorial Fund Quarterly* **62**: 475–519.

Verbrugge, L., J. Lepkowski and Y. Imanaka (1989). 'Comorbidity and its impact on disability.' *Milbank Quarterly* **67**: 450–84.

Victor, C., G. J. Westerhof and J. Bond (2007). 'Researching ageing' in (eds), *Ageing in society*. 3rd edition. London: Sage, pp. 85–112.

Vincent, J. (2003). *Old age*. London: Routledge.

Vincent, J. A. (2006). 'Ageing contested: Anti-ageing science and the cultural construction of old age.' *Sociology – the Journal of the British Sociological Association* **40**(4): 681–98.

Vincent, J. A. (2007). 'Science and imagery in the 'war on old age'.' *Ageing & Society* **27**: 941–61.

Vincent, J. A. (2008). 'The cultural construction old age as a biological phenomenon: Science and anti-ageing technologies.' *Journal of Aging Studies* **22**(4): 331–9.

Vincent, J. A., E. Tulle and J. Bond (2008). 'The anti-ageing enterprise: Science, knowledge, expertise, rhetoric and values.' *Journal of Aging Studies* **22**(4): 291–4.

Vis, B., K. van Kersbergen and T. Hylands (2011). 'To What Extent Did the Financial Crisis Intensify the Pressure to Reform the Welfare State?' *Social Policy & Administration* **45**(4): 338–53.

Vuorisalmi, M., I. Pietilä, P. Pohjolainen and M. Jylhä (2008). 'Comparison of self-rated health in older people of St. Petersburg, Russia, and Tampere, Finland: how sensitive is SRH to cross-cultural factors?' *European Journal of Ageing* **5**(4): 327–34.

WAAAM. (2010). 'World Anti-Aging Academy of Medicine.' www.waaam.orgWagner, P. (2015). 'Modernity and critique: Elements of a world sociology' in J. MDomingues (ed), *Global Modernity and Social Contestation*. London: Sage, pp. 21–35.

Wahrendorf, M. (2015). 'Previous employment histories and quality of life in older ages: sequence analyses using SHARELIFE.' *Ageing & Society* **35**(09): 1928–59.

Waidmann, T., J. Bound and M. Schoenbaum (1995). 'The illusion of failure: Trends in the self-reported health of the U.S. elderly.' *Milbank Quarterly* **73**: 253–87.

Waidmann, T. and K. G. Manton (1998). *International Evidence on Trends in Disability Among the Elderly. Report to the Office of Disability, Aging and Long-Term Care Policy*. Washington DC: Department of Health and Human Services, Office of the Assistant Secretary for Planning and Evaluation.

Walker, A. (2002). 'Ageing in Europe: policies in harmony or discord?' *International Journal of Epidemiology* **31**(4): 758–61.

Walker, A. (2005). 'Towards an international political economy of ageing.' *Ageing and Society* **25**: 815–39.

Wallerstein, I. (1979). *The capitalist economy.* Cambridge: Cambridge University Press.

Walters, W. H. (2002). 'Later-life migration in the United States: A review of recent research.' *Journal of Planning Literature* **17**(1): 37–66.

Warleigh-Lack, A. (2006). 'Towards a conceptual framework for regionalisation: Bridging 'new regionalism' and 'integration theory'.' *Review of International Political Economy* **13**(5): 750–71.

Warnes, A. M., K. Friedrich, L. Kellaher and S. Torres (2004). 'The diversity and welfare of older migrants in Europe.' *Ageing and Society* **24**: 307–26.

Warnes, A. M., R. King, A. M. Williams and G. Patterson (1999). 'The well-being of British expatriate retirees in southern Europe.' *Ageing and Society* **19**: 717–40.

Warnes, T. (2006). 'The Future Life Course, Migration and Old Age' in (eds), *The futures of old age.* London: Sage Publications, pp. 208–45.

Weiss, R. S. and S. A. Bass (2002). 'Introduction' in R. S. Weiss and S. A. Bass (eds), *Challenges of the third age: meaning and purpose in later life.* Oxford: Oxford University Press, pp. 3–12.

Wermel, M. T. and S. Gelbaum (1945). 'Work and retirement in old age.' *American Journal of Sociology* **51**: 16–21.

Westerhof, G. J. and E. Tulle (2007). 'Meanings of ageing and old age: discursive contexts, social attitudes and personal identities' in (eds), *Ageing in Society.* London: Sage, pp. 235–54.

White, N. R. and P. B. White (2004). 'Travel as transition - Identity and place.' *Annals of Tourism Research* **31**(1): 200–18.

Whitehouse, E. (2007). *Retirement income in 53 countries.* Washington DC: World Bank.

Wiener, J. M. and J. Tilly (2002). 'Population ageing in the United States of America: implications for public programmes.' *International Journal of Epidemiology* **31**(4): 776–81.

Wight, R. G., J. R. Cummings, A. S. Karlamangla and C. S. Aneshensel (2010). 'Urban Neighborhood Context and Mortality in Late Life.' *Journal of Aging and Health* **22**(2): 197–218.

Wight, R. G., J. R. Cummings, D. Miller-Martinez, A. S. Karlamangla, T. E. Seeman and C. S. Aneshensel (2008). 'A multilevel analysis of urban neighborhood socioeconomic disadvantage and health in late life.' *Social Science & Medicine* **66**(4): 862–72.

Wight, R. G., M. J. Ko and C. S. Aneshensel (2011). 'Urban Neighborhoods and Depressive Symptoms in Late Middle Age.' *Research on Aging* 33(1): 28–50.

Williams, S. J. (2005). 'Parsons revisited: from the sick role to … ?' *Health* **9**(2): 123–44.

Wilmoth, J. M. (2010). 'Health Trajectories Among Older Movers.' *J Aging Health* **22**(7): 862–81.

Wilson, G. (1997). 'A postmodern approach to structured dependency theory.' *Journal of Social Policy* **26**: 341–50.

Wilson, G. (2002). 'Globalisation and older people: effects of markets and migration.' *Ageing and Society* **22**: 647–63.

Wilson, R. W., and Drury, T. F. (1984). Interpreting trends in illness and disability: health statistics and health status. *Annual Review of Public Health*, **5**, 83-106.

Wimmer, A. and N. Glick Schiller (2002). 'Methodological nationalism and beyond: nation-state building, migration and the social sciences.' *Global Networks* **2**(4): 301–34.

Wolf, D. A., K. Hunt and J. Knickman (2005). 'Perspectives on the recent decline in disability at older ages.' *Milbank Quarterly* **83**(3): 365–95.

Wolf, D. A. and C. F. Longino (2005). 'Our 'Increasingly mobile society'? – The curious persistence of a false belief.' *Gerontologist* **45**(1): 5–11.

Wolf, H. (2002). *Globalization and the convergence of social expenditure in the European Union*. Washington DC: GW Center for the Study of Globalization.

Wolf, M. (2004). *Why globalization works*. New Haven: Yale University Press.

Woodman, J. (2007). *Patients without borders. Singapore digital edition*. Hong Kong: Healthy Travel Media.

World Anti-Aging (2010). *World Anti-Aging's Regenerative Medicine in China*. Shanghai: World Anti-Aging.

World Bank (1994). *Averting the old age crisis. Policies to protect the old and promote growth*. Washington DC: World Bank.

World Bank (2000). *Poverty in an age of globalization*. Washington DC: World Bank.

World Bank (2001). *Social protection sector strategy. From safety net to springboard*. Washington DC: World Bank.

World Health Organization (2007). *Global Age-friendly Cities: A Guide*. Paris: WHO.

World Health Organization (2010). 'What is "active ageing?"' www. who.int/ageing/active_ageing

World Health Organization (2015). *World report on ageing and health*. Luxembourg: WHO.

WOSIAM. (2009). 'World Society Interdisciplinary of Anti-Aging Medicine.' www.wosiam.org

Yeandle, S. (2003). 'The international context' in (eds), *Work to welfare. How men become detached from the labour market*. Cambridge: Cambridge University Press, pp. 15–30.

Yeates, N. (2001). *Globalization and social policy*. London: Sage.

Ying, B. and R. Yao (2010). 'Self-perceived Age and Attitudes Toward Marketing of Older Consumers in China.' *Journal of family and economic issues* **31**(3): 318–27.

Young, M. D. and P. Willmott (1957). *Family and Kinship in East London*. London: Routledge and Kegan Paul.

Zelenev, S. (2006). 'Towards a 'society for all ages': meeting the challenge or missing the boat.' *International Social Science Journal* **58**(190): 601–16.

Zheng, X., G. Chen, X. Song, J. Liu, L. Yan, W. Du, L. Pang, L. Zhang, J. Wu, B. Zhang and J. Zhang (2011). 'Twenty-year trends in the prevalence of disability in China.' *Bulletin of the World Health Organization* **89**: 788–97.

Zunzunegui, M. V., B. E. Alvarado, F. Beland and B. Vissandjee (2009). 'Explaining health differences between men and women in later life: A cross-city comparison in Latin America and the Caribbean.' *Social Science & Medicine* **68**(2): 235–42.

Index

Note: page numbers in *italic* type refer to Figures; those in **bold** type refer to Tables.

K

Kazakhstan:
  healthcare spending from public sources
    73
  pension reform **162,** 164
KOF Globalization Index 75, 75–6, 87,
  88, 97
Kohli, M. 83
Korea, Republic of:
  pension reform 160
  public spending on old age 93, 94
  retirement age increase 172

L

L'Oreal 140
labour market participation rates, of older
  people 82, 83–5, 84, 86, 183
  and active ageing agenda 169, 170, 171,
    172–4
  and globalisation 85, 87, 88
Laslett, P 26, 102–3
late modernity 37
  ageing and later life in 22–30
  see also second modernity
Latin America:
  cosmetics and cosmeceuticals 140
  family structure 120
  family, as a source of identity 121, 122
  labour market participation rates of
    older people 84, 98
  pensions reform 156, 159, **161,** 164
  residential location of older people 126,
    127
  WOSIAM membership 148
Latin America and Caribbean:
  ageing population statistics 59
  depressive disorders 66
  healthcare spending 68, 69
    from public sources 74
  pension reform 158, 166
Latvia:
  financial circumstances of older people
    99
  healthcare spending from public sources
    73
  pension reform 156
life course:
  changes to conception of in first
    modernity 11–12
  in modern and late modern societies 12
life expectancy 56, 57–8, 59, 78
  increases in 26
  see also disability-free life expectancy;
    HLE (healthy life expectancy)
lifestyle guides 28
liquid modernity 36, 124
  see also late modernity

Lithuania:
  cultural consumption spending patterns
    112, 113
  healthcare spending from public sources
    73
  labour market participation rates of
    older people 173
Lloyd-Sherlock, P. 126
LME (labour market exit), early 81–2, 98,
  168, 169, 183
localism 34, 46–8
low-income countries:
  ageing and health 65, 66
  healthcare spending 71
  life expectancy 57
  see also developing countries
Luxembourg:
  fall in pension entitlements 90

M

Madrid International Plan of Action on Aging
  (UN) 170–1
Malaysia:
  labour market participation rates of
    older people 85, 86
Malta:
  labour market participation rates of
    older people 172
  retirement age increase 171, 172
Manchester, UK, Northern Powerhouse
  48
marketing, and older people 26, 108–9
marketisation, of healthcare services for
  older people 67
Massey, D. 16
McGrew, A. 35, 43
mediascapes 38
medical tourism 138, 143–6, 180, 181–2,
  189
Medicare, USA 71
mega-cities 48
men:
  coronary heart disease 60
  increase in retirement age 172
  labour market participation rates 86,
    87, 88
  negative experiences of retirement 19
  perceptions of age of start of old age/
    ideal retirement age 103, **105**
Mercosur, South America 41
methodological nationalism 34, 37, 174
Mexico:
  labour market participation rates of
    older people 98
  medical tourism to 144
  public spending on old age 93, 94
  SAGE (Study on Global Ageing and
    Adult Health) 65

preventative medicine *see* anti-ageing
medicine
privatisation of healthcare 69–74, *72, 74,*
74–6, *75,* 77
privatisation of healthcare services for
older people 67
Proctor & Gamble 141–2
public spending:
on healthcare services *72,* 72–3, 74–6,
75, 77
on old age 93, *94, 95*

R

race to the bottom 6, 67, 68, 76, 79, 91,
93, 97, 99, 185
reflexive modernity 37
see also late modernity
regenerative medicine 147
see also anti-ageing medicine
regionalisation 34, 40–2
rejuvenation medicine *see* anti-ageing
medicine
residential care policy 17
residential location of older people 126–7,
127
retirement 17, 81
and disengagement theory 12–14
early retirement 81–2, 98, 168, 169,
170, 171, 183
in modernisation and ageing theory
16–17
as a negative event 19, 83
perceptions of ideal age of 103, **105**
in structural dependency theory 19
transformation of 83
see also finance, and older people
retirement age 15
increases in 82, 83, 168, 171–2, 175
state mandated 19, 21
retirement migration 30, 33, 124–6,
128–30, *129,* 133
Robertson, R. 30, 47
Romania:
labour market participation rates of
older people 173
rural areas, older people living in 126,
127, *127*
Russia:
healthcare spending from public sources
73
pension reform **163,** 164–5
residential location of older people 126,
127
SAGE (Study on Global Ageing and
Adult Health) 65
self-reported health *62,* 63

S

SAGE (Study on Global Ageing and
Adult Health) 65, 186
Sassen, S. 48, 50
Saudi Arabia:
index of progressivity 96
Scandinavia:
healthcare spending 68
index of progressivity 96
labour market participation rates of
older people 83
Sceptics (globalisation) 43
Scholte, J. A. 35
second modernity 10, *12*
see also late modernity
self-rated health, spatial patterns of 61,
62, 63
SERPS (State Earnings Related Pension
Scheme), UK 156
SHARE (Survey of Health, Ageing and
Retirement in Europe) 65, 128
Sierra Leone:
healthcare spending from public sources
72
Singapore:
cultural consumption spending patterns
112, 114
medical tourism 144, 145–6
self-reported health *62,* 63
Slovak Republic:
pension reform 161, **163,** 164, 165
Slovakia:
residential location of older people 127,
127
Slovenia:
HLE (healthy life expectancy) 64
pension reform 166
social democratic/Scandinavian welfare
regime 44–5, 183
index of progressivity 96
social exclusion of older people 123
social gerontology theory 2
scope of 9–10
time and space in 9
social security spending 29
Sociedad Española de Medecina
Antienvejecimiento y Longevidad 149
South Africa:
healthcare spending from public sources
73
index of progressivity 96
residential location of older people 126,
127
retirement migration 128, *129*
SAGE (Study on Global Ageing and
Adult Health) 65
self-reported health *62,* 63